Reading Biblical Narrative

READING BIBLICAL NARRATIVE

An Introductory Guide

Jan Fokkelman

Translated by
Ineke Smit

Westminster John Knox Press
Louisville, Kentucky

deo
PUBLISHING

Copyright © 1999 Deo Publishing, Scholeksterstraat 16, 2352 EE
Leiderdorp, The Netherlands

Originally published as *Vertelkunst in de bijbel. Een handleiding bij
literair lezen* by Uitgeverij Boekencentrum, Zoetermeer, The
Netherlands, Copyright © 1995 Uitgeverij Boekencentrum.

Cover design by Night & Day Design

This edition published by
Westminster John Knox Press
Louisville, Kentucky

This book is printed on acid-free paper that meets the American
National Standards Institute Z39.48 standard. ∞

PRINTED IN THE UNITED STATES OF AMERICA

00 01 02 03 04 05 06 07 08 09 — 10 9 8 7 6 5 4 3 2 1

Library of Congress Cataloging-in-Publication Data is on file at
the Library of Congress, Washington, D. C.

ISBN 0-664-22263-3

C'est la force des choses dites
qui meut l'écrivain
                    Paul Ricœur

Contents

Preface

The most widely read book in the world is not necessarily the best-read book. There are two sorts of reading. There is the sort we learned long ago, when we were five or six. The other sort is reading with understanding, receiving the text on the right wavelength.

This book advocates a creative way of reading and aims to familiarize readers with elementary but powerful insights and techniques of narrative art, which have been common currency beyond the confines of biblical studies for some generations. Those who take full advantage of them will come into personal and intense contact with the narrative prose of the Bible.

On this occasion I am writing for a broad readership: for all interested people who are without knowledge of the original languages of the Old and New Testaments (Hebrew and Greek respectively). At scarcely any point, therefore, do I make use of arguments or perceptions concerned with the original languages. To place myself in the position of my readers, I have worked with familiar translations. A translation is in essence a substitute, and as such it is a valid text in its own right.

Is it at all possible to read a highly charged series of writings such as the Bible without preconceptions? I dare to answer this question in the affirmative and address myself to readers who are prepared to embark on an adventure and to put their own views and beliefs between parentheses. When examined closely, every page of the Bible says other things than we expect.

Readers who are used to opening up the Bible will need no help in continuing. There are, however, other readers who, perhaps as the result of someone else's misuse of the Bible, will have doubt, mistrust, or some other hurdle to overcome. Since I have every sympathy for such readers, it is to them that as an encouragement I dedicate this book.

1

Preliminary exercise: a very short story

The narrative structure of 2 Kings 4:1-7

The first half of the Hebrew Bible is taken up by two extensive narrative complexes. The Holy Scriptures of the Jews (also those of Jesus of Nazareth!) start off with the five books of the Torah, the series Genesis, Exodus, Leviticus, Numbers and Deuteronomy, as they are called in the West. The word Torah means "instruction," both in the sense of a rule, specifically one set by a priest, and in the sense of "tuition." As some collections of rules have been included in Genesis through Deuteronomy, in New Testament Greek the Torah is often called "The Law." Still, the framework for the religious, civil and criminal laws remains narrative; the Torah is in the first place defined by a vast body of pious historical writings: from the beginning of the world to the moment when the chosen people of Israel are about to enter the land of Canaan, promised by God.

The next complex is called "The Early Prophets" in the Jewish canon and covers the period from the entry into the Promised Land to the great catastrophe in 586 BCE, when the tiny kingdom of Judah is wiped off the map by the neo-Babylonians, Jerusalem is captured, and Solomon's temple is razed to the ground. This composition consists of three pairs: the books of Joshua and Judges depict the arrival and settling down of the tribal community. The books of 1 and 2 Samuel cover about a century: the perilous transition from a tribal existence to the unified state governed by a king, and the reigns of the first king, Saul, and his famous successor David. 1 and 2 Kings describe the period of the monarchy, the three-and-a-half centuries from King Solomon to the end of the kingdom of Judah.

In the middle of the books of Kings the prophet Elijah and his disciple Elisha are each the subject of a cycle of stories. The Elisha series runs from 2 Kings 2, when he takes over the prophet's mantle from his master, through to ch. 13, his own death. Elisha is the main character in about ten literary units (stories). Here follows the shortest unit of the series, the first seven verses of 2 Kings 4. The numbers are those of the traditional verses, the letters indicate a division into what I will call lines, and which are usually clauses:

> v. 1a   A certain woman, the wife of one of the disciples of the prophets, cried out to Elisha:
>
> b   "Your servant my husband is dead,
>
> c   and you know how your servant revered the Lord;
>
> d   and now a creditor is coming to seize my two children as slaves."
>
> v. 2a   Elisha said to her:
>
> b   "What can I do for you?
>
> c   Tell me, what have you in the house?"
>
> d   She replied:
>
> e   "Your maidservant has nothing at all in the house, except a jug of oil."
>
> v. 3a   He said:
>
> b   "Go, and borrow vessels outside, from all your neighbors,
>
> c   take as many empty vessels as you can.
>
> v. 4a   Then go in and shut the door behind you and your children,
>
> b   and pour [oil] into all those vessels,
>
> c   removing each one as it is filled."
>
> v. 5a   She went away
>
> b   and shut the door behind her and her children.
>
> c   They kept bringing [vessels] to her and she kept pouring.
>
> v. 6a   When the vessels were full,
>
> b   she said to her son:
>
> c   "bring me another vessel."
>
> d   he answered her:
>
> e   "There are no more vessels;"
>
> f   and the oil stopped
>
> v. 7a   She came and told the man of God,
>
> b   and he said:
>
> c   "Go sell the oil
>
> d   and pay your debt,
>
> e   and you and your children can live on the rest."

This might seem an extremely simple story—wouldn't even a child get the point immediately? The prophet gets the woman out of her predicament by a miracle; that's all there is to it.

It does seem to be that simple, and we tend to conclude that this is a bit of colorful folklore, nothing extraordinary, just a piece of anonymous folk literature, possibly an instance of oral transmission in honor of the prophet.

There is much more, however, to this story. If we ask the basic question of who exactly is the *hero* of this episode, things instantly prove to be less simple than they seem. Isn't it the prophet? Before we conclude this we shall have to see if we are justified in denying the role of heroine to the widow, or how we must weigh one against the other.

However short the story may be, it is a mature and carefully structured, written composition. We meet two main characters, an anonymous widow and a prestigious man of God, the prophet Elisha. We are tempted to see him as the hero of the piece: after all, doesn't he perform a miracle?

The woman is in dire straits. Her deceased husband was their provider, and upon his death he has left a large debt. She is very poor and can pay off the debt neither in money nor in goods. As there were no social safety nets at all in the ancient world, in this precarious situation the creditor is fully justified in taking possession of the labor force represented by the sons his debtor left. This is exactly what is going to happen. One catastrophe, the death of the husband, threatens to unleash another: the boys will be slaves, and the widow is desperate. There is only one last resort: she can appeal to the prophet for help, as Elisha is the spiritual leader of the guild which her husband belonged to.

The narrator takes the shortest route to the point where he can give the floor to the woman. In one line we only get the minimum of information necessary about the woman and the nature of her action; her crying out means that her appeal to Elisha arises from distress. Next, the widow explains her problem in three lines. Isn't she the best person to do it? This opens the trajectory taken by the story, which reaches a happy ending in v. 7 with the solution to the predicament.

In both cases the narrator withdraws behind his characters, a decision on the writer's part which invites some consideration.

By having the woman speak for most of v. 1 he has refrained from formulating the problem himself, which would have been easy enough. In v. 7, too, he resists the temptation to reserve the last word for himself, leaving that to the prophet, who instructs the woman how she can now easily pay off her debt. The writer does not even consider it necessary to report that this is in fact what happens: the readers can deduce that themselves. The happy ending is a case of omission—*ellipsis* in literary terminology.

These are two extremely pertinent decisions on the writer's part. The widow is the asking party; she is best qualified to plead her cause. Having as a spokesperson someone in distress lends dramatic impact to the opening and invites the reader to follow her with sympathy. The answering party is the man of God, who knows a miraculous way out. His speeches in vv. 3-4 and 7 offer the solution to the pressing problem, so it is appropriate to grant him the last word. In this way, alternating the speakers creates a balance between the opening and the ending: the woman opens; the prophet closes. Thus the starting and the winning posts of the plot are presented: the development which takes us from misery to relief.

The writer supports this coherence of head and tail by applying a threefold or fourfold frame (*inclusio* in technical terms). Not only is there the relation between problem and solution which exactly delineates the course of the plot, but also a deliberate choice of words that create correspondences between the first and last verses, and thus perfectly round off the miniature. The first obvious link exactly indicates what is at stake in this story: it is a matter of life and death! Verse 1a tells of the husband's death, v. 7e of the life of the woman and her sons. Another set of complementary concepts comes close to this: in v. 1d the shadow of the creditor looms, but 7d mentions an easy way to pay off the debt. In this way the boys' slavery, which we may see as a second representation of death, is prevented. The taking on the part of the creditor (1d) is contrasted in v. 7 with the giving on the part of the widow: she will offer oil at the market and sell it for a good price, after which she can give the creditor what is his. She will even have enough left, and it is not for nothing that the word for that ("the rest") has been placed at the end of v. 7e. With its semantic overtones of "surplus" this very last word of the literary unit indicates that there is, after all, a good life waiting for her on the other side of this harrowing episode—an enormous relief.

One of the main characteristics of this story is that it is carried largely by the spoken word. If for the moment we leave aside the obligatory quotation formulas, as they only serve the speeches (vv. 2a, 2d, 3a, 6b, 6d, 6f and 7b), we see that this leaves very little genuine narrator's text, which moreover in three places consists of rather scant factual information; I am referring here to lines 1a, 6a and 7a which are little more than introductions. This leaves only one sequence where the narrator has the field to himself, the three lines in v. 5. This trio, however, does make a special contribution.

In his relatively long speech in vv. 3-4 the prophet has used a series of no fewer than seven predicates; strictly speaking, the speech consists of seven sentences which are nothing but instructions in the second person feminine. The woman is to collect a lot of empty vessels together with her sons and pour these full of oil from the jug that was all she had (as she told Elisha in v. 2). The writer can then decide dutifully to report the execution of all seven instructions in v. 5, but that would be rather boring; instead, he makes a selection from the instructions in 3b-4c, and tells us only how the actions mentioned in 4ab are carried out.

First two verbs are used momentarily, i.e. describing actions which are just a point in time: "she went away and shut the door behind her and her children." The collecting of the vessels has simply been left out—a barely noticeable ellipsis, a gap which readers can fill in for themselves. What follows in v. 5cd captures our attention through a radically different time aspect: "they kept bringing [vessels] to her and she kept pouring." These actions by the boys and their mother are contrasted with the regular form of narration, as they are not momentary, a single point in time, and the pouring does not follow the bringing of the vessels; here we have actions characterized by duration and synchronicity. We should realize that the three of them spend hours and hours: the boys doing the heavy work, the mother pouring. In this way, the narrator has drastically slowed down the narrative tempo at a stroke; it is a signal to the reader to take note of a scene of excellent cooperation.

Why has the writer here opted for durative forms which moreover denote synchronicity rather than sequentiality? The answer is that it is here in v. 5 that the actual miracle takes place. It takes place behind closed doors; nobody is allowed to see it, not even the neighbors who were so kind as to lend a jug. It should remain a secret—that is the point of Elisha's instruction when he ordered: "shut the door behind you and your children" (v. 4a), and this is why the narrator chose to report the execution of this action, in 5b, and left out the others.

Certainly, it is a secret, but it is revealed to us, by the writer. He is *omniscient*, as it is called in narrative theory, because he is able to see behind doors, inside heads or into heaven, and in v. 5 he lets us share in his superior knowledge so that we reach the same level of knowledge as Elisha and the widow. He allows us a peep through the keyhole, and we are completely amazed to see how that one little jug with maybe half a cup of oil just refuses to run out. In a way, the narrator has made peeping Toms of us and the virtual keyhole through which he allows us a glimpse is nothing other than the story itself.

The miracle is emphasized by another stylistic decision. Although transitive verbs are used to refer to the boys' and their mother's toil, the direct objects of both the "bringing" and the "pouring" have been left out. This double ellipsis of vessels and oil is significant: in this way, our undivided attention is directed towards the action itself, its long duration, and the cooperation between the widow and her boys.

Thus the writer, who as narrator had allocated himself so few lines, has kept the core of the plot for himself after all: it is those few hours of pouring that defy the laws of the physical universe. And this takes us to a far greater ellipsis: the character responsible for the fact that one small jug fills rows and rows of jugs, with gallons and gallons of oil, appears nowhere in the scenario! The God of Elisha and the widow is conspicuously absent in the narrator's text. A spectacular paradox, as his activity is presupposed by the text without the reader being able to pin this down to any particular verse.

The narrator's omniscience has in the meantime acquired a striking parallel in the prophet's. But how did the prophet know that things would work out as miraculously as his series of instructions already imply? The text keeps silent about this, too. Sometimes God has the strongest influence when he is notoriously invisible, and even the silence around the center of the story, the unexpressed, is inspired.

Presence and absence: these and their sophisticated interplay (their dialectics) are also central to the verses between the center and the ends on either side. In v. 2 the woman tells Elisha that apart from that one jug she has nothing. There is nothing in the house, and the reader wonders whether, for a prophet who is willing to help, there is anything to work with. This emptiness and absence finds a counterpart in v. 6 when after a long time of pouring the woman tells her boy "bring me another vessel!" The son she was addressing then answers: "there are no more vessels." The absence of any empty vessel has acquired a verbal, textual presence by a decision on the writer's part: v. 6e.

The play between presence and absence challenges us to link vv. 2 and 6. Since the middle verses, vv. 3-4 and 5, belong together according to the frequent and simple pattern of instruction plus execution, the structure of the whole now materializes: a six-part, symmetrical arrangement:

A	opening: woman formulates pressing problem	v. 1
B	dialog, prophet–woman: what have you got? Nothing.	v. 2
C	Elisha gives the woman ample instructions...	vv. 3-4
C'	... which she carries out at home, together with her sons.	v. 5
B'	dialog, mother–sons: another vessel? No.	v. 6
A'	conclusion: the prophet presents the solution.	v. 7

Thus everything falls into place. We see how the composition is governed by a *concentric* structure which could also be called a triple ring structure.

Let us check the three rings again. First, there is the relation A–A', which has already been demonstrated by several instances of *inclusio*. The woman's speech contains three lines, the same number as that of the prophet under A'. There are, however, more correspondences. In v. 1 the woman cries out to "Elisha"; she seems to be addressing a specific individual. At the begin-

ning of v. 2 the prophet is also briefly referred to by his proper
name, but no more after that. In v. 7 he is called by another
name: there the writer refers to him by his primary quality of
"man of God." So—the help Elisha gives is not a personal feat,
but a helping hand in the name of (and with the secret cooperation of) the deity. In this position, some lines after the miracle,
the label is very fitting. The speech in 1bcd itself is also marked
by a frame, though not a happy one: 1b opens with the word
"servant" and 1d ends in the plural "slaves." The one servant is
dead (and is at the same time an image for the recent past), and
the word "slaves" in the plural represents the near future for the
dead man's sons. This is a frightening symmetry, an iron vice
from which the widow sees no escape until in v. 7 the prophet
points to the way out. His speech (segment A' in the structure)
is the only and conclusive answer to the speech of segment A.

The correspondence B–B' first of all consists in the fact that
only v. 2 and v. 6 contain dialog in the proper sense: the relation of question and answer. Then there is the content: "there is
nothing, only..." versus "bring me another vessel; no, there
aren't any more." This is an ingenious meshing of presence and
absence, first in the house, and then in the text. The last words
of B and B' are identical: oil. The connection between C and
C' has been sufficiently discussed; the interplay of presence and
absence is finally also reflected in the opposition of the words
"full" and "empty," which occur in vv. 3 and 4, and in v. 6.

The ABC sequence fills 15 lines; the C'B'A' series occupies
14. This means that there is a good quantitative balance as well.
We also find this balance one level down: if we count the lines
per segment we get the sequence 4-5-6 for the "rising" first
half, and 3-6-5 for the "falling" second half. This means that the
pairs AA', BB' and CC' contain 9, 11 and 9 lines respectively.
The BB' pair seems larger, but is not, as it contains fewer words
than the surrounding pairs. In the original language there is not
much difference between the numbers of words-per-pair: in the
Hebrew text AA', BB' and CC' contain 44, 38 and 39 words
respectively. There are 29 lines in all, which makes no. 15 the
middle one. This fits nicely, as line 15 is occupied by v. 4c,
which closes the first half.

The concentric structure seems to me to be the strongest, but the story is so tightly constructed that a case may also be made for a *parallel* composition: this would be the sequence ABC//A'B'C' for the same six segments. This is suggested by the observation that the prophet gives instructions twice, in vv. 3-4 and in v. 6, at the end of the first and second halves. The dialogs in v. 2 and v. 6 just stay where they are, in the middle of their own halves, and vv. 1 and 5 neatly complement each other as word (of the problem) and action (the miracle which provides the solution). So we might also construct the following frame:

A	the woman speaks, formulates problem	v. 1
B	dialog, prophet–woman: what do you have in the house?	v. 2
C	speech by Elisha, instruction I	vv. 3-4
A'	the woman acts, a miracle saves the day	v. 5
B'	dialog, woman–sons: any vessels left?	v. 6
C'	speech by Elisha, instruction II	v. 7

This outline or labeling is more in accordance with the course of the action. The development of the plot naturally follows the linear time axis. We now notice the action takes place in two "waves." The woman pays two visits to Elisha. The first is concluded with instructions whose impact is only known to the prophet. After she has filled the vessels, she comes to see him again, and Elisha gives the final instruction which enables her to keep her sons permanently out of the creditor's clutches. The parallel structure nicely emphasizes the woman's movements: it is impressive to see how one attribute is replaced by another in the pair B-B': first there was only the jug; now we have rows of vessels, full of precious oil. Elisha's instructions have parallel openings in that both start with the same verb of movement, which is directly linked to a commandment characteristic for phases I and II:

3b "Go and borrow vessels..."
7c "Go sell the oil..."

We see how well the objects fit together: vessels and oil are exact complements. This figure itself fits well into the parallel pattern: in v. 3 the vessels come to the woman, in v. 7 she is handing out measures of oil, although at the price that suits her. She takes and she gives.

After this preliminary exercise I can repeat the basic question at the beginning of this chapter: who exactly is the hero of this story? Anticipating somewhat our theoretical discussion in Chapter 5, I will link the concept of "hero" to the concept of a "quest" or search. Usually, a story is about someone who from the outset is looking for a valuable object that is expected to make good a lack, meet a need or solve a problem pertaining at the beginning of the journey or action. Here, this is clearly the woman—she is the one with a problem and looking for the valuable object, which here primarily is finding a way to free herself from the creditor. In the second instance, this even turns out to be a concrete object: gallons of good oil which she can sell to pay off the debt. The woman is present in every verse of the piece; even if she is not acting or speaking she is being addressed by the prophet. Twice she travels back and forth; Elisha does not move a foot. The prophet is absent during vv. 5-6 and does no more than receiving and addressing her twice. He does not show any initiative either and is certainly not the person who actually performs the miracle. It is true, of course, that his knowledge has to come from God and is indispensable to her quest. In short, the woman is the heroine of this miniature. Would this also apply to the long story about the woman and her dead child in vv. 8-36, where Elisha seems to perform a miracle with his whole body?

I will round off this introduction with some conclusions. The writer's expertise makes everything run like clockwork, but this instance of narrative art is considerably less transparent than it seems at first sight. We are justified in observing a certain simplicity here, but this proves to be the result of a total and flexible mastery of form, and much more is going on in the text than the simple message to be read on the surface. A closer look uncovers a great deal of subtlety which itself casts new light on practically all aspects of the story. The text contains many figures and structures which provide frameworks for new discoveries.

What we have to learn is to read these stories according to their own rules and conventions, in an attitude of respect, and maintaining an open mind as long as possible. Creative reading is not only linear but circular as well: our attention travels back and forth while we try to link everything to everything else. This is an active attitude which from time to time requires enthusiastic puzzle-solving.

2

Introduction: the art of reading

Components I and II: language and time

In our world there are thousands of texts that have been stored and forgotten. Hundreds of these are texts of some substance, as they have great literary quality or form part of the normative texts of a religious community. Yet, we cannot say anything sensible about them until they become available to us and we are able to understand the language in which they have been written. You can only say that these texts have meaning if you recognize right away that their meanings or contents are hidden or potential. In short, a text only starts to function when it receives attention—only then does it affect someone. Without a reader a text cannot operate; it is no more than a silent shadow.

The relation between text and meaning is not a simple one. The supposition that "there is meaning in it" or that the text "contains" meaning in a similar way that a cup contains coffee is incorrect. The cup may simply be poured out without the contents being affected, but in the case of a text this is quite different. The word "exegesis" (Greek for "leading out") is misleading if we see meaning as a fixed and objective string of data which we have to coax out of a text. In reality, a text only speaks when a listener comes along. A text becomes alive and starts to speak only from the moment when we start to listen, and in proportion to how well we are listening. As loyal readers we, of course, want to respect and adhere to the words and structures of the text, but our action of reading, understanding and making connections is essential to these words and structures. Reading is certainly not passive, nor a form of easy consumption, even though our body seems to suggest this when we are lounging in our armchair. Reading is a specific mental ac-

tivity; it is *the action of conferring meaning to a text*. While reading,
I am myself structuring the living or speaking text. Thanks to
the reader's bestowal of meaning, the text moves from its dor-
mant state to the state of speaking subject; what was only latent
and potential now becomes patent and actual.

A story or a poem can only come into its own or blossom
through the channel of a competent reader. This has consequences for our responsibility. As the meaning of a text is only
realized through the mediation of the reader, our responsibility
for its meaning is greater than the text's own. Moreover, this
meaning is realized in the here and now; we confer meaning
around the year 2000, not in 800 or 500 BCE. This may seem
obvious, but it needs to be stated clearly. The effect of bestowing meaning on one's own readings and interpretations has
hardly, if at all, been taken into account by established Bible
scholarship (the so-called historical-critical school), which assumes its own attitude to be self-evident. This approach sets out
to "understand the Bible texts within the framework of their
own time," according to the slogan characteristic of these scholars. This attitude conveys a totally different message: the text
comes from far away, dates from a long time ago, and is rooted
in a radically different culture. Thus, there is a three-fold alienation which has discouraged many Bible readers, students of
theology, and future preachers.

It is true that the text of the Bible comes from the Near
East, that it is almost 2000 to 3000 years old, and that it originated in a culture which differed greatly from ours, both mate-
rially and spiritually. These differences should not be underesti-
mated; yet these distances are only half-truths, and if you treat
them as unshakeable axioms they will quietly turn into lies and
optical illusions. There is a greater, more important truth,
which is that these texts are well-written. If they are then so
fortunate as to meet a good listener, they will come into their
own without having to be pushed into the compartments "far
away," "long ago" and "very different." As products of a deliberate and meticulous designing intelligence they have been
crafted to speak for themselves, provided there is a competent
reader listening closely. They are, after some training on our
part, extremely able to reveal and explain themselves.

The living text

The text being read is the living text. The writer has been dead for centuries, as have been his audience and the society which formed the original environment (the context) for this literary production. Whether an oracle or a story of war, a Gospel or a lamentation, from the moment it entered the world and was distributed—"published" is too modern a notion—the Bible text started on the long and irreversible journey away from its origin. The very same holds for texts in general, and for you and me: once we are born, the umbilical cord is cut and the journey through time, space and culture commences, which is our life—away from the cradle, the year of our birth and the social context in which we started.

It is only natural that the Bible text should have quickly freed itself from its origin. The current rather infelicitous phrase is that the text has been *decontextualized:* maker, audience and context have long been lost. Of course, the writers knew that this was to be the fate of their stories, laws and poems—assuming for the moment that they were not born yesterday. Reading the Bible "within the setting of its own time?" A lofty goal, but in the first place this is a perilous enterprise since the setting is not there any more—it was lost about two thousand years ago. Secondly, it is hardly a viable undertaking, as we are not Israelites. The publication of a text implies that its umbilical cord is cut; from then on, it is on its own. Now, good texts can indeed manage alone, as from the beginning they have been designed to outlive their birth and original context by a long way. The writer knows that he cannot always accompany his text to provide explanations, clear up misunderstandings etc. He has to let go of his product completely; he should leave it to his poem or story to take care of itself on its own. So he decides to provide his text with the devices, signals and shapes with which it can withstand the onslaught of time and guide the reading activities of the loyal listener.

Left to its own devices by the maker, the text goes in search of a competent reader. Once it appears, the text travels through constantly changing times and contexts, always meeting new audiences and always subject to new and different views. As there are always new readers with ever different intellectual capacities, the meanings which they confer on the text constantly change, too. In this way you might even say that a text does not remain the same throughout the ages but, being a living (i.e. read) text, itself also constantly changes. It acquires an ever-growing history and ever-richer contents. Some texts die, by getting lost. Again, the similarity between text and human being is strong: we, too, make that journey. We are the same as ten or thirty years ago, and at the same time different. We have accumulated experience, which has enriched us—unless, being trapped in grief or bitterness, we consider ourselves impoverished.

The art of reading

The maker has written his text with the express intention of being outlived by it. Therefore, we, for our part, should not lock the Bible's stories and poems within the horizon and context of their origin. This is an artificial and one-sided approach, a reduction. It would be interesting to know more about the writer, his purpose (if different from publishing the exact text that we have from him now) and his circumstances, but none of this is actually essential.

What is essential? That which the text itself provides, the world it evokes and the values it embodies, and then, the confrontation, the interplay, the friction and sometimes the clash between all this and the reader's world and values. This book's motto, a quote from the philosopher Ricœur, means, translated literally: "it is the power of things said that moves the writer." And just as the maker of the text has been gripped and driven by the idea he wished to put into words, his readers may be driven and gripped by the same thing. The writer has been directly inspired by "things said," and the fact that he published his text proves that he was satisfied with the way he has rendered and shaped them. If we have sufficient training in the rules and structures embodied in his work, in turn we too can relate directly to what was said, on the basis of the power and instructions within the medium of the text form.

Under the scrutiny of the good reader, the world evoked by the text arises every time. It is a world in words which appears before our mind's eye, and a world which is evoked in our present. Contact and commitment precede the rational consideration that the biblical text has originated at a triple distance. They also precede the approach which attempts to read a story or poem as an early Christian or Israelite would have done, 19 or 26 centuries ago. The resolve to project oneself into a person from that distant past is a noble one, but it does not get us anywhere compared to the power of what is said and the here-and-now of our contact with the text. The text only lives in and through the process of acquiring meaning.

The use of the word *sense* in English shows an ambiguity which aptly illustrates the reader–text relation. You can say: this text (or this explanation) makes sense (= offers a good explanation) as well as: we try to make sense of this text (we try to find an explanation, i.e. to understand this text). The ambiguity is telling: meaning originates on both sides. There is a fusion of a speaking subject (the text) and a listening subject conferring meaning (the reader) which is hard to fathom or describe. The meaning of the biblical text emerges from a dialog, which is located in the field of intersubjectivity, as hermeneutics (the science of interpretation) would have it.

We can also show the productive contribution of the reader as subject from another side. When we open a book, we are no longer neutral or objective. At that very moment, we have already expressed a *value judgment,* which is simply that we assume or expect to find something useful in that book. Opening a book is an action based on a choice; it is an action preceded by a decision. Next, a reading takes place, and that process of bestowing meaning will be the more successful, the more talent, education and sensitivity we are able to contribute and make subservient to our contact with the text.

We, as readers, need not be ashamed of our subjectivity, since the text cannot come to life through any other channel. This does not mean that we are at liberty to do anything we want to the text and subject it to the wildest speculations. We may do that, but we will then disqualify ourselves right away as interpreters; we would be indulging ourselves at the cost of the text. If we want to be good readers, we will be busy preserving a balance while reading, by constantly being aware of our own contribution and our propensity to read things into the text, slant the text, overemphasize specific meanings, and allow ourselves to be led by our imagination. Good readers control their subjectivity: they do not deny it and know they need not be ashamed of it; on the contrary, they are able to employ it in a disciplined way for the good of the text.

Whoever says the Bible is old, remote and strange pushes the text too far away and as a result ends up with a formidable problem, namely whether the Bible "can still mean something for modern man." This, however, is a problem that people have created themselves by way of the three-fold alienation; it is unsolvable because it is a phantom problem. In reality, the Bible is very close—we have opened it, and already have expectations or assumptions about the values stored or presented in it—and its meaning takes shape thanks to our mental activity and the imagination we bring to the text. It is our own commitment that creates the field of intersubjectivity. After that, the question about the "relevance" of the Bible has largely become spurious.

Component I: language

Both sides of "meaning"—the reader who bestows it, and the text which "has" it—are reflected in the two questions which form the starting point for a sensible reading, and which are characteristic of a *natural attitude* towards any authoritative text. The first question we ask of a Bible text (and a lot of other valuable texts) is: what is it saying? What exactly is it telling me? The question which accompanies this one is also a sign of a positive attitude, one of trust: May I assume there's a message in its structure? This indicates a mentality which strongly differs from the anxious striving for objectivity, the fear of making mistakes and the fear of criticism from colleagues which has marked and constrained some scholars. Then there are the questions which should receive less attention, and a lower place in the order, carrying as they do an undertone of suspicion and a barely disguised longing for certainty: where does it come from? What was the writer's intention? Has it by any chance been put together from diverse materials? Which situation is it addressing? These questions have been persistently asked during the last two centuries, and they are legitimate enough, but they were asked by Bible scholars who had no idea of the unique mode of being of the literary text, and who never got around to training themselves in the conventions and rules of the texts themselves.

I will go back to the first question, and give it a slightly different emphasis: *what* is the text saying? In the approach and method of reading proposed by this book, this question is answered by way of an apparent detour, by asking: *how* is it saying it? This shift of focus towards the "how" is an important characteristic of this guide. During our meeting with the widow, her distress and the never-ending stream of oil from her little jug, we were constantly pinpointing and testing formal and stylistic devices, and seemingly avoiding the question about the contents. Why is this shift from the *what* to the *how* necessary?

There are three important reasons, two negative and one positive, why it is sensible and productive always to ask the same question about every story or poem, inside and outside the Bible: how exactly has it been constructed? The negative reasons dissuade us from giving a direct answer to the question: what does it say? Anyone who tries is confronted with two lethal pitfalls. In our spontaneity, in our desire to know, or because of our need for certainty, we constantly run the risk— whether during our first or our thirtieth reading of the story— of thinking: I've got it! So this is what the story is about! In our naivety we fancy we have recognized what the text says, but what took place inside us is rather something like: we picked up a number of signals from the text and in our minds grouped these into a theme or point, without keeping an open mind for various signals not yet perceived. In this way, we have formed a picture of the whole which tends to become fixed. Such a reading, however, is only partial. The theme or point that we think we have seen the first few times we read the story, threatens to harden and petrify, and then to control and above all limit all our later readings. We often inflict the same fatal process of partial observation and premature interpretation on our fellow human beings.

Moreover, right from the start we are unconsciously subject to the influence of our expectations, prejudices and religious beliefs—a series of temptations which together make up pitfall no. 2. A lot of Bible exegesis is little more than a confirmation of the writer's long-established convictions. With some twisting and pushing our loquacious mind usually manages to fit the text to our pre-formed mental patterns or even unconscious desires, and then maintain with the best of intentions that our ideas are straight out of the Holy Scriptures.

How can we avoid these pitfalls, then? Much is already gained if readers are willing to subject themselves to regular checks, and ask questions such as: what is the subject of my secret fascination? Which conceptions do I have about God, human beings and the world, which guide me and limit me in my contact with this specific text? Has my reading fallen victim to such and such particular hobbyhorses of mine? Even more is gained when one learns (a) to consciously destroy the image one has formed of a person or text, and start again from scratch, so that one can (b) adopt the attitude of a complete beginner, and become fresh and unspoilt again. In short, our basic attitude is of primary importance: it can guide us, stimulate us, limit us and paralyze us, and positively or negatively it determines the process of bestowing meaning on the text.

It is not easy always to be creative and alert, and reveal or identify one's own preferences; even with very open people it goes wrong often enough. Fortunately, we get some support in our aim to remain fresh and self-critical. This support comes from what I called the third reason why we should ask about the *how* rather than the *what*. This positive reason is the essential fact that the stories in the Bible are products of literary design, right down to the smallest detail, and usually very subtle, too. Related to this is the essential requirement that they should be taken completely seriously in their literary mode of being. It is a requirement which indicates what the reader's task is, and again proves that the meaning of the story originates only from the dialogue between ourselves and the text.

Language as art

Literary design implies that the writer has learnt how to handle his material, and is adept at exploiting all its possibilities. Where the visual artist works with paint, clay, or bronze, and as a craftsman penetrates deeply into the secrets of his materials, the writer uses language. It is a good starting point for us as readers to realize that whatever a text does, it does through language. All meanings or contents in the Bible which are conceivable or could be even remotely relevant can only exist by means of language; they have been created in language or are evoked by language. Good readers will, in a way, follow in the writer's footsteps by loving language and handling it creatively. They like to fit jigsaw pieces together when reading, and to pinpoint how in the little piece about the woman with her jug of oil the polarities of life and death, debt and repayment, widow and prophet, reporting and direct speech manifest themselves as specific language signs.

The Bible reader who is dependent on a translation will lose sight of some details. This is a pity, but not fatal. In a book which by definition has to leave Hebrew and Greek aside, I cannot demonstrate the sophisticated word plays and phonetic patterns regularly used by the narrator to underline his points. I cannot appeal to the effects of rhyme and alliteration, and some word repetition disappears in a translation as well. This means that I will have to leave out almost all references to the style in the original. It cannot be helped; at levels above that of phonemes and word formation there will still be enough linguistic material to observe for us to remain in the narrator's tracks. In a translation we can still observe how sentences are grouped, who is allowed to speak when, how the narrator presents his subject matter, what is the valuable object which the hero is after, what makes the characters tick, whether the events are dynamic enough, which reversals take place, etc.

In this book I try to trace which rules and conventions guided the writer and can be pinpointed by us in the text as they are embodied in the text itself. The aim is to understand the stories from "within," after all, they have been designed to convey their message under their own steam. When we learn more and more about how a story has been constructed and by what means, and learn to understand what the purpose is behind all those techniques and structures, we will have penetrated deeply into the meaning and values of the text.

In this process, form cannot be separated from content. Every element of language is part of a system of signs, and is either itself a carrier of meaning—the most obvious example being the word—or it is for example a structural element (for instance the rules for sentence structure) and in this way also contributes to the shaping of meaning. Conversely, all content which the writer may possibly have wanted to include in his story and convey to his audience can only be conceived of, and can only exist, by virtue of the forms of language, style and structure which he selected for it. Thanks to the mastery of style and composition to which the beginning of 2 Kings 4 bears witness, the simple word "dead" links up with "live" at the end of the story, and obliquely acquires contact with the distress of the widow, and the slavery threatening her boys. It occupies the stylistic device of the "frame," and hence also contributes to the delineation of the literary unit, and marks the conclusion of the whole, given in the dual concept of problem and solution. In short, it functions on various levels at once. There is no form without content, and no content without (being carried or indicated by) form.

David's talent for metaphor

The power of language may be illustrated by a short exercise with 1 Samuel 17, the long story of David and Goliath. Everyone knows what happens there. Two armies face each other, ready for battle, and the armored giant Goliath, the Philistines' trump card, is standing in the middle, blustering. The young shepherd David is the hero, and his aim is clear: to gain the victory by immobilizing the champion fighter who has been mocking and taunting King Saul's ranks for 40 days—a round and holy number which symbolizes the total humiliation of Israel. If, however, we take the language really seriously, and the forms of organization in which the writer presents his material, there is a lot more going on, and some important things happen which far outclass the scenes in a B-movie.

I will start with a simple quantitative observation. It takes almost half a page for David to appear and prepare himself for action. He comes from another part of the country, and is disqualified as a hero by his introduction in vv. 12-15: he is much too young; his father Jesse has only sent his three eldest sons to the front; the youngest (number eight in line) is not up to that by a long way. He merely has to take his brothers some provisions (vv. 17-19). The camera registers his arrival from v. 20; from that moment we again view the battlefield, but this time mainly through the eyes of the young man, vv. 22-27. His eldest brother snaps at him (v. 28)—another indication that David does not belong to the category of able-bodied men. And when David reports to Saul and tells him he wants to enter the arena against the Philistine, the writer also has the king speak words of disqualification, v. 33:

> But Saul said to David: "You cannot go to that Philistine and fight him; you are only a boy, and he has been a warrior from his youth!"

This sounds sensible; moreover, it is well-meant. The speech has been rather subtly constructed by profitably exploiting both aspects of "youth." Saul uses it in a positive sense with reference to Goliath as a professional soldier, and negatively with reference to David. But Saul does not know what the reader has been told in the first half of the previous chapter (1 Samuel 16), which is that this young man has been anointed by the prophet Samuel and is destined to become the new king. So we follow this exchange critically, and detect some irony: here speaks the present king, who is doomed, and he is trying to keep God's candidate from what will be his biggest success, the humiliating defeat of Goliath!

David hardly needs our help, as he is quite capable of defending himself through language. His answer leaves Saul little choice than to tell David in his own way to go ahead. David's speech is long—a decision on the writer's part which is already suggestive—and has a special status. It is a story within the story and, unlike a regular story, does not describe one unique event, but recurrent incidents and habits: David tells the king about his practice as a shepherd.

> David replied to Saul: "Your servant has been tending his father's sheep, and if a lion or a bear came and carried off an animal from the flock, I would go after it and fight it and rescue it from its

mouth. And if it attacked me, I would seize it by the beard and strike it down and kill it.

Your servant has killed both lion and bear; and that uncircumcised Philistine shall end up like one of them, for he has defied the ranks of the living God. The Lord," David went on, "who saved me from lion and bear will also save me from that Philistine."

The main point about this mini-story (vv. 34-37) with its verb forms denoting repetition in the past is that its message forges a metaphoric link with the situation around Saul and David: the battlefield and the challenger who in everyone's eyes is invincible. There is only one person who has a different view, and he is working on his qualification as a hero through a speech full of self-confidence.

The following paragraph (vv. 38-39) is another one of good intentions not working out. David is allowed to try on the king's own armor, but it's no good. Of course not, the reader who has some sense of irony and symbolism thinks, why would the doomed man's cuirass fit the chosen one? A little later, Goliath sees a young man wearing shepherd's gear coming towards him. We can imagine his surprise, so the writer does not waste time telling us that. We do get his words, and again the writer employs two levels of knowledge. What we, listening together with Saul, have heard David say about wild beasts, Goliath does not know about. Without the faintest notion that even as he speaks them his words undergo a radical change in meaning, he calls out to David (vv. 43-44):

"Am I a dog, that you come against me with sticks?" The Philistine cursed David by his gods; and the Philistine said to David, "Come here and I will give your flesh to the birds of the sky and the beasts of the field."

Goliath thinks he is asking a rhetorical question to which everyone knows the answer: of course he is not a dog. David and his audience (Saul and we readers) know better. We take this question seriously and discover: yes, Goliath is a dog. If only he knew he is now facing someone with experience in eliminating lions or bears!

The contrast between the two camps, Israel against the Philistines, with which the story started, lies at the level of the writer's material; it is no more than subject matter. A much more important opposition has materialized in the meantime, one containing a paradox. Whilst the soldiers of both camps are after each other's blood and no one thinks he has anything in common with the other side, all those present on the battlefield are linked by a single ideology: the vulgar faith in weapons. The Master of Ceremonies for both camps is the champion in the middle, who by showing off his mighty armor embodies this conviction and drives it home to everyone watching. The writer has reserved no fewer than eight lines in the exposition for the famous weapon inventory: vv. 4-7. But then, the real opposition rises up in the middle of the chapter—an opposition of one against the rest. David is an exception, as he does not subscribe to the general ideology.

Whereas the Israelites let themselves be intimidated by the appearance of the giant and embrace the faith in weapons as ardently as their enemies do, David stands apart thanks to a metaphoric view of reality, whose origin he will later reveal personally by showing himself once again to be a master of language. David keeps his cool, and sees in the arena something totally different from what everyone else sees: a wild animal. This creative vision has far-reaching consequences. He eliminates the champion with a shepherd's practiced shot: with sling and stone.

We have all been brought up on the idea that Goliath was hit in the forehead. This, however, is unlikely. In the first place, it is strange that he does not collapse, or fall backwards as a result of the impact of the projectile. He falls face down on the ground. This not only means a physical fall, but at the same time, in a symbolic and religious sense, a prostration: without realizing it, he now worships the God of his opponent. Moreover, from the reliefs of Ramses III of Egypt we know that in the eleventh century BCE the Philistines wore sturdy helmets which certainly covered their foreheads. Finally, there is a point of language. In v. 49 we read that the stone that comes whizzing from David's sling "penetrates [Goliath's] *mitschô.*" This Hebrew word actually means "front" and thus is less specific than "forehead." Now, the same word has been used earlier in the story, in the plural form (*mitschôt*), and appears, of all places, in the weapon inventory. From time immemorial this has been translated correctly by "shin-guards" or "greaves." For v. 49 no other meaning is necessary at all!

What exactly happened? Twenty years ago, a spectacular theory about this has been published by a writer who died young, on behalf of her father, an American rabbi; it is time this became more widely known. David slings the stone right above the shin guard into the knee joint of Goliath's armor. As a result, this part of the armor is locked, so that the warrior is suddenly unable to bend his leg. This proves fatal, as according to v. 48 he has just started moving. Walking towards David with clumsy tread, he is hit, and hampered by the knee joint which will not hinge anymore, he has a nasty fall—on his face, as a natural consequence of his own movement. The correct translation of v. 49 would be that David "put his hand into the bag; he took out a stone and slung it; it struck the Philistine in the greave. The stone penetrated above the greave, and he fell face down on the ground."

This version offers a brilliant advantage, as Goliath now proves to have been incapacitated at the exact spot where his strength is situated—remember the weapon catalog and its length! A formidable irony at the expense of this colossus. What seemed to render him invincible has now proven fatal to him. His advantage, the massive armor, has turned against him thanks to David's cool eye and steady hand. The result of what can hardly be termed a fight has by this reading been given a point that is much more precise, much more compelling, and, as we shall see, much more in line with the theme presented by David the orator.

The narrator continues the irony: Goliath now lies on the ground powerless, sprawling under the weight of his own armor, and is then decapitated by his own sword: David has come running and has quickly seized it, v. 51. Goliath's knee in the literature of Old Israel is what in Greek literature is Achilles' heel, his only weak spot, and in the German *Nibelungen* epic the small spot on the hero Siegfried's back.

David saw something different than everyone else, because he looked with metaphoric creativity. He saw Goliath as a wild animal, so that the warrior's fate became that of a wild animal, struck down by an experienced shepherd. And yet, all this happens within the language: first, David gives his mini-story about sheep and mauling animals; next, Goliath unwittingly links up with this through his words about dog, birds and wild beasts. The metaphoric creativity is a product of linguistic creativity. David's language provides a re-description of reality, which makes reality itself different: no longer threatening, and manageable.

The use of metaphorical language goes even further, as we are now also able to transform the sheep. In the same way as the flock was saved thanks to the shepherd's intervention, Israel and its hosts are saved by the performance of the one person who did not let his imagination be paralyzed by the macho behavior of the other side. Thus, David has qualified as a shepherd on a higher level as well: he is called to look after his people.

That is not all, because David in the meantime has passed another test as master of language. The writer opts for David giving his most fundamental speech in vv. 45-47, i.e. before the duel can get under way. Again, David qualifies as an orator; he chooses the armored colossus as his audience for the self-confident words with which he announces Goliath's demise. Ironically, Goliath receives the dubious honor of being the first recipient of David's secret: the revelation of the source of David's metaphoric vision. And his birds and animals are taken from him by David:

> David replied to the Philistine: "You come against me with sword and spear and javelin; but I come against you in the name of the Lord of Hosts, the God of the ranks of Israel, whom you have defied. This very day the Lord will deliver you into my hands. I will kill you and cut off your head; and I will give the carcasses of the Philistine camp to the birds of the sky and the beasts of the earth. All the earth shall know that there is a God in Israel. And this whole assembly shall know that the Lord can give victory without sword or spear. For the battle is the Lord's, and He will deliver you into our hands."

Thus, the writer makes David the character who in everyone's hearing, including the readers', is allowed to give a fundamental lecture in counter-ideology. David enlightens everyone, even before the ultimate act. The duo "sword and spear" is contrasted with the seemingly ridiculous duo "sling and stone," and this *skandalon* (to use a New Testament word which has everything to do with powerlessness) gets at the real point: apparent power has been destroyed by apparent powerlessness. Twice, David's speech results in true knowledge, and it is there for everyone who wants to listen. In this way, a character within the story has been allocated the task of formulating a profound message at an early stage, before the readers can work out their own. So, David's words are a kind of self-explanation of the story; the power of language has, as it were, been raised to a higher power in David's two decisive speeches, the one about his flock, directed at the king, and the one about the true and invisible liberator, directed at Goliath: "the LORD of Hosts" (as both a modern translation and the King James Bible put it). Thus, the power of language respectfully points to the power behind the scenes as its source.

Component II: time

Language bears an essential relation to time, as the words follow each other. Whether we are speaking or listening, writing or reading, words can never sound simultaneously. Narrators have learned to make the most of the consequences. A good narrator will manage to transform the limits imposed by time into opportunities and advantages.

The nature of its raw material, language, makes literature a time-bound art. Narrative art even turns this into a matter of principle. A story contains so many intimate and intricate relations with time that we should start by distinguishing at least three kinds of time, if we want to avoid total confusion. After this analytical stage there follows the final test, a form of synthesis which focuses on the question of whether we are able to handle and connect these various forms of time, and can make them function in a literary and artistic way.

I will start with the distinctions. A story is itself a finite chain of language signs and takes time: this is narration time or discourse time. You could measure this form of time with a clock, but this would not be very useful as people differ somewhat in the time they need to read or recite a story. Hence it is convenient to express the length of narration time in the number of words. A simple example: the Hebrew text of the creation story (i.e., up to Gen. 2:4a) contains 474 words which cover the very first working week.

This takes us to the second type or form, narrated time. This is the time or period covered by the text, and within which the events take place which are thought to be worth relating: the time *within* the story. The very first story of the Bible is an exceptional case where we can pinpoint the narrated time exactly: the week that is mentioned. Moreover, every paragraph covers one day. We also find a simple fourfold example in the New Testament: the gospel is the story of Jesus' life, the duration of that life is roughly the narrated time. Viewed a little more closely, Luke starts half a year earlier, as for his starting point he chooses the announcement of the birth of Jesus' precursor, John.

The narrator is not obliged to provide indications of narrated time, but he is quite capable of it. Whenever we hear this kind of information it is always important. In Judges 19 we are told explicitly that the Levite hangs around in Bethlehem for four days and a half, and what happens after that is described practically hour by hour, with the setting of the sun as an important point of reference. When the terrible night of Gibeah has ended, the narrator is equally clear about its opposite, the dawn. The story of Jacob's birth is carefully marked off by two measures: when Isaac marries he is 40 years old, 60 when he becomes a father. Sometimes we have to do some arithmetic: when someone goes from A to B, on foot or riding a donkey, we can estimate the traveling time by consulting an atlas.

The third type of time is not always relevant, but we cannot be sure of that beforehand. This is the actual sequence of the narrated events. Usually, the narrator reports most events in the order in which they occurred, thus respecting chronology and its linear axis. Yet even in such an early form as Hebrew narrative art it does occasionally happen that the writer deliberately abandons this type of sequence. He has two options: looking forward, or looking back.

The former option is less frequently used, as it usually does not contribute to dramatic tension. If it does occur, the writer has pressing reasons. For instance, I will discuss below the

striking case of 2 Sam. 17:14 where the writer deems it necessary to reveal to us from behind the scenes what God has decided about Absalom's revolt; weeks (i.e. of narrated time) before the prince is defeated we already hear that he is going to
lose. As the battle between the troops of the expelled king and
his son's army is reported in ch. 18, that text would seem the
natural place to reveal that God himself had influenced the outcome. "Natural" here means: in conformity with the chronology of the revolt itself and its development.

The other possibility for escaping from the chronology is
regularly employed, albeit seldom to any great extent. This is a
technique which every film and video watcher knows as the
flashback: looking back in time. We see or hear the story of
character X who is 20 or 60 years old, and suddenly on page N
the "normal" course of the action is interrupted because the
writer or director wants to tell us what happened 10 or 200
years earlier in the family, village, etc. Obviously, such a flashback is always there for a purpose, but one often forgets to ask
the slightly trickier question of why it should occur exactly
here, on page N, and how its meaning is related to the adjoin-
ing pages. Certainly, this is a question of temporal dynamics,
but often the answer is also revealing as to thematic structure.

Saul's long last hours

Here I will mention one example of disturbance of the chronological order; this is at the same time the most spectacular example of anticipation (prolepsis) which I know in the Old Testament, and an extensive one at that. The entire chapter, 1
Samuel 28 (which strictly speaking starts at v. 3), is such an intervention. It is about Saul's last night, just before he himself,
three of his sons, and thousands of his soldiers will be slaugh-
tered by the Philistines. What strikes us immediately is the fact
that the writer has separated Saul's last night from his last day,
although these periods form a natural unit (a 24-hour day).
Saul's last day is not described until ch. 31, two units later than
one would expect.

During his last night the desperate and exhausted king visits
a medium in order to get some idea of his fate. He does manage

to make contact with the prophet Samuel, who from the other side of the grave implacably persists in condemning Saul. The prophet repeats that by failing to destroy the Amalekites (see 1 Samuel 15) Saul has not obeyed God's instructions, and announces "Tomorrow you will be with me." Saul understands that his last hour has struck and, devastated, falls to the ground.

When we then read the chapters surrounding this story, i.e. chs. 27 and 29, we notice that these are two tightly connected stories about David. David is here concerned with his problems as a vassal of the Philistines, the very power about to destroy Saul. Why then has this closely knit pair been separated by wedging in ch. 28 between them? What happens to David and the Philistines in ch. 29 takes place a few days before the night of ch. 28, which is why 28 is a prolepsis. In 29 the Philistines have only reached their meeting point near the coast, and they still have to march to the eastern part of the plain of Jezreel. When two days later they pitch their tents there, these are observed with terror from the northernmost slope of the mountains of Ephraim: Saul has arrived there on the low table mountain Gilboa. Saul's observation is reported in 28:5, whereas in ch. 29 the Philistines have only reached Aphek, in the coastal plain.

The same process is repeated around ch. 31. Why has the story of Saul's death not been linked to that of his last night, but been wedged in between the stories about someone else? It is placed between ch. 30 and 2 Sam. 1:1-16, which also form a distinct pair by placing David opposite Amalekites. The beginnings of an answer become visible when we make a diagram. From 1 Samuel 27 we count six narrative units, four of which are devoted to David who in the South-West is waging war against a band of Amalekites, and two to Saul who about 70 miles to the north is battling against the Philistines; they make up two groups of three:

This is a remarkable arrangement, and the creative reader tries to detect the reason behind it. The figure of two triangles results from the radical decision to separate (*disjunction*) three pairs which are naturally linked: 27 + 29 belong together as they present David as the vassal of the Philistine king Achish; 30 and 2 Samuel 1 belong together because David first defeats and kills a group of Amalekites, and a few days later executes a single Amalekite who has told him a mixture of truth and lies about Saul's death. It is curious how Saul and David are each on the war path, but separated in space, and that both of them become entangled with neighboring tribes with a nasty reputation in Israel and with which the other has had difficulties earlier.

The meaning of all this will only become clear to us as advanced readers if we are willing to do some homework and check the explicit indications of time which the writer has scattered through this sequence of six stories. I will skip the details for the moment and come straight to the fascinating result. Combination and deduction yield the outcome that David defeats the band of Amalekites in ch. 30 on the very same day that Saul, three days' march away, engages in battle with the Philistines and is defeated. The underlying time scheme results in a concurrence (*synchronism*) which conveys its own message: the victory by the chosen David coincides with the defeat of the rejected Saul. The separations (disjunctions) which the writer inserted in three pairs of stories provide him with the conjunction he needs for his theme: these stories are now side by side as chs. 30 and 31! The meaning of this is that the story of David's victory now borders on the story of Saul's fall. They should be adjacent, as they occur simultaneously.

Saul is defeated by that very enemy who formally is a friend of David's but yet does not mar David's reputation. David defeats that very enemy, the Amalekites, in battle against whom Saul met his final rejection by God. The synchronism shows conclusively that the conjunction in time is also a conjunction of theme, a conjunction of Providence. It vividly paints how the ascending line of David and the descending line of Saul are inextricably linked and coincide at one point in time.

Narration time versus narrated time

Time is an ingredient at every moment in the story. Every sentence in the story takes time (narration time), every sentence has some relation or other to the narrated time, and then there is the constantly shifting relation between discourse time (narration time) and narrated time. It is almost always worthwhile paying attention to the relation between these two forms of time, as this may indicate what is really important.

The narrator can simulate keeping in line with narrated time, so that the ratio between narration time and narrated time seems to be one to one. He creates this illusion mainly with speeches. When the writer has David speak to Saul, or character A to character B, this almost always takes the form of direct speech. In this way, the suggestion is that the characters are quoted literally, and these seemingly accurate words usually sound so natural that we tend to believe that this speech was probably spoken in "historical" reality just as it is given in the text. An attractive illusion.

In the information from the writer himself, the so-called narrator's text, the ratio between discourse time and narrated time is rarely one to one. Moreover, this relation usually shifts very quickly. The narrator is constantly manipulating the narrated time, stretching it, condensing it (for instance by summarizing), and then suddenly he will skip an episode. Sometimes the interplay of discourse time and narrated time is halted. This happens when the writer addresses us directly with information, comments and explanations. All the time he is drawing up an inventory of Goliath's equipment, there is no progress in the action; "the story is not moving." During the weapon show narrated time stands still.

In 1 Samuel 27 we hear that the refugee David enters the service of King Achish, and that as a vassal he is given a small town called Ziklag as his residence and home base. Then in v. 6 the writer notes: "that is how Ziklag came to belong to the kings of Judah, as is the case to this day." This sort of information does not form part of the action; again the clock of narrated time has been stopped for a moment, and thus the discourse time/narrated time ratio has been momentarily paralyzed. Is this piece of information an interesting historiographical tidbit? On the contrary, more likely a joke on the writer's part! Is there anyone on earth who could fix a day and year for "this day?" The writer here breaks with the detached position implied in the act of narrating, by breaking the time frame of what is narrated: suddenly and rather brusquely he draws a line between the distant past, the time of David, and "this day" of... whom, exactly? Our first suggestion would be: his own present, and the present of his first audience. But like all his colleagues he does not reveal when and where he lives, and the present of "this day" moves further along every day. Moreover, the writer knows that his first audience is just as mortal as he himself and will be continually replaced by new readers...

In these separate and easily recognizable sentences, where the narrator does not follow events but provides information and explanations, we have a kind of direct contact with him. We become conscious of his voice and his part in the whole. Usually, however, the writer hides behind the stream of the action and is eminently capable of creating the impression that events tell themselves. In that standard situation, discourse time and narrated time are in a state of permanent interplay, competition and friction. I will conclude this chapter with an example of this, which also shows the importance of a correct understanding of time.

The hundred years of Abraham

In the narrative cycle devoted to the first patriarch, roughly Genesis 12–25, the round figure "100" is handled in such a way as to provide us with a grip on both discourse time and narrated time. The actual story in Genesis 12 does not show a young man or a child as a future hero, but introduces Abram (as his name is until Genesis 17) when he is already 75 years old! Then in 25:7 we read that at his death he was 175 years old. These two figures indicate that the narrated time covers exactly 100 years. This might be a coincidence, were it not for the fact that this cycle devotes a lot of attention to aspects of time.

This cycle of stories is structured by means of 13 explicit designations of time scattered over the various narrative units, in 12 verses. The exceptional aspect of this string is that it consists of exact specifications of age, mainly pertaining to the hero and his wife. For the benefit of those interested I will give the references here, with my apologies for the dull figures: Gen. 12:4; 16:3 and 16; 17:1, 17, 24, 25; 21:5; 23:1; 25:7, with at the beginning and end the ages of father and son (Terah 11:32 and Ishmael 25:17). The middle of a string of 13 items is the seventh, and this position proves indeed to be a pivotal and meaningful center. The writer has indicated this through various linguistic and stylistic signals. The verse in question is 17:17 which immediately stands out by containing *two* indications of age, for both husband and wife, and which is moreover a true poetic line of two half verses, spoken by the harassed and incredulous patriarch in answer to the announcement by God that he, an old man already, will yet have a child:

> Can a child be born to a man a hundred years old,
> or can Sarah bear a child at ninety?

Jews and Christians tend to adopt a rather one-sided view of this patriarch by concentrating only on his good sides; to them, he is the Founding Father of the faith. To me, the idea of the real Abraham's despair at God's promise of a numerous progeny, in Genesis 15–16, and here in 17 his unbelieving and cynical mirth at the absurd idea that this should yet come to pass, is much more engaging. I defend Abraham as the Founder of understandable and recognizable disbelief.

The number 100 not only governs narrated, but also discourse time. The composition of Genesis 12–25 contains an extensive middle section (five chapters, in fact eight literary units) which is devoted to Abraham's 100th year. It opens with two announcements from the deity: Isaac's birth, plus the destruction of Sodom and Gomorrah, Genesis 18. This conjunction of individual life and collective death is realized in reverse order: the cities and their region are destroyed in Genesis 19, Isaac is born in 21.

This broad center is well marked through a combination of designations of age and other temporal indications. Its boundaries are carefully delineated. Here is the remarkable border line at the beginning of the complex:

16:16 Abram was eighty-six years old when Hagar bore Ishmael to Abram.
17:1 When Abram was ninety-nine years old, the Lord appeared to Abram.

Here we have the last verse of ch. 16 and the first of 17. They are right next to each other, in a seemingly harsh juxtaposition, as if the numbers are about to clash. Here, at a stroke 13 years of Abram's life have been boldly skipped. A long period of narrated time is covered by zero discourse time! This daring hiatus, however, is no testimony of incompetence. It functions as the first demarcation of the central panel of life and death.

Exactly because of its disbelief, thinly disguised mockery and despair, the one-verse poem spoken by Abram in the middle of ch. 17 lends extra power and depth to the miracle of the coming child. After Isaac has been born (21:1-7, at the end of Abraham's hundredth year) and the neighboring Philistine king surrenders to Abraham's prestige (vv. 22-33), the last verse of Genesis 21 in turn mentions time:

21:34 And Abraham resided in the land of the Philistines a long time.

In the text that immediately follows, the beginning of Genesis 22, the boy Isaac has already reached the stage where he can carry wood and ask his father awkward questions (22:7)! So, there is also a considerable hiatus of narrated time between chs. 21 and 22; it leads me to believe that this gap has about the same length (in narrated time, in years) as the gap between 16:16 and 17:1. This would make Isaac 13 years old.

What is related next in Genesis 22 is hair-raising. Finally Abraham has a natural (not adopted) son, and now God orders him to sacrifice the child! It is clear that the writer in this way presents and accentuates the theme "progeny by miraculous means" one last time. He does this by way of a paradox, as God's command makes us think: has everything been in vain then?

Thus, a short period of narrated time (only a year in the life of the hero) is covered by a large amount of text, i.e. a lot of discourse time. This reveals much about the theme and purposes of the text. What is more, the shapes of time form the key to the structure of the Abraham cycle. The structure of the composition as a whole can be found in the section 'The next 110 stories' at the back of this book.

Translations

A translation is made for people who cannot read the text in its original language; hence, a translation is a complete and real replacement. I take that very seriously, as this book was written for readers who have no knowledge of Hebrew and Greek. This is a situation in which most native speakers of English find themselves, and in principle there is nothing wrong with it. In order to put myself completely in that position, I have looked at the original text as little as possible and have written this book almost entirely in reference to translations.

Not everyone realizes that a Bible translation is a full and independent text in itself. This applies especially to the advocates of the so-called *idiolect* translations, who have the illusion they can only remain faithful to the Bible if they translate the text in a largely or even extremely Hebraist idiom—which usually means extremely literally. The idiolect aim is based on a sort of optical illusion: the only readers who can appreciate the (apparent) faithfulness of such a rendering are those few who are conversant with the original language, but it is exactly those people who by their knowledge of Hebrew are able to do without a translation, and who realize only too well how much of the sound, style and rhythm cannot be conveyed in any way. People who are dependent on a translation are by definition unable to see, let alone appreciate, in how far an idiolect translation does justice to the original text. There is one exception I know of: a very good rendering which succeeds in sticking remarkably close to the original is Robert Alter's translation of the book of Genesis.

A vast array of new English translations and paraphrases of the Bible are now available. The most readable among the reliable translations would be the following, in chronological order:
(a) In the first place the King James Bible (=the Authorized Version) must be mentioned: an intellectual monument, over 375 years old, which has had an enormous influence

on the development of the English language and which to many people—albeit mainly older churchgoers—is still *the* Bible.

(b) Then there is the influential revision of this translation: the Revised Standard Version (RSV), 1946–1952, now itself updated in the New Revised Standard Version (NRSV) (1989).

(c) The best-selling New International Version (NIV) (1978, revised 1983) is the most popular version in many churches.

(d) Finally, there is the Jewish Publication Society's 1985 translation of the Hebrew Bible. When citing texts from the Bible I have mainly chosen translations from this version, sometimes with minor adaptations; sometimes I have made a translation myself on the spot if this was necessary for my argument.

3

Twelve stories at a glance

The practice area

Before we start thinking about making a plot and pointing to a hero, or about the story as an arena where various points of view engage in combat, we should come to some arrangement about the texts to be used. There are many, and it would be very awkward if during the discussion in chapters 4–10 readers had to leaf frantically through their Bible translations all the time, looking for the examples which I might get from anywhere. Which is why I propose to focus our attention and demarcate a practice area consisting of twelve representative stories. The books of Genesis and Judges provide us with two each, and the books of Samuel and Kings each furnish four. From this series of twelve texts I will draw in the following chapters the examples I will use to clarify and bring to life the rules and insights of narratology. As a result of this strategy, the reader who has read and digested chapters 4–10 will have studied these twelve biblical stories from all angles, and will thus be able to develop an overall picture with some depth.

I will first introduce these twelve stories to the reader by way of short summaries, with here and there some background information, sometimes finishing on a stimulating question. These introductions should however not be taken as substitutes for the texts themselves; your own reading action is of essential importance. I strongly recommend you to start off by reading through (a number of) the selected chapters yourself, and ponder these; in this way, the narrative rules and perceptions that I will present a bit further on, in a reasonably systematic order and constantly illustrated with examples from the practice ring, will be much more meaningful. Your own concentrated reading will enable you to get acquainted with these rules and perceptions at a much deeper level. What is more, the encounter with the biblical narrators will then yield a lot of enjoyment. Enjoyment and fun should not be regarded with suspicion: stories thrive on it and presuppose it, in the sense that every good narrator knows that the art of captivating one's audience is the beginning of wisdom. Only when he captures our attention does he get the chance to teach us specific knowledge and values.

You will find many of these narrative basics and techniques will also come in useful when reading contemporary novels and stories, or when critically watching and analyzing movies. If you have a VCR you can train yourself in narratological technique: by repeatedly playing specific episodes you will understand much better how a producer uses time and space, how and why he[1] makes his characters appear and disappear, and what methods and tricks he uses to make his themes register with the viewer. Movie-making is, after all, another way of telling a story along the line of the linear axis of time.

A. Genesis 27-28:9, *Rebekah and Jacob deceive Isaac and Esau*

The story. Isaac is old and wants to give his firstborn Esau his blessing. Rebekah overhears this and conspires with Jacob, whom she disguises. Jacob receives the blessing and leaves for Haran in Mesopotamia in order to find himself a kinswoman; Esau loses.

Context. This is the penultimate section in episode I of the Jacob stories. These started in 25:19-28/29-34 with two short stories, about Jacob's birth and his burning ambition to be the first in line. Before the birth of the twins Jacob and Esau, Rebekah received an oracle (a poem, four half-verses, 25:23) with a sting in the tail: "the older shall serve the younger;" this word of God controls the cycle almost as a program. With a bowl of lentil stew Jacob cajoles his brother, coming in famished from the hunt, out of his birthright (Hebrew: *bᵉkora*). Here in 27 it is the blessing that is at stake (Hebrew *bᵉraka*). In 28:10-22 God reveals

---

[1] Or she, if the producer happens to be a woman.

himself in a dream to Jacob on his flight from Canaan, and promises him his support.

Two questions. Is the behavior of mother and favorite son in Genesis 27 justified by the oracle? And who exactly is the hero of the story: Jacob, his mother, or both? Look at the characters' entrances and exits.

B. Genesis 37:12-36, *Joseph in Dothan: sold by his brothers*

Context. Joseph is the favorite son of Jacob, his elderly father, and in vv. 5-10 has prophetic dreams about a royal future; his brothers cannot stand the spoilt brat. The macro-plot of the complete Joseph story, in Genesis 37–50, is to a great extent determined by the text of the dreams. After he has been sold to Egypt, Joseph becomes a slave and has to spend years in prison before he draws the attention of the court and rises to prominence as the interpreter of Pharaoh's dreams. Having become a vizier, he plays on the guilty conscience of his brothers, who have been driven to the Egyptian granaries by famine. Their remorse breaks his harsh manner; he makes himself known to them and sends for his father and all his family, so that they can live in Egypt and survive the famine.

The story. Here in 37:12-36 Joseph is visiting his brothers, who are grazing their sheep way up in the North. They want to kill him, but Reuben and Judah are opposed to this idea. They do get rid of him, however, by selling him to a caravan traveling to Egypt. They lead their father into thinking he has been devoured by a beast.

C. Judges 4, *Deborah and Barak defeat Sisera and his chariots*

The story. The prophetess Deborah appoints Barak as the general whose army, mainly recruited from the tribes in Galilee, is to shake off the Canaanite yoke. The battlefield is the plain of Jezreel, not far from the Tabor. God confuses the enemy, and Sisera flees. Although Barak is chasing him it is the woman Jael who takes in Sisera, lulls him to sleep, and kills him.

Tricky question. Who is the hero or heroine here? One, or two characters, and what is the reason for assigning that role to them?

D. Judges 19, *The outrage in Gibeah, a gang rape*

The story. A Levite travels after his runaway concubine and lets himself be wined and dined by her father in Bethlehem. Traveling back with her, he has to spend the night in a town belonging to the tribe of Benjamin. The local rabble lay siege to the house where he is staying and want to have their pleasure of him. The Levite gives them his concubine to rape, and the next morning finds her body on the threshold. When he gets home, he cuts her body into twelve pieces and sends these to the tribes of Israel.

Questions. Think about the role of time and space on this perhaps blackest page in the Bible. And how has the Levite been characterized?

E. 1 Samuel 9-10:16, *Saul goes after his father's asses: the prophet Samuel instructs him and anoints him king*

The story. The farmer's son Saul is sent out by his father to go and find the asses that have gone astray. After an abortive search Saul goes to consult a seer. This is Samuel, who to Saul's utter astonishment puts him at the head of a cultic feast, instructs him extensively about his future during the night, and anoints him the next day. Samuel makes predictions that come true when Saul returns home. The spirit of God permeates him and gets him into an ecstatic trance. "Is Saul really among the prophets?" the bystanders wonder.

Context. This long and brilliant story forms part of the episode 1 Samuel 8–12, which marks a political turning point in the big complex that covers Joshua through to Kings. This act in five episodes tells us how an era of tribal society ends and how the monarchy is instituted in Israel—a transition to a new constitutional form which is a sensitive issue, if only because God

himself and his prophet Samuel equate the people's request for a
king with idolatry. The five units, chs. 8; 9:1–10:16; 10:17-27;
11:1-13 and 11:14–12:25, have been composed according to the
pattern ABABA. The A-sections (i.e. 8; 10:17ff. and 12) deal
with popular assemblies, where the discussion develops between
the people and the frustrated judge Samuel, who to his dismay is
commanded by his lord to allow a king after all. In the B-
stories, i.e. 9:1–10:16 and 11 (the relief of the town of Jabesh),
we meet the character of Saul who, spurred on by the Spirit, is
off to a good start.

Question. When reading the account of Saul's comings and goings for yourself, try and work out how the various meetings are
engineered; can you distinguish different stages, for instance
taking as a starting point the verbs of movement and their ar-
ticulating function?

F. 1 Samuel 17–18:5, *David overcomes Goliath*

The armies of Israel and the Philistines are facing each other,
and in the middle the awesome warrior Goliath, who for forty
days has been taunting Saul's ranks, occupies the stage. He is a
strapping fellow wearing impenetrable armor. From Bethlehem,
a young shepherd arrives, bringing provisions for his big brothers in the army. This is David, who immediately upon seeing
the giant wants to enter the arena, against the will of the king.
He receives permission, gives a speech about it being not weapons but God who would decide the outcome of the battle, and
eliminates Goliath with sling and stone. David cuts Goliath's
head off with his own sword. Jonathan, the heir to the throne,
has watched in admiration and gives David his tunic and weapons as a token of his recognition.

G. 2 Samuel 3:6-21, *Abner leaves Ishboseth and makes a pact with
David*

The story. Abner is the strong man in the small Trans-Jordanian
state that is all that is left to the house of Saul. A dispute about a
woman causes him to break with king Ishbosheth and he decides to bring the ten tribes under the rule of the king of Judah,

David. David agrees, on one condition: as a symbol of the transaction he wants to have his former wife Michal (one of Saul's daughters) returned to him. And so it happens; the pact is concluded in Hebron, the capital of Judah.

Questions. Do you see any connections between the shifts in fortune that befall Rizpah and Michal? How does David behave towards Michal, when she is handed over?

H. 2 Samuel 24, *Census and plague: David buys a threshing floor*

The story. David has the misguided idea of conducting a census, and will not listen to Joab who tries to dissuade him. God sends the prophet Gad to the king; David has to choose between three punishments: famine, plague or exile. David chooses the plague. When half the country has been struck down by the epidemic and Jerusalem is next in line, God commands the Angel of Death to stop. Meanwhile, David has confessed his guilt and begged for mercy on behalf of his subjects. Acting on a hint by the prophet David buys a threshing floor on mount Zion (the very spot where the Angel had halted) from his subject Araunah, builds an altar there, and makes sacrifices to God. The plague has ended.

I. 1 Kings 1, *Two factions warring over the throne: Solomon succeeds as king*

The story. King David is very old and has so far not done anything about naming a successor. His ambitious son Adonijah cannot wait any longer, and wants to proclaim himself king at a banquet with his supporters. At the last minute, Solomon's faction intervenes through Nathan the prophet and Bathsheba. They use their influence with David, who states on oath that Solomon is to be his successor. This prince is crowned in a great hurry, and when Adonijah's party discover that they have been effectively outdone they fly terrified in all directions. Solomon admonishes Adonijah to keep quiet.

Context. The chs. 1 Kings 1–2 form both the conclusion of the David stories and the opening of Kings. The triangle Nathan–Bathsheba–Solomon, opposite the king, was already present in the stories presenting David's moral fall (his adultery with Bathsheba and the contract killing of her husband Uriah), 2 Samuel 11–12. Solomon is the second child of Bathsheba and David, and has been legitimized by the prophet. Nathan's intervention in favor of Solomon is no big surprise: when the prince was born, he had on God's behalf given him a nickname meaning "beloved by Yahu" (2 Sam. 12:25); this is a hint to the reader that a great future awaits Solomon. Nathan is the important prophet who:

(a) in 2 Samuel 7 pronounces a great oracle of salvation, in which God makes a solemn promise to David that his house will be a lasting dynasty,

(b) but who also sees himself forced in 2 Samuel 12 to pronounce a great oracle of doom, which announces retributions for David's crimes of adultery and murder.

For the overall composition from 2 Samuel through to 1 Kings 2 it is essential to read these three texts (1 Kgs 1, 2 Sam. 7 and 2 Sam. 12) in relation to each other. The positive oracle is largely nullified by the negative oracle, and in 1 Kings 1 the prophet shows himself not above party politics.

J. 1 Kings 13, *The word of God, through true and false prophecies*

Context. After Solomon's death the unified state of Israel is split in two; God legitimizes the schismatic Jeroboam through the prophet Ahijah. His realm will be Israel in the narrow sense, the ten tribes without Judah. Jeroboam establishes his own cult by two golden calves, one in the North and the other at his southern border, in Bethel; God condemns this.

The story. A "man of God" from Judah appears at King Jeroboam's side when he is making sacrifices at Bethel, and speaks a command of God to the altar that causes it to disintegrate. The angry king becomes the victim of a portent (a withered arm) and needs the intercessory prayers of the man from Judah to recover. When the latter starts the journey back home, he is accosted by a colleague (always referred to as "old prophet") from Bethel, who invites him for a meal and even claims to have been instructed to do this by God himself. The Judean gives in; his host then has to pronounce a condemnation of his action, through an oracle of doom. The man from Judah continues his journey and is killed by a lion. The prophet from Bethel, his host, travels to the spot and observes that the lion does not touch the dead man and his ass. He buries the man from Judah in his own grave.

Questions. What is wisdom for the man from Judah, when the colleague addresses him? What is the narrator's attitude towards the two men of God? Do you think the old prophet from Bethel is let off fairly? What, after v. 10, is the "valuable object," and who is looking for it?

K. 2 Kings 2:1-18, *Elisha the great prophet after Elijah's ascension to heaven*

The story. The Elijah–Elisha relationship is one of master and disciple. Now that Elijah's task is finished, Elisha and the guild of prophets know that God will take Elijah away. They set off together on foot for the river Jordan, the disciple not leaving his master's side. Elijah makes the waters part with his mantle, and after they have crossed Elisha asks Elijah for a double portion (as inheritance) of his spirit. He witnesses how Elijah is carried up to heaven in a chariot with fiery horses. Taking up his master's mantle, Elisha in turn strikes the Jordan with it so that the waters part when he goes back, westwards. The throng of prophet–disciples observe this. Some of them look for Elijah's body, contrary to Elisha's advice; it is in vain.

Question. Who exactly is the hero: one of them, or both? What are the reasons for your decision?

L. 2 Kings 4:8-37, *A mother fights for her child, Elisha raises it from the dead*

A wealthy woman married to an elderly man prepares a permanent guest room in her house, which the prophet Elisha can use

when he is travelling in the area. Elisha wants to give her something in return, but she does not need anything. He perseveres
when he hears from his servant Gehazi that she is childless, and
announces the birth of a son to her.

Having grown up, the boy dies one day while working
among the reapers. The mother puts his body in Elisha's bed in
the guest room, and resolutely sets off to rouse Elisha. She finds
him on Mount Carmel and does not leave his side. After a fruitless treatment by Gehazi, who is not able to retrieve the child
from the dead, Elisha himself appears at the bedside and succeeds, after a lot of trouble, in calling the child back to life,
through a combination of petitionary prayer and magic ritual.
There is an intriguing description of what he does with his
body.

Questions. What is the exact relation between the prophet and
the woman? What do you think of his contribution? Is he the
hero, or is it the woman?

4

The narrator and his[1] characters

When we open up a story, we hear as it were a voice speaking to us. This is not the voice of the historical and unique individual that was the writer, that one person who around 800 or 500 BCE wrote about Moses or Solomon. What we hear is the voice of his *persona* (a Latin word that amongst other things means "mask"), the narrator. The narrator is a pose, an attitude. One could call him an offshoot or a sub-personality of the writer. The people from ancient Israel who are responsible for the texts that, in translation, we now have in front of us have systematically omitted all references to their identity then and there. The prose writers have remained anonymous, and wanted to remain anonymous. The only exception (Nehemiah, in whose story an "I" figures) only serves to confirm the rule. And whether we turn to Exodus or to Judges, it does not take us long to see that the writers are talking about events that took place in what was also for them a distant past.

Whoever writes a story establishes himself as the narrator, choosing the position of narrator. What does that mean? The narrator draws those lines and selects those details, right down to the smallest, that suit him. He is the boss of a complete circus. He is like a juggler who keeps a lot of balls in the air at the same time. He structures time, sketches space, brings characters on and takes them off again, misleads the reader at times, and enforces his point of view through thick and thin. Meanwhile, he also has to comply with a few basic requirements for communication: first of all, his story must remain attractive so that he

---

[1] It is possible, but very unlikely on sociological grounds, that the biblical author in a given case is female. Nonetheless, the sex of the author is not significant for the present discussion, and the reader may wish to think of the narrator as possibly female.

retains the public's attention; it should be easy to follow (have *followability* as the technical term would be) and it should present the great diversity of data (people, acts, words, motives, points of view, intentions and everything else) in such a way that his view of what is narrated remains plausible and probable. In this way, the text becomes convincing; all the time, the narrator is striving to appear convincing. In this respect, he practices the art of rhetoric. The original definition of rhetoric is still rock solid: the art of convincing with words. This is why a sound narratology is largely a form of rhetorical analysis.

The narrator is a veritable ringmaster. When he wants to have a camel in the text, he just puts one in. When he does not feel like letting a character speak, we only hear his voice, and so only get his view of things. In 2 Kgs 4:1 he decides to have the widow speak as soon as possible, but on the first page of the Bible, another narrator has God wait for four clauses before he is allowed to speak four syllables. These are "let there be light," and are followed by the confirmation on the part of the narrator, "and there was light," so that we can be sure God's command worked out all right. It is a splendid move: the light is the first of all things to be created, and it comes into being solely through God's words. In this way, John would be proved right when he opened his Gospel with the intriguing and masterly: "In the beginning was the Word."

The first sentences of the Bible immediately betray one of the main characteristics of the narrator: he is *omniscient*—but in a literary rather than a theological sense. The writer of Genesis 1 tells us about events at which nobody was present, and yet he tells them with authority. This authority is a result of his position as narrator. In other places a narrator may, if it suits him, look in on the council of heaven, or inside the heads of his characters, God included, or inside their hearts: not long after the start of the biggest project in history, "the Lord regretted that He had made man on earth, and His heart was saddened," as it says in Gen. 6:6. The narrator knows because he knows, and he knows because he says it, and maybe he only knows when he says it; it is not necessary to consider such a statement "historically reliable" and assume a prior phonecall from the Holy Ghost to the writer.

The writer's license and authority

The biblical writer usually draws his material from events and characters in national history, but is not overly concerned with the strict requirements that historiography has to meet in the 20th century. His work is governed by poetic license, and I will illustrate the far-reaching consequences of this liberty with an example that to a good listener may be fairly shocking.

Taking a census is a taboo in Old Israel. What could move a ruler to do such a thing? Would he not then be a God-forsaken bureaucrat who wants to determine his people's well-being, instead of trusting the God of the covenant to do that? In 2 Samuel 24 David's policy provokes God into striking the country with the plague. But where did the king get the idea? This is what the writer of the Samuel books has to say: "The anger of the Lord again flared up against Israel; and he incited David against them, saying: 'Go and number Israel and Judah.'" Texts like that immediately raise the question of what motivates God. Is he indeed a schemer whose goal it is to strike a people with the plague, who devises some subtle machination to this end and uses David as his puppet? The answers to these questions are less important than our being sufficiently alert and unbiased to ask them and put them as bluntly as this.

Now this chapter is one of a series of texts from Samuel and Kings that sometimes have been included, practically unchanged, in the work of a later writer, the books of the Chronicles. The so-called parallel text about the census and the plague we find in 1 Chronicles 21, with, however, two touch-ups. The writer defers the sentence about God's anger until v. 7, and he now starts the passage as follows: "*Satan* arose against Israel and incited David to number Israel."

This is rather a jolt: the older text, from Samuel, tells us that it is God who drives David to madness; the younger text (c. 400 BCE) states that it is Satan, and this radical contradiction is found within the one Bible! What can it mean? In the first place, we note that the later writers have not deemed it necessary to adapt the alternative text to their point of view by deleting the word "God" and replacing it by "Satan." At the same time, however, the later writer is still completely free to compose his own text and coolly change God to Satan. This says everything about

poetic license, and it is a pointed hint to us as readers not to fall
into the trap of racking our brains about the question that is as
desperate as it is fruitless: what is the historical truth? Nor
should we be so stupid as to play off one writer against the
other, as this gets us nowhere. What we should do is understand
that it suits the writer of the composition Joshua through Kings
to pin the suggestion on God, whereas it suits the Chronicles
author to push Satan forward as the firebrand.

One writer's image of God is totally different than that of the
other, and the same goes for the image of David that is por-
trayed, which in Samuel is quite different than that in Chronicles. The fact that David is a tough criminal (as the juicy stories
in 2 Samuel 11 and thereabouts show) is conveniently absent
from Chronicles, which holds David in high esteem. With
regard to the episode of the plague, the writer of Chronicles
obviously did not like the thought of God playing a shabby little
game with the illustrious David. On the other hand, the view of
God entertained by the Samuel author does leave room for
dubious tricks. Not surprisingly, this writer does not pretend to
fathom God's actions.

It is our task to leave the different versions as they are; we
are not required to deliver a final judgment, pronouncing one
author right and discarding the other. This sort of "it is–it isn't"
game is unproductive. The same goes for the various "contradictions" between the four Evangelists. Mark presents his own
picture of Jesus, which is different than Luke's. Long live
diversity—there may be more than one truth...

In religion and theology mortals, including writers, are sub-
ordinate to God, as man was created by God. But we are here
concerned with narratology, and it should be very clear to us
that when it comes to story-telling, the situation is radically different. In narrative texts God is a character, i.e. a creation of the
narrator and writer. God is a language construct; Abraham is a
linguistic device; David is a portrait made up exclusively of language signs. God can only act if the narrator is willing to tell us
about it. The narrator decides whether God is allowed to say
anything in the story and if so, how often and how much. In
this way, God is no different than a donkey. In a story, donkeys

may also speak, even in a way that makes a person of some importance blush with shame—see the story of Balaam and his ass in Numbers 22–23. This highly-paid seer and soothsayer is totally unaware that an angel with a flaming sword is blocking his path until his donkey draws attention to this by opening its mouth…. There are few mortals who can outdo this animal.

Creator and creation: that is, then, the relation between the narrator and every character or form in the story. A far-reaching consequence of this unequal relationship is that we should not fall into the trap of equating the writer's opinion or point of view with that of whatever character. In Genesis 1 there is no problem: the subject matter and the elevated theme do not lead us to suspect that the narrator does not support God. But in the case of another matter of prime importance, the introduction of the monarchy as a form of government, matters are less simple. This issue is examined from many angles in the Old Testament, both religious and political, and pops up time and again as a barely manageable problem; the central text is 1 Samuel 8–12.

This passage opens with the people's request for a king, a question put to Samuel. The prophet, soon supported by his Lord, thinks the idea nothing less than idolatry—the worst possible offense—but it is quite doubtful whether or not the writer thinks that. We can only gauge his opinion after intensive reading and re-reading of his complete work, and a careful consideration of all sorts of subtle signals.

Samuel protests vehemently in 1 Samuel 8 and 12, and this sounds very principled. So far, almost every Bible scholar has fallen into the trap of thinking that Samuel's position is *the* truth, i.e. coincides with the writer and his point of view. Bible scholarship could have saved itself this blunder by merely noting in 1 Samuel 16 how fallible the old man is, or noticing the irony in 1 Samuel 9: the "seer" is unable to "see" with either eyes or mind that the farmer from Benjamin who addresses him in the gate of his town is God's candidate for the throne. Everything Samuel says in chs. 8 and 12 is exclusively his own view, however long and venerable his gray beard. A character's words cannot automatically be taken as proof or a sign of the writer's viewpoint.

A fallible prophet

The extent to which writer and character operate at different levels is aptly illustrated in 1 Samuel 15. Saul has been sent on a campaign by the prophet but has neglected the divine command to wipe out Amalek, the arch-enemy, completely. As a result, he is confronted by the oracle of doom (vv. 22-23, a brusque poem) which announces his final damnation. Having to pronounce this divine saying causes old Samuel a lot of problems and is painful to him: it has cost him a lot to install Saul as the first king and advise him, and he now has to forfeit this laboriously started project:

> The word of the Lord then came to Samuel:
> "I regret that I made Saul king,
> for he has turned away from Me
> and has not carried out My commands."
> Samuel was angry and entreated the Lord all night long.

It is a pity that our timid translators have diluted the text (1 Sam. 15:10-11) by massaging away the word "angry" and rendering it as "distressed" (JPS) or "it grieved him" (KJV). First, Samuel is angry, for the simple reason that God at a stroke wipes out the entire project he has worked so hard for. Next, he feels the pain, and his entreaties then, also a sign of his need for consultation with his Sender, are of the same nature—it is the same verb in Hebrew—as the appeal of the widow to Elisha: a cry for help, a cry in distress. This time, it is to no avail. In vv. 13-26 the story presents a long and painful confrontation between prophet and king. Saul finally has to admit that he has sinned, but he asks his mentor to leave him his royal glory in front of the troops. Samuel refuses, but Saul presses him so strongly that it becomes very difficult for the prophet to keep rejecting him; and so he says:

> Moreover: the Glory of Israel does not deceive or have regrets;
> For He is not human that He should have regrets.

This sounds very fine and principled, and for a believer it is tempting to have this statement about God's essence (in v. 29) framed on the wall. But is this view of the Godhead true? What is more: does Samuel mean what he says? The "problem" is here indicated by the key word "regrets." Mortals are turncoats, but God is eternal and unchangeable, Samuel claims. Unfortunately, this view is doomed from the outset; wasn't it God himself who just before this (in v. 11a) revealed to the prophet: "I regret" making Saul the first king! This contradicts what the prophet says in v. 29. One character seems at odds with the other.

The narrator does not abandon us to this perplexing situation. He allows himself the last word (v. 35) and declares authoritatively:

> Samuel never saw Saul again to the day of his death.
> But Samuel grieved over Saul, because Yahweh regretted
> that He had made Saul king of Israel.

Here we have the third and decisive use of the key word "regret." The creator of the text, the writer, here authoritatively declares through his narrator that God did have regrets, and thus authorizes (!) the words of his character God in v. 11. In his view, God can certainly change his mind, and in this he is in complete agreement with (the narrator of) Gen. 6:6 or Jonah 3:10 and 4:2.

As to Samuel: he spoke about constancy and unchangeability because for him this was the quickest, and theologically impressive, way to put an end to the insistent pressure from Saul. We need not accord his words the status of principles, but should understand them as an utterance that suits the moment, a unique and delicate situation. Samuel would not be the last cleric to overwhelm and brush off his audience with pious cliches.

This fingering exercise in 1 Samuel 15 shows that a character cannot overrule its maker. The narrator is at a level of communication that is essentially different than, and higher than the characters'. Consequently, you might even say that there is not even a contradiction between the view "changeable," expressed by the writer, and the statement "unchangeable" by the prophet. Those two statements would only conflict if they were on the same level.

The narrator's comments

Sometimes the writer gives away what he thinks of his character's point of view. He can decide to support or even adopt his character's words. The opening of 1 Samuel 8 is given to the narrator's voice:

> When Samuel grew old, he appointed his sons judges [i.e. rulers] over Israel.... But his sons did not follow in his ways; they were bent on gain, they accepted bribes, and they subverted justice. (vv. 1 and 3)

Equipped with this knowledge, and consequently biased by it, we then hear, in vv. 4-5:

> So, all the elders of Israel assembled
> and came to Samuel at Ramah, and they said to him,
> "You have grown old,
> and your sons have not followed your ways.
> Therefore appoint a king for us, to govern us like all other nations."

Here we have a collective character speaking, the elders of the nation. Their speech consists of two considerations, and the controversial request. Does the writer consider this wrong? The word "so" alone indicates that he thinks their visit is justified: the sad business of corruption is an empirical fact. Moreover, it is immediately obvious that their two considerations are given in the same order and same wording as vv. 1 and 3, which are the narrator's responsibility. As part of the narrated world the elders do not know that their creator used those words to address us, one level above the story. Their using the same words ("grown old ... not followed your ways") as their creator is also a deliberate choice on the part of the narrator, who in this way indicates that the elders represent the facts faithfully and confront Samuel with them. This in turn means that there is a good chance that the writer does understand the desire for a different type of constitution, despite the fact that being "like all other nations" should not really be a spiritual goal for the chosen people. The writer has certified the elders' view through his narrator. Who knows? He may well have a completely different opinion of the monarchy than the angry and disappointed prophet and his Lord...

I note that there is an essential, even radical difference between narrator and character. This is a hierarchical difference, as the two parties move on totally different levels. In terms of communication, the narrator is above the narrative material and outside the story, as the transmitter of a message of which we are the recipients. The characters only live inside the story; they are part of that world that by virtue of a string of language signs is said to have existed then and there. They are themselves language signs. Characters communicate with each other, but cannot escape from that level and address the narrator or us.

One of the prophets somewhere asks the rhetorical question whether it is possible for a piece of pottery to argue with the potter. Of course it cannot, and so it is with the narrator and a character in a story. A striking example of such an impossible debate that in principle is doomed to failure can be found in 1 Samuel 31 and its immediate sequel, 2 Sam. 1:1-16.

The persuasive powers of the Amalekite

In the final chapter of 1 Samuel the narrator reports the battle between the Philistines and the Israelite army, which costs King Saul and three princes their lives. In his last hour, Saul asks his arms-bearer to run him through, so that the enemy, the detested uncircumcised, will not commit sacrilege by making sport of him, the Lord's Anointed. But because of this very same taboo around the king—his office is sacred—the arms-bearer refuses. The only course left to Saul is to fall on his sword, and thus there is an end to this tragic character's tough resistance to his doom. Three days later, a hireling from Saul's troops appears in David's camp in the South-West, hands David the dead king's crown and armlet, and addresses him as the new ruler. This self-appointed messenger is an Amalekite who brings David a report of the war and Saul's death. He claims to have stabbed Saul to death himself, to finish him off, at the king's request. The objects he is carrying prove that he is the first with the news of the defeat.

What, then, is the truth about Saul's end? The well-informed reader knows that ever since Exodus 17 the Amalekites are a detested people, which already puts the messenger's story in a bad light. A decisive and watertight narratological proof, however, is the fact that the narrator was the first to get in his own, and by definition authoritative, report of Saul's death as a suicide. Fortified by this observation we listen to the Amalekite again, and this time we can smell what drove him to it: to appropriate a part for himself, and take his news scoop to the coming man, in the expectation of a generous reward for this delivery service. Just to be sure, the writer has David return to this confrontation in 2 Sam. 4:10; it becomes clear that David got wise to the man after he had received more information.

The Amalekite's long and clever report, 2 Sam. 1:6-10, is hard to disprove, certainly on a first reading of it. This is because this mercenary must have been present during Saul's last minutes. In principle, his report is an authentic eye-witness account, as he has seen Saul speaking to his arms-bearer, and either heard or deduced what the king was asking for: a mercy blow. He then got the idea of changing two details in his picture of the battle. He scrapped the arms-bearer and sub-stituted himself in the position near Saul, and he replaced the arms-bearer's "no" by his own "yes." The narrator cleverly establishes the link—a case of substitution—through the word "fear." In 1 Sam. 31:4 he tells us the arms-bearer refused because he "feared greatly." His fear is of a religious character; the young Israelite does not dare to break the taboo on the king. In 2 Sam. 1:14 a shocked David asks the Amalekite how he dared to lift his hand against the king. Literally, the text reads: "How [is it possible that] you did not fear to lift your hand and kill the Lord's Anointed?" This creates a contrast between fear/not-fear (= the arms-bearer's not daring, and the mercenary's daring) that draws our attention to the clever substitutions the messenger has woven into his report.

Two clearly demarcated lies within a framework of sheer truth from an eyewitness! The result? The Amalekite thought that being a stranger he would not be subject to the religious law that protects the king, and consequently could safely pose for David as the man who administered the *coup de grâce*. A fatal miscalculation that costs him his head. David has the man exe-cuted immediately, probably on the grounds of the following consideration: if an Israelite is not allowed to touch the king

because his office is sacred, this would apply even more to a
foreigner. This is part of a diabolical ambiguity between David
and the messenger, which turns into a matter of life and death.
This ambiguity has been subtly expressed by its occupying the
exact middle line of the story. There, the Amalekite tells David
how on the battlefield he said to Saul: "I am an Amalekite." To
his mind, this statement of identity implies two signals: to Saul
(three days earlier on the battlefield) it hints, "I am allowed to
give you the final blow," and to David (now his audience in
Ziklag) it sends a comparable signal: my status as mercenary
enabled me to fulfill the king's wish. David, however, is not
fooled and shortly afterwards one stroke of the sword puts an
end to all expectations of a generous messenger's reward.

Deceit

Readers of biblical narrative are sometimes faced with a thorny
puzzle. The characters are quite capable of lying and deceit—
how do we find out about it? The majority of these situations
can be classified as one of three possibilities:

   a. The simplest option is for the narrator to make things
easy for us and tell us in so many words about any deceit going
on. He lets us share in his omniscience or prior knowledge.
When Esau has been sent off to prepare a game dish for his old
father, preparatory to receiving his father's blessing (Gen. 27:1-
4), the writer changes the scene and tells us that Rebekah has
overheard this plan. Next, he immediately shows us how she
warns her favorite, Jacob, and conspires with him, so that he,
disguised as Esau, can appear before Isaac and in this way steal
the blessing (vv. 5-10 and 11-17). From the moment that he
appears before his father, there are two parties with a shocking
difference in knowledge: Isaac and Esau do not know anything
about the fraud and are the big losers; the other party includes
the duo in possession of all the facts, Jacob and Rebekah, and
beyond this, outside or above the story there is a similar duo
with prior knowledge: the narrator and we, his audience. So,
we watch Isaac's groping for the identity of his visitor from his
innocent and ignorant perspective, but also from the perspective
of the scheming couple. In vv. 18-27 this becomes an

embarrassing struggle for certainty in which the old man needs almost all his senses: his eyes are not functioning any more, his ears tell him he hears Jacob's voice, his sense of touch tells him Esau, and finally smell and taste will have to decide: it must be Esau, the blind man decides. A painful spectacle.

Another example of the writer saving us trouble is Genesis 37. The way in which he focuses and directs our attention is sometimes comparable to the panning of a camera. In vv. 12-17 the camera follows Joseph who is on his way to his brothers. Next, however, our view makes a 180-degree turn: the narrator now has us watch the brothers, and reveals in v. 18: "They saw him from afar, and before he came close to them they conspired to kill him." From this point, the plot of "Joseph in Dothan" takes on the shape of a true conspiracy. Again, there is the unequal level of knowledge: Joseph approaches innocently, but we have prior knowledge.

b. Often, we do not immediately discover whether we can take characters at face value, or whether they mean what they say. This takes us into the situation we often experience in our own life: unable to gauge another person, we are forced to compare words with actions, and have to reach an interpretation or a conclusion by way of often laborious combination and deduction. It is exactly the same with the characters in the biblical story. If they speak pretty words while committing atrocities, we take our cue from the latter. In Genesis 34 a girl is raped in the town of Shechem, and her brothers, the sons of Jacob, are livid. They are bent on revenge, but decide to take recourse to higher politics: they speak with honeyed tongue during negotiations with the king of the city state, to lull him into a sense of security. Then, in the night, they strike and massacre the entire population of the town.

c. If the writer considers it important that we should not be misled by pretty talk, he may decide not to play hide-and-seek any longer; he leaves his role, does not partake any longer as narrator in the stream of the sub-actions and tells us himself, in the voice of the narrator, that something is a lie. This is what happens in Genesis 34 when Jacob's sons are buttering up the king of Shechem, Hemor. Concerned lest we, too, allow ourselves to be misled, the narrator tells us in v. 13: "Jacob's sons answered Shechem [the prince, and the rapist] and his father Hemor—speaking with guile," etc. The words "with guile" are an intervention, a typical hint from the narrator to us.

Or take the obscure situation in 1 Kings 13: a man of God from Judah has performed his task in Bethel, by pronouncing an oracle of doom against the cult Jeroboam has high-handedly set up, and can return home pleased with himself. An old prophet from the town invites him to his house, and claims that it is God himself who told him to do so. This gets us into an awkward position. How can we know whether the old man is lying? Will we get around at all to the question, what possesses him or what his intention is? These are the same pressing questions as the man from Judah is faced with at that moment, and he chooses the wrong option! The writer has decided to give us all the facts. About the claim that God himself had instructed the prophet in Bethel to coax along the man from Judah, he now has his narrator say in a lightning interruption: "he was lying to him," at the end of v. 18. He needs to clarify the situation, as otherwise we would be totally confused by the unexpected sequel: the prophet from Judah does not survive; a few hours after the visit he is killed by a lion, but his lying host is hardly punished. I shall come back later to the question of whether there is a justification for this.

What are the characters saying?

The vast difference in status and authority between narrator and character is accompanied by a difference of immediate impor-tance to the reader: a division into two types of text. The main text is the narrator's, and all words spoken or thought by char-acters have been embedded in this. Character text, whether monologue or dialogue, is "only" embedded text and is opposed to narrator's text. More than 95% of the narrator's text is reporting on a usually distant past, and is governed by a string of verbs, every one of which is in some form of preterite or other. In the case of dialogue, this is quite different. Characters are mainly concerned with their own present: of course, it is their life. What to them is their own life is to the narrator a string of language signs that he has to present credibly.

Characters are in principle just as ignorant and insecure, arrogant or sad, just as smart or vicious or ironical or excited as we are in our own lives. We remember the widow: she is under pressure from a creditor. That is her present, and that is the distress she communicates to Elisha. Speeches and dialog are a type of text totally different than paragraphs referring to a distant past, which you can arrange in any way you like.

The other speeches in our *pilot story* show that the character's text not only contains many forms of the present tense, but often also commands and wishes. This means that speech is often about the imminent future, and this is something the narrator himself can never manage. Characters may say that they want to have this or that, or want this or that to be done in such-and-such a way. Speeches are often excited or dramatic. The Bible does not contain one single instance of *small talk*; almost every word by a character is existentially revealing or rooted: the speaker is totally committed to the matter under discussion.

How different is the writer's comfortable position: looking back on a distant past, arranging words and actions in a way that suits him, having all the time to change and fine-tune his subject, secure in the advance knowledge of which theme he wants to elaborate on and which tone he wants to use to create the proper atmosphere. The narrator manipulates his material at arm's length, always keeping a certain distance. This yields the great advantages of overview and order. The narrator has a powerful grip on his subject matter and his creation; the characters have as little grip on their lives as we have. What holds for the reality of people of flesh and blood also holds for the characters in the world-in-words of the biblical story: there is more passive experience and suffering than positive action.

During the reporting, relating the course of events as it were, the narrator is totally unnoticeable. He is hiding behind the events so that it appears as if they narrate themselves. This illusion is exactly what the narrator aims for: he uses it to suggest objectivity. The writer is an illusionist.

The narrator's text

The writer's hand, however, can be seen in that small portion of narrator's text where he departs from mere reporting, i.e. narrating in the strict sense of the word. It is our responsibility to make the most of these sparse signals, as they offer a direct view of the writer's scale of values, long hidden, and of his ideology and point of view. I refer to the moments when we receive information (e.g. description), comments, explication or a value judgment from the writer. These four forms of intervention visible from outside have the common characteristic that the action stops momentarily, or, to put it differently: the narrated time is interrupted and put aside.

Information. The finale of the book of Judges (chs. 17–21) is precisely demarcated by the statement: "In those days there was no king in Israel; every man did as he pleased." We find these two sentences in their entirety in 17:6 and 21:25, the final verse of the book, and in the first sentence framing the threshold to a new story in 18:1a and 19:1a. What is said here has no momentary aspect; it summarizes an entire era and thus betrays the narrator's perspective. The second sentence is quasi-neutral, but there is very little chance that the writer intends to use it in a neutral sense. He has already equipped a number of stories in Judges 1–11 with a threshold made up of formulaic language, saying: "The Israelites (again) did what was offensive to the Lord."

This happens in 2:11, the opening of a paragraph full of verbs indicating repetition in the past tense (especially close to v. 18) that contains the writer's agenda for the book; 3:7 as the start of the paragraph 3:7-11 that serves as the model for the cycle of apostasy–tyranny–deliverance; 3:12 as the start of the story about the liberator Ehud; 4:1 as the start of the story about Deborah, Barak and Jael contra Sisera; 6:1 as the start of the Gideon episode, and 10:6 as the threshold to the drama of Jephthah.

These thresholds enter into a dialog with the framing words of the finale, so that the question rises whether "do as you please" is actually any different than "doing what is offensive to the Lord." Answer: unfortunately not, as the finale is full of materialism, crime, egoism, confusion, anarchy and misery, and thus serves as the gloomy backdrop for the first section of 1 Samuel, chs. 1–12, culminating in a powerful central authority (the king!) in Israel.

In another case, information guarantees that Reuben's reputation does not suffer too much in the conspiracy to liquidate Joseph. In Gen. 37:18-20 the conspiracy is described, and then Jacob's eldest son, who feels responsible, is given the following two verses by the narrator:

> But when Reuben heard it, he tried to save him from them. He said: "Let us not take his life." And Reuben went on: "Shed no blood! Cast him into that pit out in the wilderness, but do not touch him yourselves"—intending to save him from them and restore him to his father.

What comes after the dash is remarkable because it is not a full new sentence from the narrator, but a short clause, a declaration of purpose that as narrator's text does not belong to the words preceding the dash—these, after all, are character's text. Only after we have grasped the meaning are we able to put the quotation marks in the correct position. We also note how the short paragraph has been framed (twice "save him from them"), and that the narrator is omniscient: he is able to see into Reuben's heart.

Information also constitutes 1 Sam. 9:9. At the moment that the important word "seer" appears—this turns out to be Samuel —the narrator interrupts the almost finished conversation between Saul and his servant with a statement that betrays a great distance in time and is an overview on the narrator's part. This is about a custom:

> Formerly in Israel, when a man went to inquire of God, he would say:
> "Come, let us go to the seer,"
> for the prophet of today was formerly called a seer.

One function of this fact revealed to us in an aside is that in this way we are prepared for Samuel's new role as prophet; until now he had been a "judge" [i.e. an administrator]. Another important aspect is the introduction of the root "to see." Samuel does not see much; everything that is really important God has explicitly to whisper into his ear, cf. 9:15-16, a striking instance of a flashback. Another joke in v. 9 is that the writer knows as well as we do that his "today" is constantly shifting; it cannot be fixed to the period when the text was written, however much historical-critical scholars might want it to.

Description. The description of people, thoughts, landscapes and buildings can take up many pages in modern narrative. In the Bible it is extremely scarce. If the narrator leaves the action for a moment and tells us of a woman that she is "fair of face," this is never just because of this quality in its own right. He will only mention something like that if it is going to be a factor in a plot. Consequently, he will usually allocate this sort of observation to a character: in Genesis 12 the Egyptians notice that Sarai is beautiful, which has unpleasant consequences for her lawful husband: she is taken from him. In 2 Samuel 11 David looks down from the roof of his palace and sees a beautiful woman bathing nude; the end of v. 2 contains the description proper. Everything he then fails to stop himself from doing (adultery, murder, and the disastrous aftermath of these capital offenses: inner turmoil, repression etc.) will conclusively ruin his life.

The book of 1 Kings opens with objective information from the narrator:

> King David was now old, advanced in years, and though they covered him with bedclothes, he never felt warm. [On the advice of his courtiers] they looked for a beautiful girl throughout the territory of Israel.
> They found Abishag, the Shunammite, and brought her to the king. The girl was exceedingly beautiful. She became the king's attendant and waited upon him, but the king was not intimate with her.

Here, the contrast between her beauty and the fact that David was not capable of making love to her any more is important—he was that old. Is that all? Far from it. Abishag is in an extremely ambiguous position, which is played out for all it is worth by the narrator and his character Solomon in ch. 2. After all, she both has (physically) and has not (sexually) shared David's bed, and nobody can tell the difference, except of course ... the omniscient narrator! After the Solomon party has won the struggle for power, the beaten candidate Adonijah, who has been warned by Solomon to keep quiet, is stupid enough to ask Bathsheba (Solomon's mother, of all people) to request her hand for him from the king. Solomon (loving brother and king) is quick to interpret this as proof that Adonijah still has not given up his claims to the throne, and has him killed. Beauty is here, again, clearly a factor in a plot.

Values, finally, are so important that I have set aside a complete section for them in Chapter 8.

5

Action, plot, quest, and hero

When we read a novel or watch a movie, we often let ourselves be guided primarily by the action. This word usually has a broad spectrum of meaning, and justifiably so. It is a productive concept for narrative art in the Bible as well, but it is necessary as well as illuminating to distinguish between "the action" and the *sub-actions*. These often occur in sequences, populating sentence after sentence, and are indicated by the predicate (verb).

An example will clarify this. The action (in its broad sense) of "Joseph in Dothan" is, in a nutshell, as follows: Joseph is sent out by his father to go and see how his brothers are doing; they conspire to kill him and throw him in a pit; after some deliberation, they sell him as a slave, so that Joseph ends up in Egypt. This can be put in even fewer words: Joseph has to go and see his brothers, but when he finds them he is humiliated and sold to Egypt. The concept of "action" goes hand in hand with the notion of grasping the story at a glance or making a summary.

The sub-actions, on the other hand, are as it were the infantry; they are responsible for the details—but these details are of course the actual business. An example of such a sequence follows here. I have chosen the moment after the brothers have made their plan and Reuben has come out against bloodshed, Gen. 37:23-24. I am largely following the JPS translation, but I will show the structure of this bit of narrator's text typographically by printing each clause on a separate line:

When Joseph came up to his brothers,
they stripped Joseph of his tunic, the ornamented tunic that he was
    wearing,
and took him
and cast him into a pit.
The pit was empty; there was no water in it.

We have here a simple sequence of four sub-actions: the first is still intransitive ("to come," a verb of motion), but after that the game is up for Joseph and he becomes the direct object—in both senses—of his brothers' scheming. They get three sub-actions with a transitive verb as predicate, but that does not make this simple sequence a pedestrian set of lines. In the second line there is an apposition that, merely by being there, stops the narrative pace for a moment and reminds us of how the elderly Jacob had dressed his favorite son in an elegant, multi-colored garment (with all its connotations of princely garb); it is this sort of preferential treatment that has made the brothers see red. In a minute, with some relish they will dip this smart coat in blood, and send it back to their father. Finally, there is the fifth line, which contains description instead of action. At the moment Joseph lands at the bottom of the pit, the narrative tempo practically grinds to a halt: a short break enables us to consider Joseph's new position, and to realize how completely overwhelmed he must be feeling by the course events have taken.

Many biblical stories consist of a well-planned combination or alternation of report and speech: there are some sequences of sub-actions presented by the narrator, which alternate with sequences of clauses containing direct speech, i.e. character text. A clear idea of this sort of combination contributes much to a good understanding of the text as a whole, and of the various themes. This is why I would recommend readers who would like to dig a bit deeper to type out the entire story, line by line, indenting all direct speech by one or two spaces. Character text is, after all, embedded, and in this way, you can see immediately how the text is divided into the two types of language. Moreover, in this typed or printed text it is now possible to draw as many connecting lines as you want, to color in key words and other forms of repetition with a felt-tip pen or crayon, etc. This sort of kindergarten work often leads to new insights.

Actions

I return to the concept of "action." This is very broad, as it includes highly divergent elements:

a. The first component is "actions" in the strict sense: the deeds the characters perform, which can be either intransitive, as for instance movements (Joseph came up), or transitive, in which case they touch on somebody else (his brothers cast *him* into the pit).

b. Characters lead just the sort of life people in extratextual reality, like us, do. They endure more than they actively achieve, and more often than not this "enduring" equals "suffering." The Latin word *passio* means both, experiencing and suffering; it is opposed to *actio,* which could serve as the label for component *a.* In short: the action of a story mainly consists of action and passion; in our language the latter aspect is more often expressed in the *passive* form than it is in the Bible. It is more lively and forceful to say "they cast him into the pit" than "he was cast into a pit." It also has more character: unlike passive forms, active forms do not hide where the responsibility lies, which is often important to the narrator and his scale of values.

c. Acting in the strict sense, enduring, and suffering are economically supported by descriptive and explanatory sentences, in which the narrator offers some background, sketches a situation, or reveals motives or purposes. They are likely to occur more frequently at the opening; thus, Genesis 37 already offers so much background in verses 1-4 that Joseph's treatment at the hands of his brothers in Dothan is no surprise any more. The hero is introduced in v. 2: we are told Joseph's age and the fact that he helps his brothers when they are tending their flocks. The end of v. 2 not only nominates Joseph as the hero, but also as the villain: he discredits his brothers towards Jacob. We are certainly justified in expecting their father to buy this, because v. 3 now reports: "Israel (Jacob's new name, which marks him out as a patriarch) loved Joseph best of all his sons, for he was the child of his old age." This is background plus motivation. The final straw for the brothers, however, is the following: "he had made him an ornamented tunic." This line still belongs to the preliminary stage: it is a short flashback that epitomizes the father–son relationship, but at the same time efficiently introduces an attribute that (a) is roughly handled by the furious brothers, both in v. 23 and in vv. 31-32, and (b) ends up, covered in blood, in the hands of Jacob, who then draws the wrong conclusion and plunges into mourning. In an opening chapter that is loaded with tensions, this attribute brings together motives of love and hate at one and the same point, which is always attractive to a narrator. And then, the fact that an entire family is torn apart by emotions is reminiscent of Genesis 27.

d. Finally, the broad concept of "action" also includes processes. The Levite of Judges 19 wants to go home after a long stay and will not listen to his host, who says: "The day is waning toward evening; do stop for the night." He leaves in the afternoon and before long gets himself into trouble: "They were close to Jebus, and the day was very far spent." And when he has decided where he wants to seek shelter (in vv. 11-13), it says: "The sun set when they were near Gibeah." The natural process reported here is part of a system of exact coordinates of time and space; it has far-reaching consequences, which I shall examine in the next chapter.

Selection

For each sub-action that has found its way into the text ten or more have been left out. The series that we see is a radical selection, and when we understand what it is that governs the writer's choice, we will have found the main point of access into his linguistic work of art. Our understanding will increase considerably if we are able to retrieve the writer's criteria for rejection (omission from the text) and selection (inclusion in the text). Every word that the writer allows to participate has a relation to his vision and themes. At the same time, his task was to allot each detail its correct position along the linear axis. We find ourselves confronted here with *the plot*.

The plot is the main organizing principle of a story. It provides a beginning, a middle and an end to the course of action. This seems overly simple, but it is in fact extremely productive: it is the brilliant opening statement by the father of literary theory, Aristotle, in his *Poetics*. Admittedly, he was referring to the structure of tragedy, but his observations about coherence apply to all story-telling. The plot provides the head and tail we need to hold on to, and thus determines the boundaries of the story as a meaningful whole. These boundaries then, in their own way, draw the horizon of our correct understanding of the story: within it, the reader is looking for the connections between everything and everything else.

Beginning, middle, and end: here we have three stations or benchmarks. However, what is a plot exactly? One of the most illuminating answers is to picture the plot as a course that is run. Thus, we can describe the course of the action, that is the course of events in a story, as a *trajectory*. The full-grown story begins by establishing a problem or deficit; next, it can present an exposition before the action gets urgent; obstacles and conflicts may occur that attempt to frustrate the *dénouement*, and finally there is the winding up, which brings the solution of the problem or the cancellation of the deficit.

Beginning, middle, and end, however, are more than linear entities. Their value or meaning is not purely quantitative; they are no mere instantaneous photographs along the axis of objectively proceeding time. They have been carefully attuned to each other, which is not surprising as they themselves are deliberate products of selection. Inspired and guided by a specific vision, the writer "sees" what would be a meaningful whole within the material he is working on, and how to delineate this whole. The trajectory he creates occupies a certain amount of narrated time, for instance the time taken up by a journey (think of Joseph's being sent to Dothan, or the Levite who goes to collect his wife in Judah). Such a stretch of time, however, only becomes functional and meaningful if it can be demarcated and fleshed out through the prism of a specific thematic field. Of course, the plot basically follows the chronological order of the narrated events themselves, but it is not *only* defined by a time interval of a certain length, and not even *primarily*. Trajectory and plot are in the first place determined by a vision. Before I go any further I will illustrate this with an example. The narrator may decide to relate a thousand and one things about the day Joseph comes to his brothers, by means of as many sub-actions; but what would be the point? If he likes, he can fill an entire page with a description of the landscape, brother A's mood and brother B's clothes, but he leaves that out. Nor does he tell us that Reuben cut his nails yesterday and that his big toe hurts because he stepped on a thorn. Why not? Because it is pointless. Why *is* it pointless? Because it is not *relevant*.

All right, but what—you may well ask—*is* relevant? It is the writer's vision or agenda that determines what is relevant. He wants to relate how the subject of the search—Joseph had been sent out to find his brothers—becomes its object, and how he is humiliated and eliminated, permanently, as it seems. To this end, he arranges some dozens of sub-actions, makes deliberate choices as to who (only Reuben and Judah) is allowed to say what, and at which moment exactly. The rest is silence: no descriptions of the weather, what the shepherds look like, or the other myriads of details. His criterion for selection is the plot. The plot is an organization of the action in such a way as to result in an *ingenious combination of the "horizontal" and the "vertical" arrangement*. The horizontal organization is the seamless succession of clauses along the linear axis of time, a succession that pretends to cover the chronology of the narrated events. The vertical organization results from the writer's vision, who is on a plane above his subject matter and only includes (along the same linear axis!) what contributes to his thematics and to the ideological unity of the story. The biblical narrator only uses details if they are functional to his plot.

Quest and hero

The concept of "trajectory" becomes more concrete and vivid when we illustrate it by means of two other fundamental entities, *quest* and *hero*. The trajectory in an independent story is often a search or "quest" undertaken by the hero in order to solve or cancel the problem or deficit presented at the outset. The hero is the subject of the quest, and he proceeds along the axis of his pursuit: he is on his way to the object of value that he wants to acquire or achieve.

This valuable object is not always physical, and the search operation is not always literal. In Genesis 27 the valuable object is the paternal blessing, i.e. a unique and special speech act of great power, through which Isaac marks the son who receives it as the leader of the new generation. The story is a game in which the blessing is the prize. In 1 Samuel 17, a text about a war that threatens Israel's survival, the valuable object is also obvious: disabling the armored giant. Whoever conquers the protagonist wins the war.

Joseph in Dothan

In Genesis 37 neither quest nor hero is simple. The literary unit "Joseph in Dothan" starts with vv. 12-18. Joseph is the hero, and it is he who executes the quest. The problem is that of the father who sends Joseph out: his sons are far away, and he wants to know how they are doing. The quest started in this way is that of Joseph; as the searching agent he is the hero. Soon, however, there is an end to his position as the subject and acting character. From v. 18 onwards, our attention is directed towards the brothers. This move of the camera is an ominous one, as it is motivated by a radical reversal: now it is the brothers who are hatching a plan and proceed to action. They usurp the plot and give it the color and significance of a veritable conspiracy. They, too, have a quest: we'll teach our little brother a lesson, let's just kill him, shall we? During the exposition, Reuben, as a speaking subject, proposes a change of plan, and shortly afterwards the plot takes a decisive turn as Judah's proposal is put into effect. Thus, Joseph has changed from subject into object, and it is no coincidence that we do not hear another word from his mouth. The literal search on Joseph's part—who actually gets lost for a moment, in vv. 15-17—is eclipsed by the figurative one manned by the brothers. Joseph's quest fails, since Jacob, who sent him, does not receive a report from Joseph about them. Theirs, however, succeeds, and does result in a report. It is the message about Joseph, which needs no words: it is the sight of the bloody coat that makes the old man think Joseph has been killed.

Why does Reuben appear twice, and what is the significance of the fact that he finds the pit empty? There is also a striking repetition: the terrible message "a savage beast devoured him" not only occurs in v. 20, but is repeated *verbatim* in the middle

of v. 33. What is the point of that? Everything falls into place
when we discover the structure of vv. 18–33:

A		18-20	conspiracy by the brothers: kill Joseph! *"A savage beast devoured him!"*
	B	21-22	speeches by Reuben: no, throw him into the pit
	C	23-24	brothers cast Joseph into the pit
	D	25	a caravan passes by
	X	26-27	proposal by Judah: sell Joseph
	D'	28	Joseph sold to caravan
	C'	29	Reuben finds the pit empty, rends his clothes
	B'	30	and mourns; speech to his brothers
A'		31-33	they deceive Jacob with the coat, Jacob concludes: Joseph must be dead. *"A savage beast devoured him!"*

There is not only linear progress, but also circular coherence,
which has been made possible by the narrator's grip on his material. He was able to develop this grip through his vision: I will
start with the brothers' conspiracy against Joseph, and I will
conclude with the mini-conspiracy they plan against Jacob by
deliberately deceiving him with the coat. I can emphasize that
by putting the fatal clause about the savage beast first on their
lips, and then have the same words spoken by their father.

The reader notes that the sentence about the animal in v. 20
only has the status of an intention, that Joseph and Jacob are in
the dark as to this (they do not hear it) and that the narrator
takes us into his confidence, so that we have the same level of
knowledge as the brothers. The plot does not run as expected,
since it is first twisted by Reuben, and next by Judah; at the
conclusion, however, there is the surprise that, upon seeing the
bloody coat, the father chooses the very words which, unknown
to him (unlike us and the brothers), constitute the lie that the
brothers planned to spread, of course in order to effectively hide
their own responsibility. Since Jacob is not contradicted after v.
33, his conclusion "Joseph devoured" remains, and the old man
is steeped into unstemmable mourning which is to last many
years. Through our prior knowledge, we know who is responsible for this cruelty. Meanwhile, Joseph in his turn does not
know what is happening at home: he has long since been trans-
ported south as a slave.

The repetition of the utterance "A savage beast devoured him!" is spectacular, as the clause both is and is not the same. Whereas the choice of words and their meaning remain unchanged, the sense and the value of the utterance have been changed and expanded in an intriguing way: the context has been drastically altered; it is a different character speaking the clause, and the truth/untruth ratio has been shifted. Its positioning in v. 20 and v. 33 is one of the supports of the ring structure and, through being part of A and A', marks the boundaries and thus the conclusion of the section devoted to the conspiracy, vv. 18-33.

The concentric structure also shows how Reuben, Jacob's firstborn who feels responsible towards the father (end of v. 22!), is useful at first but eventually sidelined; we see him empty-handed next to what was his idea: the empty pit. Thus, his contribution in vv. 21-22 is reduced to the level of a nice leg-up for Judah and his crucial idea. Yet, the writer does pay him a compliment: by having him mourn and especially by introducing his clothes, too, as an attribute—Reuben rends them as a sign of mourning—he places him next to the grieving Jacob, who does the same after v. 33. Elements B and C (speech and action) are mirrored in the winding-up, where C' and B' offer action and speech.

The ring structure takes us to the center, the central member X that has no counterpart and conveys the unique message about Judah's prominence. It is Judah who gets to speak the most words, and it is his proposal that is executed. He easily eclipses the firstborn, which is no more of a coincidence than the writer's drastic decision to introduce a digression in Genesis 38, an excursus with, as its subject, Judah again.

This extra attention for Judah, during which a kid again becomes part of a mix-up (38:17 and 20), clothes serve as disguise, and the *dénouement* consists of a recognition that causes a great shock (vv. 24-26), sets him up for his major role as the brothers' spokesman in Genesis 44, and prepares us for Judah's crucial speech (44:18-34) at the Egyptian court. The point of this ardent and desperate plea is that he, Judah, should be allowed to take the place of Benjamin who is in danger of being taken hostage by the viceroy (the as yet unrecognized Joseph). His

speech is by far the longest in Genesis 37–50, moves Joseph to
tears, and has the result that the viceroy sheds his "disguise" and
makes himself known to the perplexed brothers: "I am Joseph!"
Chapters 37, 38 and 42–45 employ the attribute of clothing and
various forms of disguise, i.e. not-being-recognized; all the time
recognitions take place, which makes these stories fit perfectly
into a tightly constructed cycle.

In search of the hero

I will now go round the practice area in order to show how
much clarity and force is added to the stories by a correct application of the concepts of hero and quest. There are various texts
where pinpointing the hero is not that simple, but where every
time it is the very exercise of weighing the pros and cons with a
fine sense of proportion that, paradoxically, will help us best to
determine what are the exact requirements a character has to
meet in order to qualify as hero. Just for the record, I would
simply note here that a character (M/F) can be the hero in a
narratological sense, but a villain in a moral sense. A solid and
law-abiding citizen offers less scope to the narrator than a crook
or a loser. Thus Jacob, being a practiced deceiver, is a perfect
candidate for both labels. And what should we think of the
Levite in Judges 19? As far as ethics and sensibility go, he is
hardly distinguishable from the riffraff of Gibeah...

As narrative art is very flexible, there are few rigid laws gov-
erning it. As far as the hero is concerned, we will come a long
way by checking if three conditions are met: Is the hero the
subject of a quest? Is he/she mostly or permanently present in
the text? Finally, does the hero or heroine show initiative?

(A) Rebekah and Jacob deceive Isaac and Esau

For one paragraph in *Genesis 27-28:9* we think that Isaac and
Esau are in line for the position of hero, because, as the father
sends and the son goes out, they have a quest in common that
should result in the ceremony of the blessing for the firstborn.
The second paragraph, however, contains a surprise: Rebekah
has eavesdropped on the two and makes her own plan, to the

benefit of her personal favorite Jacob. So a second line is drawn: that of the counter-quest. These two characters see that it is now a race against time: who will be the first to get to Isaac with a lovely dish of meat? Interestingly enough, their counter-quest aims at exactly the same object of value as that of Isaac and Esau: the paternal blessing.

Who, then, is the hero of Genesis 27? The pair Rebekah–Jacob, since they win the race and Jacob, disguised, indeed receives the blessing? (Just a stray moralizing thought: are we as readers not rewarding crime too easily?) This would be correct if all we had was vv. 1 through 30a (the moment when Jacob leaves, satisfied). These, however, constitute only half of the long episode. After the middle, a real problem arises in the shape of a furious Esau who plans to take revenge on his twin brother. Rebekah sees this and acts shrewdly. She makes a virtue of necessity by getting Isaac to do the dirty work. She asks him to send Jacob away in order that he can find a kinswoman to marry in Haran. And so it happens; Esau, who had already got himself sidelined in a religious sense by an exogamous marriage (26:34; check what his parents think of this in v. 35!) can only conclude that for the second time he has lost crucial ground, 28:6-8.

Isaac and Esau have become the tools for the cunning plans made by Rebekah and Jacob. For one moment, the initiative was with the father, but it is negated and eclipsed by Rebekah's. Moreover, in the second half the mother takes an original initiative that is realized. Again I ask: are Rebekah and Jacob, who win two races, not the hero as a couple? This brings me to Jacob's part, which is less than admirable. In the first half, he is only carrying out his mother's scheme; he can still maintain he is only finishing a difficult job. In the second half, however, he is no more than the character who is sent, according to the mother's plan and the word of the manipulated father, and he flees the danger. At the level of the chapter as a whole, that leaves Rebekah victorious, the real heroine. This is mainly due to the factor of initiative; as regards the moral dimension, we are left with a gnawing question: are Rebekah's actions not justified because in this way she helps to fulfill the prenatal oracle? This word of God in 25:23 was the exact power center of the opening story, and had this sting in its tail: "The older shall serve the younger!" I leave it to the reader to answer this question; it is a variation on the well-known problem whether the end justifies the means, or any means.

I have challenged Jacob's status as a hero for the single story. At the next two levels up, however, Jacob again claims the position of hero, because the act of the play that includes Gen. 25:19-34 (two short stories: oracle and birth of the twins, the birthright sold for a dish of lentil stew) and Genesis 27–28 (the long story of the deceit, plus the short story of the dream and revelation at Bethel) mainly focuses on him, and does form part of the cycle (Genesis 25–35) that is wholly devoted to him. Seen in this light, Genesis 27 is only a station in the macro-plot of the entire Jacob cycle. In the next chapter, we will see that Genesis 27 has a remarkable structure that also affects the question about the hero.

(B) Deborah and Barak defeat Sisera

The problem at the beginning of *Judges 4* is quickly discovered: oppression by the Canaanites, which triggers the quest for the liberation of Israel. This combination of war and liberation is a feature of many stories in Judges, Samuel and Kings, for instance in Judges 6–8 (Gideon), 10–12 (Jephthah), 1 Samuel 4, 8, 13–14 and 17 (each chapter contains battles against the Philistines) and the wars against the Aramean kings in 1 Kings 20, 22 and 2 Kings 3, 6–7.

Here in Judges 4 it is not long before a formidable candidate for the position of heroine enters the stage: Deborah, the only woman judge in the Bible and the only one who is a prophet. In vv. 6-7 she pronounces the trajectory and the aim of the quest in the presence of Barak, and wants to send him out as a general. In this way, she invites Barak to become the subject of the quest and offers him the chance to gain the glory of victory. From a military point of view, however, this man is no hero:

> But Barak said to her: "If you will go with me, I will go,
> but if you will not, I will not go."

This does not sound too good; he seems so faint-hearted that Deborah almost has to hold his hand. For Deborah, this puts a totally different perspective on things:

"Very well, I will go with you," she answered.
"However, there will be no glory for you in the course you are taking,
for then Yahweh will deliver Sisera into the hands of a woman!"

Thus a short but revealing conversation in vv. 8-9. The reader, who does not yet know how the war is going to end, is convinced at this stage that the woman who will apprehend Sisera must be Deborah herself, as there is no other candidate. With her speech about the glory falling to a woman, she would thus forcefully stress her own position as subject of the quest and as a heroine.

Things, however, will turn out very differently, and we will find that we have been cunningly wrong-footed here by the narrator. As the positions of the two armies are still being discussed (vv. 10-13), v. 11 presents a piece of intelligence that at first we do not know what to do with: about one Heber who is an ally of Sisera and his king. The positioning of this verse has a subversive function which for the moment remains hidden, as it prepares us for the appearance of Heber's wife Jael. After v. 16 the section about the large collectives is finished. While the Canaanites are being scattered in defeat, Sisera leaves his chariot and flees ignominiously. The camera follows him—note how v. 17 takes up where v. 15b left off—and we enter the second half of the story. The aftermath of the battle has been exclusively reserved for individuals. Sisera seeks shelter with Jael, who receives him cordially. The visit ends rather gruesomely: she drives a pin into his head while he is sleeping. The narrator has not prepared us for this; on the contrary, the information he gives in v. 17 makes us exactly as unsuspecting as Sisera about the allies Heber and Jael—we share his perspective. For us, the surprise is complete, but Sisera cannot feel it any more. In v. 20 he had unwittingly authorized his destruction, by prompting Jael to turn away any pursuers with the words "Nobody is here." He has become the nobody from his own speech.

Only afterwards do we realize that Jael must have decided to defect, for reasons the writer does not disclose. Israel admires her change of allegiance, and honors her by an expressive hymn in 5:24-27. The final scene is given to Barak, vv. 22-23. All that is left for him is to note that his opponent has already been destroyed, by ... a woman. With him, the reader now also notices that Deborah's prediction in v. 9 has acquired a different content: the woman at whose hand Sisera was to fall turns out to be Jael instead of Deborah. Judges 4 is an ingenious construction about two men from opposing camps, who both cut a foolish figure with two strong women. The position of heroine falls to Deborah and Jael. They complement each other, as Deborah figures only in the first half, Jael only in the second. Hidden in the background there is another hero, who made Deborah clairvoyant: she has divine foreknowledge when she foretells the glory of a woman (= Jael). It is this hero, too, who instantly decides the battle in v. 15a: "And Yahweh threw Sisera and all his chariots and army into a panic before the onslaught of Barak." This is the only instance of the writer bringing Yahweh on stage. In the end, all the inspiration and courage shown by Deborah is due to him.

(C) The outrage in Gibeah

From the point of view of plot analysis, *Judges 19* is extremely interesting, as it is a case of a quest that fails. The problem at the outset is at the same time the gap that needs to be filled: the Levite's concubine has deserted him. His quest, which consists in getting her back and requires a journey there and back, seems to be successful. He is allowed to take her home, but on the return journey she dies, after a night of terror in Gibeah. The Levite comes home with her body, 19:28-29, and the quest has failed. This is not, however, the end of the story: the Levite cuts her body in twelve pieces, which he sends to the twelve tribes, and reaps bewilderment all around; in v. 30 we hear the country's reaction. In this way, he lifts the case on to a higher plane, that of national justice and national well-being.

The Levite did traverse a circle by retrieving the woman, but at the moment his quest got stuck, he defined a new and much

larger problem, and he defined it before the nation. The gang
rape is a blatant violation of the law, and if the whole of Israel
does not redress this with a fitting punishment, the crime may
taint the entire nation and bring down the wrath of the deity.
The assembly of the tribes at the beginning of ch. 20 marks the
start of a new quest. The tribes form a coalition and ask the
tribe of Benjamin, of which Gibeah forms part, to hand over
the group of rapists. When the Benjaminites refuse, the coalition
decides that the tribe as a whole should pay the price. An absurd
civil war breaks out, in which at first Benjamin wins a battle
twice (20:17-26) but is eventually defeated. At the moment that
the coalition is about to attain its goal, the annihilation of the
tribe of Benjamin, they recoil, frightened by their own vindic-
tiveness, so that it suddenly becomes necessary to stage a veritable abduction of virgin women in order to resuscitate the
remnants of Benjamin.

However ill-considered and chaotic the moral and religious
actions of the tribes in Judges 20–21, in a strictly narratological
sense they are the hero of the new quest, which is only ended in
21:6-7. This shows that a hero can also be a collective person-
age. In the final section, a new quest comes up for a moment, as
the coalition wants to give Benjamin another chance. What is at
stake this time is life, the exact opposite of the coalition's first
goal: the annihilation of Benjamin. As to ch. 19, we may note
in retrospect that the incident in Gibeah functions as the fuse in
the powder keg of chs. 20–21.

(D) Saul anointed king on the road

The long story of *1 Sam. 9:1–10:16* is a showpiece with many
different characters, and a rewarding subject for plot analysis.
There are no fewer than three quests. The opening is simple:
the farmer Kish sends his son Saul to look for some asses that
have gone astray. This is a literal search, Quest One (hereafter:
Q_1), of which Saul is the hero. I now jump to 9:15ff. where we
meet the seer/prophet Samuel in his own setting, and learn that
God is preparing him for the arrival of Saul. Samuel is awaiting
him, and knows he has to anoint the Benjaminite king. This

makes him the subject of Quest Three (= the prophet looking for the candidate for the throne), hereafter Q_3.

When we take another close look at the nature of Q_1 and Q_3 and compare the two, we notice that actually there is no logical and necessary connection between a farmer's looking for his animals, and a prophet's waiting for the right candidate for anointment. The former seems a trivial, private matter hardly worth recording, while the latter is important material for real historiography. The narrator links Q_1 and Q_3 in a masterly way through Q_2. I will now take a closer look at the text segment in question, vv. 6-14, and state the writer's technical problem: how can I bring a random farmer and the spiritual leader of the nation together on one plane? He does this by introducing indispensable informers who in their spontaneity do not realize how vital their contribution is to the installation of the first king. They are one boy (Saul's servant), and a group of girls who have come down from the town to draw water. These characters are also anonymous.

The first quest has failed. Saul and his servant have searched the hill country for days, to no avail. So, in 9:5 Saul is about to give up, but his servant has an idea: why not go to the town up there, and ask the man of God for advice? Saul refuses, but the servant is remarkably persistent and manages to persuade Saul. This is the origin of Quest Two: they try to approach the problem from a different angle, but they now have to find "the seer," who so far has also remained anonymous. Q_2, then, is to find the seer. As soon as this aim has been stated, the girls appear, descending the hill that Saul is climbing. Their relatively long speech (vv. 12-13) contains a lot of information that will later turn out to be relevant, as they mention a sacrificial meal at the cultic high-place, with Samuel as the indispensable officiating priest. At this moment, only (the character) God and the narrator know that Saul is to be the guest of honor at this cultic meeting on the hilltop. The girls press him to hurry, and Saul indeed runs into the prophet just when he is leaving the gate, v. 14. At that moment, Q_2 has succeeded and is eliminated, but at the same time Q_1 and Q_3 become alive and operational: the farmer can now ask for clairvoyant information about his asses (which he soon gets: v. 20), while the prophet can take care of his guest and initiate him into his unexpected destiny. Suddenly, Q_1 and Q_3 are merged; a brilliant reversal, as subject and object of Quest One exactly coincide with object and subject of Quest Three. Saul finds the prophet at the same moment as the prophet finds Saul. In the next chapter I will show that in the end Saul is the hero of the long story as a whole, as he not only occupies two quests as subject and may also be considered the valuable object of Q_3, but is also the only character to be present in all scenes.

(E) Abner leaves Ishbosheth for David

Second Sam. 3:6-21 takes us to the tiny state that is the sole remnant of Saul's kingdom. His weak son Ishbosheth rules in the Trans-Jordanian region, but the strong man of the regime is Abner, the general. When his king rebukes him about a woman, he has had enough, and decides to deliver the Northern Kingdom— ten tribes, in theory—to the king of Judah, David. The argument in vv. 7-11 constitutes the exposition, and is about Saul's concubine Rizpah; this puts her in a triangle together with Ishbosheth and Abner. After this, the plot starts, which largely coincides with Abner's quest: how do I deliver the tribes to David? Although Abner is the hero, he is also the asking party. David is much more powerful: he stays where he is and moreover makes a heavy demand that the Saulite state has to meet. Again, this concerns a woman; it is Saul's daughter, to whom David was married for a short time but who was taken from him. To David, she is a pawn on the chessboard of national politics: if he can have her back, Abner will have proved his loyalty, and at the same time the possession of the princess will raise the legitimacy of his (David's) kingship over the whole of Israel. Without her, he will be no more than an upstart in the eyes of many. Michal has been made a symbol of the transfer of the tribes, and there is no noticeable personal feeling for her in David. She is handed over to him after having been cruelly torn from her husband Paltiel in vv. 15-16. A diagrammatic representation of how the women are being juggled about would look as follows:

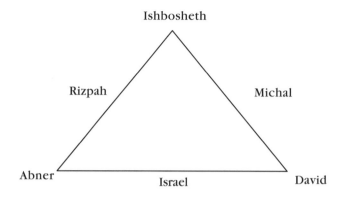

The potentates are in the corners; the objects of exchange (two women and a nation) are between them along the sides and are subject to shifts. Ishbosheth ends up as the big loser; yesterday the concubine Rizpah was taken from him, today he has to give up his sister, tomorrow he will have lost his country and his position. Abner is the great initiator: he initiates the first and third shifts, and monitors the second one, the delivery of Michal as demanded by David. It is David who gains the most here: he gets the princess back, which at the same time symbolizes how he now becomes the guardian of the entire nation. This story lends a unique shape to the intimate connections between sex, power, and politics.

(F) Two factions at war over David's throne

First Kings 1 is another long story, which becomes complex on account of the large number of characters who, divided into two groups, are active in two places simultaneously. The problem is that David is very old, and has not settled the succession. This spurs prince Adonijah, whose ambition and vanity are strongly reminiscent of the rebel Absalom, into action. For the moment, he is the hero, and his quest—to seize power—seems to be advancing according to plan, as, surrounded by his associates, he gives a banquet that is to seal his coup. The Solomon party raises the alarm, led by Nathan the prophet and David's most influential wife, Bathsheba, Solomon's mother. They are the heroes of the counter-quest, and manage to persuade David to make a pronouncement that at a stroke radically turns the tables.

Again, there is a race against time, as in Genesis 27. Adonijah's party is celebrating just a few hundred yards from the palace, near the spring of Rogel. Therefore David, together with the rival faction, organizes a coronation of Solomon at the spring of Gihon, just below the palace. Thus Solomon beats his brother to the crown, who is suddenly in danger of being found guilty of high treason. Solomon falls far short of qualifying as the hero, as everything is done for him and he is always the object—even the grammatical object—of discussion, transport, etc. The hero is his faction, which raises the alarm and gets busy; he himself shows no initiative at all. The beautiful structure of this varied episode, with its pivot (v. 30) of David's authoritative decision that changes everything, is discussed in the next chapter.

(G) *True and false prophets*

First Kings 13 opens with an exposition in which God, through a prophet who has come from Judah, opposes the altar of King Jeroboam. With the support of the prophet Ahijah, Jeroboam had separated the North from the House of David, but is now operating an illegal cult in Bethel. During the exposition (12:33–13:10), the anonymous man of God from Judah is the subject of the quest, which consists of putting a curse on the cult (through a prediction, and carrying out a destructive sign), and in this he is successful. All this, however, is only a prelude.

The story proper is in vv. 11-32 and quickly presents us with a nasty problem. An old prophet in Bethel invites the Judean to his home for a meal, and states that God himself instructed him to do this. The Judean, who just before resolutely dismissed a similar attempt at reconciliation by the king, now rises to the bait, which will cost him his life. Thus, a counter-quest has started that reeks of temptation. Apparently, the prophet from Bethel is prepared to go to great lengths to get the man of God into his house. What is he after? I would guess it is prestige, and it is at the same time an attempt to placate the Judean after all, on behalf of Jeroboam's regime. For the entire section of vv. 11-32 the prophet from Bethel is the hero of this second quest.

To our minds, the two men do not meet their deserved fates. The man who did good work against the detested altar, and who brushed off the king by pointing to his own instructions (go straight home after business), pays with his life for letting himself be taken in by the colleague from Bethel. The deceiver who lied (thus v. 18) about God's word, becomes, to our surprise, a vehicle for God's word in vv. 20-22 and pronounces an oracle of doom against his guest. An hour later, the Judean is killed as he continues his journey home, but his remains find a place in the grave owned by his host, with the result that 200 years later this grave is spared during the religious purge under King Josiah—thus 2 Kgs 23:16-18.

We can get a clearer understanding of the fate of these two prophets, one from the south, the other from just across the border, when we acknowledge that there is a hidden but razor-sharp competition here about true and false prophecy. Who is right? And first of all: how was the Judean man of God to know that the man who invited him was lying about God? Did he have a realistic option of refusing him, as he had done the king? He should probably have kept strictly to his own task, which undisputedly had come from God, and realized that this command certainly would not be cancelled or contradicted by God himself. In short, he should have been utterly obedient. Now that he has caved in to the prospect of a convivial drinking session (remember the Levite of Judges 19?), another hero appears in the arena where true and false prophecy are at loggerheads. This is the Word of God, which employs various spokesmen, but which always reaches its destination, even though this has to be accomplished through the mouth of a prophet who has just lied to a colleague.

(H) Elisha after Elijah's ascension to heaven

Our first thought in *2 Kings 2* is that of course Elijah must be the hero—isn't he awarded the unique honor of being taken up to heaven? No, this consideration is based solely on content, and is refuted by the opening clause. The curious thing about 1a is that in the first phrase the ascension figures as something already known—these first words are no more than an indication of time. The first main clause refers to the journey undertaken by Elijah and his pupil, and the temporal clause treats the ascension as something which is nothing new to those concerned (Elijah and Elisha, and the throng of prophets following them): "When Yahweh was about to take Elijah up to heaven in a whirlwind, Elijah and Elisha had set out from Gilgal." We cannot help noticing how well-informed all these prophets are, when in v. 3 the narrator lets us in on an exchange where the prophets ask Elisha: "Do you know that Yahweh will take away your master from over you today?" Elisha answers that he knows it, too.

The two holy men travel a route to the east that is shown to us on the map: Gilgal—back to Bethel—Jericho—Jordan. Elijah had wanted to travel alone, but he does not get the chance. Three times the narrator has Elisha use strong language: this is the oath in vv. 2/4/6 by which he swears to his master that he will not leave him. Apparently, he is determined not to; why? The truth comes out after Elijah, in a final display of divine power, has divided the river with his mantle (v. 9): Elisha wants to receive a double portion of Elijah's spirit, i.e. his divine inspiration. This request reveals that Elisha (no relation!) assumes the role of Elijah's son, and wants to inherit a firstborn's portion: under the law of succession, the eldest son receives a double share. No wonder Elisha should cry out at the *moment suprême*: "Oh father, father! Israel's chariots and horsemen!"

It is now clear who is the hero, and of which quest: 2 Kings 2 is already a story about Elisha, because he, the disciple, now wants to become the master, at the exact moment when his master disappears. And so it happens. He witnesses a miracle in v. 11, as a chariot of fire and horses of fire take Elijah away from him, up to heaven. Now that he sees it with his own eyes, he knows that he is, in fact, the successor accepted by God, as Elijah had determined earlier (v. 10). Elijah's departure is the axis of the story, around which are placed Elisha's seeing and not-seeing-any-more (vv. 11-12). The next ring consists of vv. 8 and 14: Elisha takes up Elijah's mantle, and divides the waters of the Jordan just as his master had done on the way up, so that to the throng of prophets following events from a distance

(another ring, vv. 7 and 15) it is now also quite clear who is
their new leader. The conclusion of the unit confirms this,
when Elisha is confronted with some skeptics who still find it
necessary to go and look for Elijah's body in the rough Trans-
Jordanian terrain. As it is their problem, Elisha sensibly leaves
them to it and manifests himself as spiritual leader; the narrator
grants him the last word in this final paragraph, with its comical
mini-quest (vv. 15-18).

(I) A mother fights for her child

I conclude with *2 Kgs 4:8-37*, where Elisha twice performs a
miracle, and where again we are tempted to think that the great
prophet is the hero. Again, however, this consideration, based
on content, is wrong. A first signal that we are on the wrong
trajectory already occurs in the exposition, when the woman
from Shunem makes it clear that she does not need any favors
from the prophet (jumping ahead for a moment: be sure to link
v. 16 with her bitter reproach in v. 28!).

The exposition covers vv. 8-17 and already brings on all the
actors. The quest is the woman's, as her goal is to have a guest-
room permanently available for the man of God in her house,
and she has the initiative. The prophet wants to do her a favor
in return, but prefers to speak with her through his servant
Gehazi (see especially vv. 12, 14-15 and later on v. 36)—a slightly
disagreeable form of indirect contact. Moreover, being a child of
his time the prophet suffers from the traditional notion that
every woman considers motherhood *the* fulfillment of her life,
and without paying attention to the fact that she is not very
interested, he announces that she will have a child. So it
happens, and in certain respects this outcome resembles a
counter-quest in which the prophet forces his plans through.
The circumstance of her husband's being old (and who
knows—she herself could be 50 already) is an allusion to
Abraham and Sarah who had a child when this had long been
impossible from a biological point of view (Genesis 17–21).

The story's central part covers vv. 18-37. The child dies, and
the father appears indolent (if not sluggish, v. 23). The desperate
mother has to cope on her own, but she fights like a lioness. All

action is initiated by her. She knows that the only remaining chance to get her child back is Elisha's power to work miracles, and she sets off in a hurry. She finds him on Mount Carmel and will not let go, in much the same way as Elisha behaved towards Elijah in ch. 2. She, too, swears: "As Yahweh lives and as you live, I will not leave you." This is a poignant detail: to have a *dead* child but to swear on the *lives* of the two male authorities, with the implicit message that the prophet should not attempt now to wriggle out of it. First Elisha tries a solution through his servant, but of course Gehazi is just as good at doing miracles as you or I (vv. 29 and 31), so that the great prophet will really have to make an effort himself. With his body he works a kind of healing that succeeds just when all hope seems lost.

The woman is the real hero. Twice the initiative rests with her, she is continually present in the text, and she devises the preliminary quest (and is rewarded with young life). Some 15 years later she is forced with her back to the wall, but immediately takes action and resolutely and alertly completes the trajectory of the second quest, truly a life-and-death struggle. She shows the prophet his responsibilities in v. 21, when she carries the dead child to the guest-room and puts it on Elisha's bed. And through her oath, she makes sure that he is going to try himself. It would be a gross error to view 2 Kings 4 as a naive or primitive story about wonder-working; on the contrary, the good listener discerns subtle criticism of the man of God. She is a woman of character.

Assistance and opposition

I will conclude this chapter with a brief discussion of *helpers and opponents*. Now that we have learned to discern the axis of pursuit, we are able to position the remaining characters correctly in relation to the quest. They are on the action axis, and are usually few. They are seldom neutral; in fact, the question whether they further or obstruct the action is often enlightening. If we see Rebekah as the heroine of Genesis 27, it is clear that Jacob is her helper. In his case, this function with respect to plot or quest coincides with his position as beneficiary. In the first half, his brother and father are unwitting opponents—of course only in relation to the plot. The father is partly a helper, in so far as he wastes his blessing on the disguised son. In the second half, Esau is clearly an opponent, and Isaac is transformed into a helper through Rebekah's wiles. In 1 Samuel 9–10 the prophet Samuel obviously functions as helper, in relation to the journey that turns an unsuspecting farmer into a surprised, but secretly initiated candidate for the throne. I trust readers will find it easy to develop this distinction for themselves.

The narrator may, however, decide not to use a simple black-and-white contrast but may opt for ambiguity, two examples of which I mention here. The man of God from Judah and the old prophet from Bethel, the duo from 1 Kings 13, are in the interesting gray area. In relation to the straightforward quest of the Word of God that creates and changes reality, they both have merits as well as demerits. A more intriguing use of ambiguity occurs in 1 Samuel 17 as regards Saul. On his way to the arena where he is going to slay Goliath, David has a conversation with Saul. In vv. 31-40, the king offers him his armor to wear in the fight. Saul must be a helper—or is he?

No, he is not, for in the first place the king already proves obstructive by not admitting David to the arena, v. 33, even though motivated by the best of intentions. When next David argues that as an experienced shepherd he knows what to do, Saul gives in and offers him his sword and armor. David puts it on, but it does not fit him. Not surprising, we conclude, on the basis of our superior knowledge. What no one in either of the army camps knows except David—and "above" the story the reader knows, too, thanks to the narrator—is that the shepherd boy from Bethlehem has been selected by God to be the new king, and that his rise is closely interwoven with the fall of the rejected Saul (both story lines: 1 Samuel 16). Hence, it is highly symbolic that Saul's attributes sit awkwardly on David, and that afterwards Jonathan's tunic does fit him like a glove. From the start, the offer of the king's armor was doomed to failure, and the entire incident is an obstacle on the shepherd's route to the Philistine champion. It is also a good example of the irrelevance of good intentions. The conclusion is that Saul's contribution in vv. 31-40 makes him a helper as well as an opponent.

6

Time and space, entrances and exits

The power of a correct structuration

When we succeed in making a correct division of the text into its various parts, everything comes together. Two useful avenues of approach are the entrances and exits of characters on stage, and the way in which the writer employs his system of time and space coordinates.

Characters come and go

When we check Genesis 27 (story A: Rebekah and Jacob deceive Isaac and Esau) for entrances and exits, we notice a remarkable alternation that shows how meticulously this act has been put together. There are six scenes with two figures each, and these are always one parent plus one son:

A	Isaac and Esau (vv. 1-5)	A'	Isaac and Esau (vv. 31-40)
B	Rebekah and Jacob (vv. 6-17)	B'	Rebekah and Jacob (vv. 42-45)
C	Isaac and Jacob (vv. 18-30)	C'	Isaac and Jacob (v. 46; 28:1-5)

This distribution of characters seems to be a decision about form. Shouldn't a correct exegesis be concerned with content? So far, I have studiously avoided the terms "form" and "content," and will wholeheartedly continue to do so. As it is, this duo is not very useful. The impression they give of a neat dichotomy is misleading. A literary approach can only flourish if we realize that all form affects content, and that all the content you may imagine for any story of quality can only be seen and discussed if it has taken some form or other. Form and content are so inextricably linked that they are difficult concepts to handle. Take, for instance, the tight design we notice in Genesis 27.

The ABC//A'B'C' pattern consists of a parallelism of two trios. Moreover, the "content" side of a "form" that always links one parent to one son is quite remarkable: the family quartet has been torn apart, right through the middle.

The mother who is in control both times occupies the center, and her "sending" is highly effective, unlike Isaac's in paragraph A. Try and consider to what extent A' is the fulfillment of A. Notice also that the blessing, which is the point of the story in C, acquires a strange extension in C'. There, God's promises to Abraham and Isaac are recapitulated by the latter, and passed on, again, to Jacob. Apparently, Isaac has reconciled himself to the *faits accomplis,* as he does not show any grudge about the deceit. Maybe he is consoling himself with the text of the prenatal oracle.

The parallel symmetry has an irrefutable validity, but there is another symmetry that is linked far more directly to the content, and closely corresponds to our plot analysis. The same six scenes may also be arranged in a concentric pattern. For me, this ring structure is more powerful than the parallel model:

A   Isaac sends out Esau
 B   Rebekah instructs and disguises Jacob
  C   Jacob before Isaac: receives the blessing
  C'   Esau before Isaac: receives counter-blessing
 B'   Rebekah's marriage plans for Jacob
A'   Isaac sends Jacob to Haran

A fascinating implication of the A-A' correspondence is that Isaac both times consciously relates to the son-to-be-blessed. Because of the deceit, however, this is not the same person both times! An exchange has taken place that in turn reflects the contrast at the basis of the relation C-C'. The advantage of the concentric model is that its labels exactly fit the terms of the plot analysis: in A-A' we see that the father, as sender, opens up a trajectory, and already indicates what is to be the object of value; in C-C' we see that he is the character who hands over the valuable object, while B-B' makes Rebekah's central position very clear. She mediates in both halves, thus enabling us to get from A to C. The link between C and C' is very apt, as these two paragraphs are based on the opposition between what each son receives: blessing and counter-blessing. This opposition has been carried over into the choice of vocabulary. The Hebrew proposition *min* means "from," but is ambiguous: it means both "being part of" and "away from, separated from." This ambiguity is perfectly exploited by the writer, through the words of the old father. The blessing given to Jacob, expressed in poetic lines, among other things says in v. 28:

> "May God give you *from* the dew of heaven
>   and *from* the fat of the earth,
>   abundance of new grain and wine."

Verse 28 is a so-called tricolon, as it has three parallel members. In v. 29 Jacob receives confirmation as well as an expansion of what the prenatal oracle (25:23) had said about old and young. Below, I quote its two verses (here: poetic lines), indicating by indents that each is a bicolon (a whole consisting of two half-verses):

> Let peoples serve you,
>   And nations bow to you;
> Be master over your brothers,
>   And your mother's sons will bow to you.

What does this leave for Esau, who misses the boat in vv. 31-34? He asks this question himself, v. 38. There, the writer uses the other side of the preposition *min* and has Isaac say:

> See, your abode will be [far away] from the fat of the earth,
>   and [far] from the dew of heaven above.

This is exactly the reverse side or the complement of the real blessing—Esau is even reprimanded for being too late. Not until the end of v. 40 is the loser shown light at the end of the tunnel.

Time and space: Joseph

The drama of Joseph in Dothan (story B from the practice area, Genesis 37) only sparingly uses explicit indications of time, and compensates for this with a wealth of data about space. The two paragraphs preceding the brothers' conspiracy, vv. 12-14 and 15-17, direct our attention towards Joseph's journey. The goal of his quest has been set by the father who sends him out. By

means of the italics, I have marked the inclusions that form a
simple but effective frame around the paragraphs.

> One time, when his brothers had *gone* to pasture their father's flock
> *at Shechem*, Israel said to Joseph: "Your brothers are pasturing at
> Shechem. Come, I will send you to them." He answered: "I am
> ready." And he said to him, "Go and see how your brothers are and
> how the flocks are faring, and bring me back word." So he sent
> him from the valley of Hebron, and [Joseph] *came near Shechem.*
>
> A man *found* him wandering *in the fields.* The man asked him,
> "What are you looking for?" He answered, "I am looking for my
> brothers. Could you tell me where they are pasturing?" The man
> said, "They have gone from here, for I heard them say: Let us go to
> Dothan." So Joseph *went after* his brothers and *found* them *at
> Dothan.*

At first sight, these two fragments do not seem at all remarkable.
A closer look, however, yields a different insight. The paragraph
of departure is framed by the name of the town Joseph is making for, and by the complementary "going" and "coming." At
the end the names of Hebron and Shechem are close together,
indicating start and finish of the journey, and moreover hinting
that Joseph will have some way to go, about three days' march.
The father's attention focuses on the well-being of brothers and
flock. The question of how the contact between this young man
and his brothers will work out raises some misgivings. As early
as v. 4b we have been told that they had fallen out, and it is
there, too, that we find the first *shalom,* indicating that nothing
positive is said by the brothers any more. And here we have the
father asking Joseph to bring him back a double *shalom* (well-
being) in the shape of a positive "word"! We will have to see
whether this quest will succeed at all.

The second paragraph is a well-rounded story in thumbnail
size. At the opening, Joseph has lost the way, which given the
context is a poor show; could it be a bad omen? At the end of
the paragraph, everything is all right, as he has been helped on
his way by a passer-by and he reaches the place where he wants
to be, in Dothan. The short intermediary quest has apparently
succeeded. The incident between the beginning and the end,
however, is intriguing. In the first place, the boy is searching;
this is to no avail, and he is "found." Secondly, by not saying

that he comes upon a man, but rather that the man comes upon *him*, the text underlines a curious reversal that is not very favorable to Joseph. He is the object of someone else's finding, which aptly illustrates how badly lost he is. And of course we know what will follow: he will be the object and victim of his brothers; Reuben will not get the chance to "restore him to his father" (as he wanted, v. 22b), and what will be restored to father is a bloody coat with an apparently unambiguous message! Here in v. 16, Joseph is the requesting and dependent party—he has no notion of what is really happening in the evil outside world. This adds a symbolic surplus value to the mysterious stranger who has to show him the route towards pit and slavery. "To have lost one's way" is an expression we, too, use figuratively.

The next two paragraphs, Gen. 37:18-22 and 23-24, have also been marked by spatial terms. In both segments, the opening contains an opposition between "far off" and "close by." While Joseph is still a long way off, the writer has the opportunity to let us overhear the conspiracy. After he has arrived, however, a rapid succession of actions (23b + 24) quickly flushes Joseph down a hole; there is no time for discussion now. The elements D and D' from the diagram I gave in the previous chapter, i.e. vv. 25 and 28 that form the first ring around Judah's decisive proposal and both mention the caravan, have also been spatially marked. They end in a sort of rhyme as they both indicate the new destination by a spatial term: Egypt. (The sequel to this is the final note of v. 36, plus 39:1, which picks up the thread exactly where it was left off in 37:36.)

Saul on his way to Samuel

The text of *1 Samuel 9-10* (story E) contains a striking number of explicit indications of time and space; these add up to more than 60, and refer to Saul's journey outwards and back and the stages in his remarkable quest. These indications are regularly accompanied by verbs recording the hero's movements.

I will pursue the function of the verb of movement a little further. Within a story, the situation is exactly the same as in the extra-linguistic reality: when character X moves from point A to point B, this takes time, and space as seen by traveler and spectator changes. In the linguistic or textual reality, the verb of movement is a flexible mediator, easily and discreetly arranging a fusion between narrated time (the time within the story) and narrated space (the world evoked). This truly makes space and time almost inseparable dimensions of one and the same coordinate system. If my understanding is correct, this would be no surprise to the theory of relativity or quantum physics.

I will now consider the fusion of terms for time and space in 1 Samuel 9–10. Many of them highlight the boundaries of paragraphs and story sections. I have selected a very special quartet, each member of which constitutes a threshold and presents a sometimes ingenious combination of time and space: vv. 5, 11, 14b, 27. In v. 11 and 14 we notice instances of synchrony (simultaneousness): people "happen" to run into each other in this or that significant place, and the converging movements are synchronous. These four passages each consist of one pair of clauses, and have been carefully attuned to each other:

threshold 1 = v. 5a
When they reached the district of Zuph,
Saul said to the servant who was with him...

　threshold 2 = v. 11
　As they were climbing the ascent to the town,
　they met some girls going down to draw water,
　and they asked them...

threshold 3 = v. 14b
As they were entering the town,
Samuel came out toward them,
on his way up to the shrine.

　threshold 4 = v. 27
　As they were walking toward the end of the town,
　Samuel said to Saul...

I will just note a few connections. In 1, 2 and 4 we see the combination of coming and speaking. Each first line contains an observation of space. Thresholds 3 and 4 complement each other because of the inward and outward movements, which have been recorded with the precision of stage directions. The complementary movements up and down in case 2 also occur in case 3. The boy in 1 corresponds to the girls in 2. Not only does the original Hebrew employ the same nominal root for boy/girl, but in both cases the characters are anonymous, yet indispensable to get Saul and Samuel together, as they propose and initiate Quest Two—see the previous chapter of this book.

In combination with the many other indications of time and location, these data help us to arrive at a well-founded structuration of the story. A diagrammatic representation of the nine parts would look as follows:

A	introduction: new hero, something missing, search fails	vv. 1-4
B	servant proposes new excursion: to the seer	vv. 5-10
C	group of girls: catch the seer on his way to the sacrificial meal	vv. 11-14a
D	God informs Samuel, conversation 1 between Samuel and Saul: various anticipations on the part of the prophet	vv. 14b-21
E	Saul honored at the head of a cultic feast	vv. 22-24
F	conversation 2 between Samuel and Saul, at night	vv. 25-26
G	anointing of Saul, privately; Samuel foretells signs, instructions	vv.27–10:8
H	Saul ecstatic on his way back, proverb	10:9-13a
I	return, conversation with uncle	vv. 13b-16

The two blank lines serve an articulation into three parts: journey there—reception—journey back. The reception covers sections C-G, that is, the broad center, with Samuel as the host, but the prophet is absent in AB and HI. However great his contribution to content, with his divine knowledge and his ability to make predictions, he is not the hero. This is Saul, who as the only one among a dozen characters is present in each of the nine paragraphs. The concept of the quest is also an argument in favor of this view. The first quest, finding the asses, is only seemingly less important, and remains valid while Quest Two is on (vv. 5-14) and Three fascinates us (9:15–10:8).

Let me recapitulate the indications in the text. In 9:20 the seer does say that the animals have been found, in order to reassure the hero and direct his full attention to his new career. Consequently, for a moment we think that Q_1 is finished. In 10:2, however, Samuel predicts that Saul will receive confirmation from unexpected quarters that the animals have been found (note how the father's worrying from 9:5 reappears here!), and even then the writer does not abandon Quest One: in the final verses 10:14-16 an uncle asks Saul about them, and there is the dry wit of Saul's answer in v. 16 with which he satisfies his uncle regarding the asses, and at the same time keeps completely silent about the most important part, his kingship.

The conclusion echoes the opening: the father had a name and exercised the usual total authority over the son, but when the prophet, on God's authority, determines Saul's life there is an anonymous uncle who remains ignorant, to symbolize that Saul is now embarking on a radically different career where the old family authority does not count any more.

When we take a closer look at the space, the nine scenes prove to have been arranged in a compelling order. We find an underlying structure of concentric symmetry, which shows that this long story is based on an *itinerary* of the hero's: the route of his journey.

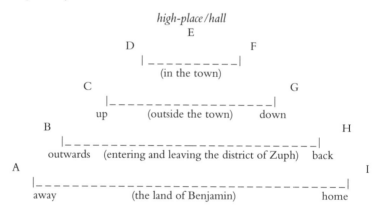

The man who left his house at the beginning of this episode returns to it after about a week, but he is not the same man any more. He has changed in an essential respect. On the way back the Spirit of God entered him, which for a few hours even took him into a prophetic trance, among a great crowd of prophets (a kind of dervishes). The writer beautifully brings out this transformation by showing us in 10:10-12 how other people, ordinary citizens, watch the spectacle in amazement and spontaneously react:

The people said to one another:
"What's happened to the son of Kish?
Is Saul really among the prophets?"
And somebody answered:
"Who is their father?"

The form of the last line is immediately striking, as the answer is phrased as a question, with roughly the meaning of: where do these guys belong? They fall outside the stable structures of the community! Moreover, the word "father" makes this a subtle stage on the line that runs from the almost omnipotent father Kish to the anonymous uncle who has been sent off with a flea in his ear. Finally, the writer underlines the exceptional aspect of Saul's new status by even breaking out of the frame of narrated time to tell us that the incident has been preserved for posterity in a proverb: "Is Saul really among the prophets?"

Adonijah or Solomon?

The story of 1 Kings 1 (practice story I) has an extremely varied cast. It must have been quite a challenge for the writer to mold his material into an elegant shape; the arduousness of this task can be deduced from the inventory of characters and details below. I have grouped them into two columns, in order to show how the competition between the two warring factions works out. The middle column contains various aspects and entities, with on either side the corresponding proper names from the appropriate faction, or the realizations of these aspects in text or language.

Adonijah	*(prince/candidate)*	*Solomon*
Abiathar	(priest)	Zadok
Joab	(general)	Benaiah
Judean courtiers	(servants)	"loyal soldiers" (vv. 8, 10)
Jonathan	(name in vv. 11–14//41–48)	Nathan
Haggith	(mother)	Bathsheba
guests	(faction)	"calls" + direct objects, vv. 28, 32
old, cold, passive	(David)	decides, commands
chariot + runners	(attribute)	rides the king's donkey

(cf. 2 Sam. 15:1)

Rogel	(spring)	Gihon
in vv. 50-52, for	(mortal danger)	in v. 21, for the Solomon
Adonijah		faction

The lists shows that both camps are very well equipped, with figures of authority such as priest, general, a following at court or in the army, as well as royal attributes. From this point of view, it is certainly not immediately obvious who is going to win this contest. Why exactly would the balance tip in favor of Solomon? Again I could say, on the basis of "content": because of the authority of the great prophet Nathan, the same character who pronounced the great oracle of salvation in 2 Samuel 7, and who on God's behalf gave the surname Jedidiah to the child Solomon (2 Sam. 12:25). Instead, I would rather look at "form" again, i.e. those decisions that determine structure, and the sense I can glean from that structure.

The first half of the chapter has been articulated in such a way that there are no less than three speeches, of exactly equal length—twelve (!) lines each—and all presenting the same worrying message: Adonijah is seizing power at this very moment! Next, their rhetorical climax follows, which is compellingly presented but cannot be proven in any way: the contention that at one time my lord the king swore an oath that Solomon was to succeed him! This stream of arguments and manipulations is twice poured out over David, vv. 15-21 and 24-27. After that, the writer shows us what it is all about. What does King David think? This is the structure, with its unique center, and again there are nine scenes (after the introduction, vv. 1-4, which describes David's weak condition):

A	Adonijah prepares his coup; his faction and Solomon's	5-6 information 7-10 action
B	Nathan warns and instructs Bathsheba	11-14 speech
C1	Bathsheba: speech to David	15-16 entrance 17-21 speech
C2	Nathan: speech to David	22-23 entrance 24-27 speech
X	David: OATH to Bathsheba: Solomon will succeed me!	28 entrance Bathsheba 29-30 oath

		31 Bathsheba's gratitude
C'1	David issues commands	32 entrance Z, N, B
		33–35 commands
		36–37 consent
C'2	commands executed: coronation	38 descent
	of Solomon	39 ceremony
		40 ascent
B'	Jonathan informs Adonijah and	41 fright
	his followers:	42 entrance
	Solomon king!	43–48 message
		49 fright
A'	Adonijah flees to the altar,	50 position of Adonijah
	confrontation with King Solomon	51–52 Solomon's reaction
		53 Solomon x Adonijah

Everything turns on the authoritative word of the current king, however old and stiff he may be. David chooses the most weighty and binding language available, that of the oath, and so decides the matter. In great haste, Solomon is hoisted on to a royal donkey, anointed at Gihon practically below the palace, and brought in with loud cheers. Adonijah is beaten, and the message that the priest's son Jonathan (not to be confused with David's bosom friend) brings him scares the life out of him and the party guests: who knows whether they will not be charged with high treason! 1 Kings 2 shows us that this fear was not groundless, as there the two most powerful figures in Adonijah's party are killed after all, at the command of the new king: the prince himself (after his reckless request for Abishag) and the old war-horse Joab.

The elegance of the ring structure of 1 Kings 1 is based on the solution the writer found for a difficult technical problem. He had to depict two scenes that occurred simultaneously but could only be expressed linearly in language—one thing after the other. How did he work this? He realized that Adonijah's state banquet required some time, so that he could move that scene to the background for a while, which would give him space for Nathan's and Bathsheba's wily maneuvers. Segment A, together with vv. 1-4, forms the exposition that presents us with the problem and the lack: the problem being that David has become too old, and the lack the fact that Adonijah is still not in possession of the throne; he cannot wait any longer. This first segment also contains the beginning of the action: Adonijah takes a political risk by giving a banquet that is to bring the decision.

Exactly at this point, the camera moves across and during four long paragraphs (BCXC, no less than 30 verses) shows us how the counter-quest quickly gathers momentum and manages convincingly to trounce David. After the king's oath (effectively made the axis of the composition) we remain a moment longer with the Solomon faction, which quickly creates various *faits accomplis,* with the support of the king and equipped with official paraphernalia of court and priesthood. When that is finished, the writer considers we can return to Adonijah's banquet, and he bridges the distance brilliantly through the sound of the trumpets that powerfully support the cry "Long live King Solomon!" (v. 39). Suddenly, we find ourselves at the spring Rogel, where people are scared out of their wits by the awesome noise (segment B'), and only then are given the actual news by Jonathan. In A' the two princes are finally together, but what is said only accentuates their differences: the absolute power threateningly raises an iron fist, and Adonijah, trembling, slinks off.

Between Bethlehem and Gibeah

The story in Judges 19 (practice story D) starts with a runaway wife. The writer measures how long she stays with her father in Judah, "a full four months," and then has her husband, the Levite, spring into action. He follows her and is cordially received in Bethlehem. His stay there is rather conspicuously spread out over vv. 4-9: while the Levite lives well as a guest, the writer is meticulously keeping track of the time. When will the man finally leave? Even on the fourth day, he lets himself be persuaded to stay a little longer. The gentlemen are having such a good time that the woman is nowhere to be seen—a rather ominous sign. Then, on the fifth day, something strange happens: the Levite does start his return journey, not in the morning, but in the afternoon. This will have far-reaching consequences.

We, the readers, will now have to consult our atlases and do some arithmetic. The distance from Bethlehem to Jerusalem and Gibeah is not great, only one or two hours on foot, and if you leave in good time you can make most destinations in Ephraim in one day's march. Apparently, the Levite finds it hard to extricate himself from the wining and dining on that fifth day (see v. 6), and the writer takes pains (v. 9) to describe how he finally takes his leave. How strange, though, that the Levite should only start on the return journey after the siesta, with concubine, servant and laden donkey! He will surely become stranded by the time it gets dark?

And so it happens. The writer devotes a conversation between Levite and servant to it in vv. 11–13. There are still more indications of time here, and we begin to wonder whether the night is not symbolic of disaster. Against his servant's suggestion, the Levite decides to travel for half an hour beyond Jerusalem and spend the night in Gibeah. His stay there occupies vv. 15-28, and we know the terrible outcome. If we take the many indications of time and place seriously—and they require being taken seriously by sheer force of numbers—we will be able to articulate the entire story as a journey there and back, and the structure will be found to reveal a secret that we could not think out for ourselves. From v. 9 onwards, the terms of space and time enter into a subtle collaboration, marking the following pattern:

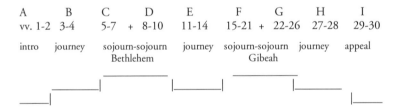

A	B	C	D	E	F	G	H	I
vv. 1-2	3-4	5-7	+ 8-10	11-14	15-21	+ 22-26	27-28	29-30
intro	journey	sojourn-sojourn Bethlehem		journey	sojourn-sojourn Gibeah		journey	appeal

We notice a symmetry that starts with a private problem (wife gone, segment A) and ends with a national problem (segment I, a crime that is broadcast in a gruesome manner in all directions). The sojourn after the journey up occupies a double paragraph, C + D, and receives a counterpart in F + G, the sojourn in Gibeah half way along the journey back. The correspondence between the two sojourns works in two directions. Going from the beginning to the end, we now notice that in Gibeah, too, the Levite is keen on men-only conviviality (vv. 21b, 22a), however different the circumstances. Working back from the end to the beginning, we see that the crime, for which he and his host are partly responsible in a hardly fathomable but certainly visible way, is by virtue of the structure linked to the callousness of the two men, which casts a backward shadow. We now understand what value label we should attach to the extensive boozing in Bethlehem: self-indulgence and materialism.

The real surprise of the story, however, is its central element, vv. 11-14. The structure itself has put this segment E in the pivotal position, so that we can give it a new label X for the unique center. We here get, carefully delineated by information about the sunset (11a + 14b), a conversation between master and servant which itself also proves to be concentrically arranged:

a	Since they were close to Jebus, and the sun was sinking,	11a
	the attendant said to his master,	11b
b	"Let us turn aside to this town of the Jebusites	11c
	and spend the night in it."	11d
x	But his master said to him,	12a
	"We will not turn aside to a town of aliens,	12b
	who are not of Israel,	12c
	but will continue to Gibeah."	12d
b'	He also said to his attendant,	13a
	"Let us approach one of those places	13b
	and spend the night either in Gibeah or in Ramah."	13c
a'	So they passed on and went their way,	14a
	and the sun went down on them near Gibeah of Benjamin.	14b

The elements a-a' are themselves concentrically arranged: in the center, there is a clause about the two men (speaking and moving, 11b + 14a); then there is a chiastic construction containing place and time (Jebus = Jerusalem plus "sun is sinking" in 11a, "sun set" plus Gibeah in 14b). This is the carefully crafted setting for a pearl: the conversation behind which the writer is hiding his scale of values. First, however, I will briefly discuss the structure of the pair b-b' and that of the center. The servant's suggestion (11cd) specifically mentions "the town of the Jebusites" and is about spending the night, while his master's words in v. 13 (separated from the speech in the center by their own introductory formula, 13a!) contain a counter-proposal. The fact that this proposal has a chiastic relation to the servant's idea is no coincidence, as the Levite opens with a line about spending the night, with a remarkably vague term of space, "one of those places," and does not give actual names until his second utterance. The Gibeah he mentions replaces the Jerusalem from the servant's suggestion, and is to be the town where, a little later, they will only just manage to find lodging.

The speech by the Levite that occupies the center of the paragraph (v. 12) contains three lines, again concentrically arranged. "Turn aside" plus "a town of aliens" in 12b are opposed to "continue" and the name of the town of Gibeah in 12d. This pair covers the rejected proposal, and the master's alternative. This leaves one line in the middle of his speech for which there is no counterpart, and which itself now takes the position of pivot. These are the words that are to define "aliens": "those who are not of Israel." Is this apposition at all relevant?

It is not for nothing that the writer has placed this unique line in the middle of the middle of the middle, i.e. has made it the center of the middle verse of the paragraph that itself occupies the middle of the nine-part composition. The central line presents us with a group prejudice on the part of the speaker: one's own people are better than strangers, so we should not ask favors from Jebusites, the Levite thinks. Maybe he considers his servant naive with his suggestion of spending the night in Jerusalem, and he rejects it on the basis of his own prejudice. The change of accommodation, however, with which he closes the conversation, has disastrous consequences. It is not the "aliens" from Jebus but the Benjaminites in Gibeah, that is, people from among the elect, who commit a hideous crime. Thus, the course of events ends on the inescapable exposure of the sad prejudice that Israelites are better persons than "heathens."

By placing this conversation in the center, the writer has indicated his real concern. This is not a specific incident, however appalling. He is not interested in gutter journalism, but through the rigorous structure of his story he opens a debate on values. He relentlessly criticizes complacency. In a way, the concentric pattern of the story reflects the selfishness and rancid group egotism of the Levite. The closedness of the symmetrical structure symbolizes what people who seal themselves off hermetically from their fellow human beings are reduced to: icy callousness.

7

The power of repetition

The dialectics of similarity and difference

Hebrew prose writers as well as poets like to use the device of repetition, and they use it systematically and deliberately. At the same time, they know very well that repetition for the sake of it soon degenerates into monotony. This is why they developed a sophisticated technique of *varied repetition,* with the primary purpose of expanding the richness of meanings and keeping all sorts of surprises in store for us.

The concept of repetition makes some demands on the modern reader. Many of us make our first tentative forays into the field of serious writing in high school, when we have to write an essay, and are immediately criticized for using the same words too frequently. This is a justified criticism, as many of a beginner's repetitions are the result of inexperience and lack of control. We often leave school with the impression that repetition is something to be avoided at all costs. Besides that, our culture is characterized much more by information and communication, so that the written word is used considerably more frequently and extensively than in the simple and relatively stable society of ancient Israel.

The Bible can only come into its own through a creative reading if we have first realized that the position of Israel's narrators and poets is almost diametrically opposed to our own, as regards the use of repetition. We, on the one hand, are intent on avoiding repetition as much as possible; the biblical writer, on the other, has received an extensive training in exploiting as many forms of repetition as possible in the interests of effective communication. In other words: in this respect, our rules for writing and our expectations when reading differ drastically from those in ancient times. The result is that we run the risk of misunderstanding and misjudging forms of repetition.

"Go down to the camp"

I will illustrate this with an example from Judges 7. Gideon has been designated by God as the liberator who is to drive the enemy, Midianites and other camel nomads, from the country. When after a great deal of shilly-shallying—i.e. protests, fear, and all sorts of fuss, patiently sidestepped by God—he has more or less reconciled himself to the assignment, God gives him the following instruction in vv. 9-11 (I am following the JPS):

> "Come, attack the camp, for I have delivered it into your hands. And if you are afraid to attack, first go down to the camp with your attendant Purah and listen to what they say; after that you will have the courage to attack the camp."

When we read this without thinking about the great difference in literary conventions, we probably consider all this repeating of "attacking" and "the camp" too much of a good thing. Moreover, the arrangement of the speech may strike us as strange: something seems to be wrong with the chronology of what Gideon has to do. This commission of God's, however, will take on a completely different profile when, assisted by the insights from the previous chapters, we pay attention to the structure of the speech and employ the Hebrew style to our advantage. Suppose the repetition here has a certain surplus value, or maybe even has some useful functions; what then? I will rewrite the passage, translating the verb of movement ("descend") consistently and literally, and restoring "hands" in v. 11b:

9b	Come, *go down* to *the camp,*
c	for I have given it into your hand.
10a	If you are afraid to *go down,*
b	first *go down* to *the camp* with your attendant Purah.
11a	You will hear what they say,
b	and after that your hands will be strengthened
c	and you will *go down* to *the camp.*

We now notice that the writer has placed the combination of "go down" plus "the camp" in strategic positions: at the beginning, in the middle, and at the end. We also notice that Gideon's hands occur in 9c as well as 11b, and thus form a ring inside the boundary lines. Finally, if we adopt a positive attitude towards the chronological ordering of the actions Gideon is asked to carry out, we will be on the track of a subtle play of variations-within-repetition that vitiate the impression of monotony.

Not all going-down is of the same kind. Verse 9c contains the so-called formula of deliverance, which occurs regularly and usually indicates that God will liberate his people from a war (see for instance Judg. 3:28, 4:7, 9 and 7:7, but also, as a counter-point, the end of 7:2!), but which sometimes indicates the very opposite (Israel as the enemy's quarry, e.g. Judg. 4:2, 6:1). This tells us that "go down" in line 9b is used in a military sense and refers to the crucial attack. However, we now have a complication. In v. 10, God recognizes that Gideon may experience fear, which is not surprising in the light of 6:22-23 and 27 (and see also 7:2-3; out of every three soldiers in Gideon's army two are afraid, and are allowed to go home immediately). Maybe Gideon can control his fear if he takes his armor bearer with him, God says. Is Gideon really afraid? The last line of v. 11 betrays that this is indeed the case, as there the story goes on to tell us that Gideon does take along his attendant.

Having reached this point, we notice that the complication ("If you are afraid to go down," v. 10) actually refers to a totally different kind of going down than that in 9b + 11c (the outer ring of the speech), and that it does not comply with the chronological order. This particular going down is actually stalking; it precedes the attack and is not carried out by Gideon's band but by the leader and his companion only. There is going down and going down. God here allows for some human weakness. If Gideon cannot yet muster the confidence that God will "deliver the enemy into his hand (= power)," it will be necessary to "strengthen his hands" first. This will give him the courage to attack, and receive the promised victory from God's hands. The sequel is spectacular: Gideon overhears a soldier from the enemy camp telling his mate about a dream he has had, and realizes how these two Midianites become terrified at the thought of an attack. This finally completely convinces him of the success of his mission. He now efficiently organizes the attack. If we read 7:15-22 carefully, we notice that under his command the three hundred do not have to inflict a single blow with the sword, and yet gain a total victory. The climax in v. 22 shows how this is possible: "For when the three hundred horns were sounded, Yahweh turned every man's sword against his fellow."

Abishai speaks

God's speech to Gideon shows that repetition is enlivened, refined and enriched by variation-within-repetition. There is an interaction between similarity (equality) and variation or difference (inequality). Another instance of this is a text containing two short speeches at a considerable distance from each other, which turn out, however, to have been carefully geared to each other. These are the words of the warrior Abishai in 2 Samuel 16 and 19, read against the background of Absalom's rebellion.

What is the situation? King David has been ignominiously put to flight by the army that is marching to the capital, Jerusalem, under the command of his son Absalom. He has to flee to the east, across the Mount of Olives, with his own standing army and a band of faithfuls. A vindictive man from the tribe of Benjamin by the name of Shimei, who is embittered about the fate of the previous king (Saul), crosses David's path and showers him with curses and stones. At this, general Abishai (one of Joab's brothers) indignantly says to his king:

16:9b   Why let that dead dog curse my lord the king?
    c   Let me go over and cut off his head!

David, however, will not hear of such violent action, and rebukes his commander: "Let him go on hurling abuse, for Yahweh has told him to. Perhaps Yahweh will look upon my misery, and recompense me for the abuse [Shimei] has uttered today." Abishai just has to swallow his anger, however great his solidarity with his king.

A week or two after this, Absalom's rebellion has failed, on a battlefield in Trans-Jordan. The prince himself is put to death by Joab personally. David can now return victorious to this side of the Jordan, to his residence. Shimei realizes that, having committed high treason, he can now expect to be executed. As soon as David has crossed the Jordan, he meets the king and begs for his life (19:20-21). Again, Abishai puts his oar in:

19:22b   Shouldn't Shimei be put to death for that —
    c   cursing Yahweh's anointed?

When we compare these two lines with the first pair in 16:9, we first of all notice great similarity: Abishai is still just as furious, and still eager to have his adversary put to death. Moreover, the connection between the two pairs is established by mirroring: the four lines cited constitute an ABB'A' pattern, as the order of cursing and death has been reversed. In this way, a chiasm of clauses has been created. A closer look, however, reveals considerable differences within these correspondences. Abishai has learned from his first brush with the king. He has moderated his choice of words a little, leaving out himself (and his eagerness to kill), as well as the abusive "dead dog." In addition, he dresses his text in a legal and religious cloak. In 22b, he adopts the passive voice, a much more impersonal construction than the active "I" of 16:9c. He uses this to suggest objectivity: is not the death penalty the only possible answer to treason? And this time he refers to the king by the religious term "Yahweh's anointed," so that Shimei's offense can be presented as sacrilege. We see how the interaction between the similar and the different creates shifts of meaning and new meanings. This play of repetition and variation I call the *dialectics of similarity and difference*.

Lines and circles

In the preceding chapters, we have already noticed more than once how clauses or paragraphs in stories were arranged according to a symmetrical pattern. The two main forms of symmetry are the *parallel* pattern, in which elements are placed parallel to each other in the same linear order and which may be written as

ABC // ABC, and the *concentric* pattern, in which the direction of elements is, as it were, towards the middle. This may be written as ABC–CBA, and it is not unusual for an element without a counterpart to assume the function of axis or center, ABCXCBA. These parallel or mirrored sequences may of course be expanded; they may contain fewer or more than two times three elements. If four elements show the order ABB'A', we have a *chiasm*. Absalom's rebellion, the long text that covers 2 Samuel 15–20, is a concentric composition of no less than 16 parts (ranging from a single paragraph to a page-long story), and hence may be written as A through H plus H' through A'. The entire sequence is given in full in *The next 110 stories* at the end of this book.

These models of parallel and mirror-image articulations occur at practically all levels in prose as well as poetry, ranging from sounds and words to clauses, paragraphs or strophes, and higher-level units (stories and stanzas). In this chapter, I am classing the phenomenon of repetition, which itself takes many different shapes and can also be applied to all textual levels, with the concept of symmetry. The instant we think of an example of a symmetrical arrangement, for instance the story of Isaac's deceit, it becomes clear that such an ABC–CBA pattern is based on repetition; what is more, it is a structural application and exploitation of repetition. This is another signal of the enormous gap between our culture and that of ancient Israel, and of the fact that it is our duty to adapt our attitudes and expectations if we really want to understand how the texts have been structured, and how they enrich life and meaning.

I will now explore how patterns of structuration and repetition strategies collaborate, starting from the question: when exactly is a scheme such as ABC–ABC or ABC–CBA valid? In quite a number of publications by biblical scholars with a literary orientation, these models are used in a rather immature fashion. As symmetries have a great attraction for intellectuals eager to master the text, it frequently happens with apprentice exegetes that they are determined to see a symmetry, which they then force through, i.e. impose upon the text, by their own verbal fireworks.

How can we avoid forcibly subjecting the text to a simplistic scheme or otherwise misguided patterns? The answer is by being self-critical, with the help of sound criteria. A structuration such as for instance ABCXCBA is valid if *(1)* demonstrable relations are present that *(2)* yield a better understanding of the text and point to new meanings. By "relations" I mean correspondences: the links indicated by A–A', B–B' and C–C'.

Now, we will meet these criteria, 1 (demonstrability) and 2 (relevance), if the symmetry by which a text seems to be determined consists in correspondences that, as forms of repetition, are based on (a) demonstrable and illustrative similarity, or (b) demonstrable and illustrative contrast or opposition, or (c) a combination of such similarities and contrasts. I will illustrate situations a, b and c one by one by examples; first, however, a word about what is and what is not demonstrable.

To my mind, there is a hard and a soft type of demonstrability. Let me remind the reader of God's speech to Gideon. In its first, middle and last lines "going down" was linked to "the camp." This is an undeniable correspondence, based on the "hard" demonstrability of strict repetition. A connection based on semantic similarity, i.e. correspondence of meaning, can be classified as a case of "soft" demonstrability. I will dig up a single example of this from the center of Judges 19, the ring structure of which I have discussed in the previous chapter (the section "Between Bethlehem and Gibeah"). The servant's suggestion was: "Let us turn aside to this town of the Jebusites, and spend the night in it." His master, however, does not agree and says: "Let us approach one of those places and spend the night either in Gibeah or in Ramah." Here, most correspondences are not literal, but still clearly recognizable. This is because Jebus and Gibeah (or Ramah) both belong to the same semantic category of place names, and because "turning aside" is not only contrasted with "approach" (by not turning aside), but also shares a category with it, that of movements of travel. In this way, there is still sufficient similarity of meaning.

Various contrasting encounters

As a composition, Absalom's rebellion is governed by the element of space: a large part of this text consists in units stationed on David's journey out and on his journey back. In 2 Samuel 15–17 David flees Absalom's coup, but after his victory on the battlefield (18), he can return victorious. On his flight, as well as on the return journey, the king has three encounters.

on the Mount of Olives, during David's flight

C	David and Hushai (who goes back as a spy)	15:32-37
D	David and Ziba (forage, Mephibosheth accused)	16:1-4
E	David and Shimei (curses and stones from Saul's tribe)	16:5-13

at the Jordan, when David returns as victor

E'	David and Shimei (who begs for mercy)	19:17-24
D'	David and Mephibosheth (innocent, refutes Ziba)	19:25-30
C'	David and Barzillai (farewell, Barzillai goes back)	19:31-40

First of all, we have here two pairs full of dramatic contrast, DD' and EE'. The same man who wished David dead and triumphantly added to the king's humiliation by hurling invective and stones at him, now again decides to confront David—but this time in order to avert his own execution for high treason. The two Shimei scenes offer various correspondences, but the first aspect we notice is that of similarity: the two men are the same. This is quickly followed in our observation by the relations between defeat, flight and humiliation on David's part, versus Shimei's swaggering and abuse (under E), and victory on David's part versus Shimei's begging and confession of guilt (under E'). These are all relations based on contrast, as a result of the political reversal on the battlefield. In linguistic terms, all these correspondences are semantic ("soft" demonstrability), however compelling they are as markers in a life-and-death conflict.

Just as semantic, but morally and politically also dramatic, is the contrast D–D' (Ziba–Mephibosheth). Ziba, the dynasty's steward who was to take care of the lame Mephibosheth (2 Samuel 9) helps the king on his flight by means of a modest but useful foraging column, and in the same breath voices a nasty accusation with respect to his master: Mephibosheth is again harboring ambitions to the throne now that misfortune has befallen David. David is in a hurry and cannot investigate the matter, but he bears it in mind. When he returns and finds Mephibosheth waiting for him at the Jordan, he naturally asks Saul's descendant for an explanation.

Actually, the man's exterior says it all. The narrator himself, never very generous with descriptions of people's appearances, begins by telling us in 19:25 that Mephibosheth has not washed for weeks, following his protector's defeat. As we see (and smell...) the signs of mourning, this information immediately establishes Mephibosheth's innocence. He exonerates himself in vv. 27-29 and has to conclude that Ziba has deceived him. This creates an awkward predicament for David: who is right, and what sort of judgment is he to pass? The king then tries rather unedifyingly to have his cake and eat it, v. 30. By dividing the lands between Ziba and Mephibosheth he passes an abortive judgment-of-Solomon *avant la lettre*, as in this way he tries to reconcile two irreconcilable entities for which he feels obliged: Ziba's material support at his hasty departure, which enables him to reach the Jordan, and the immaterial support (meaning the genuine love) plus the innocence of his best friend Jonathan's son.

The pair CC', Hushai–Barzillai, shows us in a strange symmetry the two friends of David's who on either side of the Jordan play a crucial part in the restoration of his kingship. Not only do their names rhyme (with the Aramean ending *-ai*), there are all sorts of striking similarities. Hushai wants to come with David to the east, but is refused; he is sent back to the west, to be David's secret agent in Jerusalem. Barzillai is invited by David to come with him to the west and take up an honorable position at court, but this time the king is refused; Barzillai retraces his steps and remains in the east. A brilliant signal that C and C' form a pair is the word "burden," which is nowhere to be found except in the speeches under CC'. In the first scene it is David speaking to his friend; in the second the direction of address is reversed:

15:33ff.   If you march on with me, you will *be a burden to* me.
            But if you go back to the city [...]
            you can nullify Ahitophel's counsel for me.
19:35/36   How many years are left to me that I should go up with

the king to Jerusalem? [explanation in v. 36]
Why then should your servant continue to *be a burden to*
my lord the king?

Moreover, together with the key word "burden," returning to
Jerusalem forms a chiasm that keeps the two passages tightly together across four chapters. In both cases, having a friend along
is a burden for David.

Similarity and difference

I have said that correspondences were valid if they were demon-
strably and illuminatively based on *(a)* similarity, *(b)* contrast, or
(c) a mixture of both. For a and b we can also say: equality and
inequality. The perfect case of similarity, then, would be complete identity; is that a realistic proposition? The curious thing is
that this question must be answered with both yes and no.

I remind the reader of the clause from Genesis 37 that read:
"A savage beast devoured him." These words from v. 20 are
completely unchanged when they are repeated in v. 33. Yet,
they are not the same—they are now spoken by a different
mouth: not the brothers', but Jacob's. They form part of a different situation: Joseph has been deported. Moreover, they have
a different status: first they were a plan, part of a conspiracy, and
now, coming from Jacob, they are a heartrending conclusion—
as discussed in Chapter 5 above, in the section "Joseph in
Dothan." At the heart of total equivalence, we find difference!
How can this be? When we consider this matter, the linear axis
comes to mind. Even though a writer may repeat a string of
words without any change, their sense and function cannot remain unaltered as the context has changed: they have moved
along the linear axis, and in the meantime all sorts of develop-
ments have taken place.

From this analysis it follows that no form of correspondence
can be imagined based on complete identity. Strictly speaking,
we will never come across situation *(a)* (a relation of perfect
similarity). Those that look like it, such as Gen. 37:20/33, move
to *(c)*: a mixture of similarity and difference. This takes us to the
varied and lively world of actual literature. In the vast majority
of cases, the relations that the elements of a symmetrical ar-

rangement enter into are ingenious combinations of contrast and similarity. The dialectics of similarity and difference are active everywhere.

David's encounters on his journeys back and forth, as discussed just now, are beautiful examples of mixing similarity and contrast. Every text has its own unique ratio between the similar and the dissimilar, and it is probably best to resist the temptation to capture such play in figures and accommodate its components in percentages.

8

Points of view, knowledge and values

A good story is much more than just information, but without information a story cannot be imagined, and simply could not exist. From the beginning, a story in a sense informs; every sentence takes us a bit further, and every sentence carries the stream of information further. The narrator knows this and cleverly exploits this aspect, for instance in order to create tension, to wrong-foot us, to make the linear axis (the progress of the story) subservient to his view, and so on. Usually, the way in which he conveys information serves more than one purpose at a time.

The narrator is a manipulator who hardly knows when to stop, and this at two levels. Within the story he manipulates his characters like a puppeteer. He pulls the strings with which he makes them appear and disappear: it is he who decides who does or says what, and for how long. What we are concerned with here, however, is another level, that of communication. Writer and reader maintain a sender–receiver relationship, and both are far outside the narrated world. Within this dimension, too, the narrator is an experienced manipulator. The puppets now dangling from his strings are we, his audience. With every word the writer controls, massages and manipulates us, and we are left with only the simple choice between obedience and pulling out completely. In this case, obedience means following the story. The writer in turn knows that he has to help us by seeing to it that his text, and the information it offers, are easy to follow (have *followability*).

The beginning

The first sensitive moment for the stream of information waiting for us when we open a text is the very beginning. Everything is still open, and the narrator has a host of options available. He may decide to disclose almost everything at the start, or choose to do the very opposite, or only *appear* to start off with something essential. The very first sentence of the Bible is hard to beat as an example of instant and almost total disclosure: "In the beginning God created the heavens and the earth." It is a monumental sentence, functioning as a caption epitomizing in a nutshell what happens in the first story. To a certain extent this reduces the rest of the creation story to fleshing out and providing details for this outline. There is no tension, and hardly a plot to speak of. The six days of creation are dealt with one by one, culminating in the day of rest which is called the sabbath and is declared holy. The powerful opening sentence has its counterpart in a postscript, Gen. 2:4a: "These are the generations of the heavens and the earth when they were created." Thus, the last clause of the creation story is an echo of the first. Together they provide a solid frame. The specific verb used for "to create" can only have God as its subject; it is a keyword in Genesis 1 and is completely absent from the second story. (Gen. 2:4b–3:24, the story of Paradise, is strictly speaking not a second Creation story but a closer study of the created human being, its origin and its fundamental relations with God and the world.)

Genesis 22 is another example of crucial information being revealed right at the beginning. The subject is highly immoral: a father is commanded to kill his only son as a sacrifice. In order to soften the blow somewhat, the narrator reveals to us the true character of the order, and the intention of the speaker, even before God issues the command to Abraham: it is a test. "Some time afterward, God put Abraham to the test." The omniscient narrator grants us prior knowledge of what is to come, and gives us a head start on the patriarch. It is only after passing the test with flying colors that Abraham will have the opportunity to heave a sigh of relief and conclude: Phew, it was *only* a test.

From Saul to David

An obvious thing for the narrator to do is to introduce the hero at the beginning of a narrative cycle. I am thinking now of the way in which Saul is introduced in 1 Sam. 9:1-2 (practice story E):

> There was a man of Benjamin whose name was Kish son of Abiel son of Seror son of Becorath son of Aphiah, a Benjaminite; he was a man of substance.
>
> He had a son whose name was Saul, an excellent young man; no one among the Israelites was handsomer than he; he was a head taller than any of the people.

In the first verse, we meet someone of consequence. He is not only a gentleman-farmer but can also boast a long family line, so that it is obvious he must be someone important in his tribe. For a minute, we think that he might be the hero. Next, however, we are shown picture two: his son Saul seems to have everything going for him—youth, looks and good breeding. This raises expectations with the reader, as well as the question: could "being a head taller" be symbolic for his destiny? This expectation is quickly confirmed, as Saul becomes the hero of the quest. After Saul's secret anointing (10:1ff.) and his return, the prophet Samuel summons a national meeting and announces the appearance of the candidate.

> [A]nd when he took his place among the people, he stood a head taller than all the people. And Samuel said to the people, "Do you see the one whom Yahweh has chosen? There is no one like him among all the people." And all the people acclaimed him, shouting, "Long live the king!" (1 Sam. 10:23-24)

By organizing a meeting and putting on a religious ballot (vv. 20-21) that yields the name of Saul for the throne, the prophet is playing the part of a director. With this set-up he manipulates the people in such a way that they think they "recognize" the king by his stature. The fact that he stands a head taller than everyone else is read symbolically, as a sure sign that he is destined for the throne.

The writer himself is not so naive as to agree that height is a guarantee for quality. Once Saul is doomed, God sends Samuel to Bethlehem in order to anoint a son of Jesse's as the second king, and the following scene unfolds (1 Sam. 16:4-10). The father lines up seven sons, of which his firstborn, by the name of Eliab, is the tallest. Samuel is impressed and assumes, apparently with the previous anointing in mind, that this young man must definitely be God's candidate. This is rather a *faux pas* on his part, which at the same time serves to make it clear to us that even a prophet will always be a fallible human being. God puts the mortal Samuel in his proper place with the classic words:

> "Pay no attention to his appearance or his stature, for I have rejected him. For not as man sees [does the Lord see]; man sees only what is visible, but Yahweh sees into the heart!"

Samuel believed his eyes, instead of waiting to hear a voice in his ears. He has apparently forgotten how his meeting with the first king (in 1 Samuel 9) passed off when he, the "seer," could do little or nothing with his eyes and only acquired supernatural knowledge after God had whispered this into his ears (see especially 9:15-17).

Information about Gideon kept back

Judges 6–8 is a good example of how bits of information may be distributed through the text. The beginning and the end of the short cycle about the judge Gideon beautifully show how the narrator divulges information and, later, undermines this by revelations he has initially kept from us. First we get the background, 6:1-5. The country has been occupied and pillaged for years by Midianites and other camel nomads from the East. When in distress the people cry out to God, he replies with the rather repressive diagnosis, conveyed through a prophet, that he, always their protector and savior, now has been forsaken by the disobedient Israel. The impression this creates is one of: you can sort it out for yourselves. Next, the story proper starts with the introduction of the hero, a man from the centrally situated village of Ophrah, and it soon becomes clear that through him God will after all set about liberating Israel from the occupying forces. In 6:11 we read three clauses:

> An angel of Yahweh came and sat under the terebinth at Ophrah, which belonged to Joash the Abiezrite, as his son Gideon was then beating out wheat inside a winepress in order to keep it safe from the Midianites.

The first impression is that Joash is to be the host of this visitor. His son receives no more than a circumstantial clause, and thus seems to be busy in the margin. In this way, the narrator has us on the wrong foot for a moment, as Gideon will soon turn out

to be the hero; he is designated as the liberator by God himself.
In addition, another impression is created which we will have to
correct two chapters further on: here in 6:11 it seems reasonable
to assume Gideon is a young man.

Gideon is a strange character. At one moment he is insolent
(6:13), at the next he is frightened (6:22, 27 and 7:10-12) or
vacillating, and moreover, until a fairly late stage he is skeptical.
After his commissioning as savior has been concluded with the
miraculous departure of the angel by way of the sacrificial fire
(vv. 21-24), he receives a command from God by which he can
and must prove himself as a hero: he is to destroy the altar of
Baal that belongs to his father! In his fear, he does this at night
(6:27b), as if that would help to hide his actions from sight.

Then the text leaves a gap: the narrator does not furnish any
information about Gideon's father! This leaves us with the un-
answered questions of what Joash thought of his altar being
smashed when he found out it was his own son who was responsible for this sacrilege, and how he reacted when he found
out. This formidable gap (*ellipsis*) has been left on purpose, and
can only be filled by us two pages further on. What we do hear
now, in 6:29-32, is that the people of Ophrah discover the
identity of the perpetrator and demand that Joash hand him
over: Gideon must be put to death. The father's reaction is surprising, as he staunchly supports his son, challenges Baal to
prove his divinity by fighting his own battles, and chases his
fellow citizens off by means of a bluff (v. 31). Where does Joash
find the strength to confront the entire community? The answer
is not found until much later. In the meantime, we may deduce
from his intervention that Joash has been through a dilemma
and has arrived at a clear-cut decision: to side with the furious
community and the Baals by delivering Gideon up to them, or
protect his son and break radically with the cultus of this idol.
He chooses the latter option. The question now also becomes:
how are we to interpret the fact that the father does all the dirty
work, and that Gideon does not defend himself (6:30-32)? Is
our impression correct that he takes a rather dependent position?

Shortly after this, Gideon does have the effrontery to put
God himself to a double test (6:36-40), as nothing can convince

him of his divine commission. God has his hands full persuading and pacifying this pain in the neck, but persists with great patience until Gideon finally accepts his task (7:15). The entire central unit 7:9-22 is set at night. The enemy is defeated without Gideon and his 300 men having to wield the sword once— see 7:22. He then mobilizes the neighboring tribes for the chase. Here, too, the text causes great surprise. At this stage of reaping the fruits of victory, the hero is suddenly extremely assertive and fierce, and even extraordinarily cruel (8:5-9 and 14-17) towards his countrymen, the inhabitants of two towns in Trans-Jordan. How come? So far, we have not heard anything to explain this. Next, however, there is a paragraph (8:18-21) in which Gideon has a conversation with the two Midianite kings whom he has taken prisoner and is going to have executed. From the point of view of imparting information, this passage is highly surprising:

> (18) Then he asked Zebah and Zalmunna, "Those men you killed at Tabor, where are they?" "They looked just like you," they replied, "like sons of a king."
> (19) "They were my brothers," he declared, "the sons of my mother. As Yahweh lives, if you had spared them, I would not kill you."

What we now hear from the mouth of the hero is that before the battle a fatal incident has taken place. The enemy has executed a number of Israelites (in retaliation for acts of resistance, or as an intimidation strategy, I imagine) on the Tabor hill, a prominent spot dominating the Eastern half of the great plain of Jezreel. In addition, Gideon reveals to these kings (and the narrator reveals to us) the vital information that these victims were his own full brothers. With a shock we realize that all the time he was acting as leader on God's behalf, Gideon must have been shattered, sad and furious over the loss of his brothers. The question he asks here (v. 18a) is not informative. He probably knew all along that the enemy were responsible for their deaths, but he wants to tackle their leaders about it. We then get the reaction of the two kings, which is no less than sensational: they admit that the victims had the air of royalty.

The phrase "sons of a king" is the first signal of the actual theme of the cycle: kingship. It makes us realize that the family of Joash was held in particular esteem. It enables us, upon re-

reading the story, to understand how it is possible for Joash to confront the entire community of Ophrah in 6:31, and chase away the people with a threat in order to protect his son Gideon.

We further hear in 8:20 that Gideon has a son, which gives us a different idea of his age: he is not a teenager, but a man in his prime. This makes it all the more ironic that in 6:11c he is introduced to us by way of a circumstantial clause, in his father's shadow, and also that he needs his father's intervention to escape from capital punishment (6:25-32). In short, the paragraph 8:18-21 contains all kinds of *deferred information*, which forces the reader to re-gauge, re-read and maybe re-interpret everything that has gone before.

The royal appearance of Gideon and his family is recognized from an unexpected quarter: the Midianite top dogs, two men who themselves are kings and discover that they have not helped their chances of survival by admitting the royalty of their victims. The recognition comes from a quarter that is above suspicion: if your enemy agrees that your brothers look like princes, who is going to dispute that?

Immediately after their execution by Gideon himself, the theme of kingship is unfurled to its full extent. The people request the victor to be their sovereign, but Gideon refuses in pious phrases (8:23). Yet, he behaves like a tyrant and falls victim to the glamour and lures of the spoils of war. He melts down the captured gold into an idol (a so-called *ephod*) and so lapses into a type of religion that is strongly condemned by the narrator in v. 27. Thus the wheel has come full circle, in a negative sense: just as Joash (whose name contains an abbreviation of the holy proper name Yahweh, and who consequently still worships Yahweh) at the beginning still maintained an altar for Baal in an act of syncretism, his son Gideon now on his own authority sets up a misguided cult. No wonder that after his death, people again "play the harlot after the Baals" (8:33). And what Gideon really thinks of the monarchy is betrayed by his half-forgotten son in the provinces, the impetuous Abimelech from Shechem. He establishes a dictatorial monarchy, after having created carnage among his 70 half-brothers, the sons of Gideon who as lawful heirs formed a kind of oligarchy after their father's death.

With the assistance of his mother's relatives, the outcast Abime-lech avenges himself on the father and his recognized progeny, the seventy. Judges 9 covers his reign, and its downfall, which is as disastrous as it is violent. The boundless ambition of Abime-lech, whose name ominously enough means "my father is king," exposes the desire which was smoldering in Gideon's subconscious, and is its enlargement and fulfillment.

Levels of knowledge: David's ignorance

Manipulating information implies that the writer will sometimes decide to release a surplus of facts, and sometimes to create a shortage. Sometimes he will do this in time, sometimes only after the fact. There are always good reasons for his choices, and it is our job (not always easy) to discover these.

Manipulation of the data stream is at the same time manipu-lation of knowledge. The writer may decide to grant us the same amount of insight as the character he introduces, or more, or less. In Gen. 22:1 he gave us a head start on the patriarch who had to sacrifice his child. In other situations, a character knows much more than we do and acts accordingly without our being wise to it. Gideon has known for a long time why he be-haved ruthlessly towards his own people, while we have to wait for the surprises of 8:18-20 (the murder of his brothers).

It is part of the charm of some stories that they play off vari-ous degrees of knowledge against each other, thus creating a competition between different avenues of approach or perspec-tives. Consider, for instance, the thresholds that we cross to step into the world of 2 Samuel 12 and 14. King David has acquired everything he desires, but falls for a woman in ch. 11 and has her husband eliminated in a sly and reprehensible fashion. Thus, within a short time he has committed two capital offenses, and as there is no one to correct the absolute sovereign, God himself intervenes by sending Nathan the prophet to him. Nathan tells David about a rich egoist in the country who steals his poor neighbor's only sheep, and when the king becomes angry at this and, as a judge, pronounces a condemnation of the rich man, the prophet reveals that it was "only" a parable: "That man is you!" Then follows a double oracle of doom, announcing punishments for murder and adultery, 12:7-12.

In the last sentence of ch. 11, the writer assumes the position of an omniscient narrator by telling us: "Yahweh was displeased with what David had done." In 12:1 we hear that Yahweh sends the prophet to David. Nathan's arrival and his recital of the parable employ no fewer than three levels of knowledge. At the highest level are God, the prophet and the narrator, who already know that David is to be trapped by means of a parable. At the lowest level is the king, who does not know anything of these plans, suddenly sees Nathan appear, and innocently thinks he is listening to an offense by a reprehensible materialist on which in his capacity as a judge he will have to pass judgement. In between, however, there is the reader in an intermediary position. We do know that God will not allow David's crimes to go unpunished, and we are also quick to notice that Nathan has devised a subtle strategy (or had this suggested to him by his Sender) for dealing with the king. What we do not know, however, is how he is going to do it. The function of this intermediary position is to give us a double perspective on the prophet–king confrontation. The narrator has let us in on the conspiracy, so that we have been warned. Yet, we listen with the same naivety as David; we can still identify with him.

In 2 Samuel 12, David is forced by means of a brilliant stratagem to admit his criminal acts. Tricked by the parable he cannot escape confronting and confessing his guilt. Chapter 14 is a structural parallel. What has happened? Princess Tamar has been raped by her half-brother Amnon. After two years, when the court is not paying much attention, her full brother Absalom sees his opportunity and takes the law into his own hands: he avenges her honor by killing Amnon. He immediately vanishes into exile for three years, thus placing himself beyond the reach of justice. David is torn between emotions and thus gets stuck in a deadlock between anger against the fratricide, and grief over the loss of Amnon. His chief-of-staff Joab recognizes the predicament of his king and considers it a matter of national importance that conditions should be created for a reconciliation between the ambitious Absalom and his father. To this end he sends a "clever woman" to David and instructs her to play a

widow in a Cain-and-Abel-situation. She is to try and get David
the judge to swear an oath that her only surviving son will be
allowed to live, instead of being executed for fratricide. She succeeds in this scheme; then, the woman applies David's judgment
to the case of Absalom, so that David sees himself forced to admit the prince back to Jerusalem. The court case simulated by
the woman is again a parabolic construction designed to bring
David to greater self-knowledge.

I would first like to give a new translation of the boundary
between the chapters, before I indicate the various levels of
knowledge:

(13:39) This [i.e. the murder of Amnon and Absalom's disappearance]
raised the desire in David to march out against Absalom, as he grieved
for Amnon that he was dead.
(14:1) Joab, the son of Zeruiah, recognized that in his heart the king
was against Absalom. (v. 2) He sent a message to Tekoa and had a
clever woman brought from there. He said to her: "Pretend you are in
mourning, put on mourning clothes, don't anoint yourself, and behave
like a woman who has grieved a long time over a departed one. (v. 3)
Then, go to the king, and speak to him as follows"—and Joab put the
words into her mouth.

Again, there are three levels of knowledge. The position above
the subject matter, occupied by the narrator who knows exactly
where he wants us, is the topmost, and within the story it is
shared by Joab. The general has an involved plan, for the dis-
crete execution of which he needs a well-trained person. This
will be the woman of Tekoa, whom he briefs in vv. 2-3. I
imagine that these two have discussed and practiced their course
of action thoroughly before she appears in front of the king with
her request for legal assistance. Again David knows nothing at
the moment she comes to him in vv. 4-5. Again, he thinks he is
about to hear a court case, and again he gets himself deeply involved by passing judgment (the oath he swears at the end of v.
11). We, on the other hand, know better, but we are one level
below that of the creative schemer Joab. Verse 2 raises hopes
that this time we will be fully briefed beforehand, but in v. 3
this proves an illusion: the narrator teases us by hiding the plan
behind the evasive words "speak to him as follows [...] put the
words into her mouth." At the moment the woman addresses

David, we again have a double perspective: we do not know what is coming, and identify with the innocent king who wants to ally himself with the widow and her weak position *vis-à-vis* the revengeful clan demanding the fratricide be handed over. At the same time, we know from the beginning that it is a put-up job, a clever piece of theater to confront David with himself and break through his deadlock.

Knowledge and suspense: Ahithophel's advice

A writer can ensure even more attention to his text if he creates suspense in his story. Traveling together with the hero and his quest, we readers wonder whether he will succeed; at various stages along the hero's trajectory the narrator can increase suspense by presenting us with open-ended situations where much is at stake.

The decisive moment during Absalom's rebellion (2 Samuel 15–20) is at the same time the most thrilling. This occurs when David has hurriedly withdrawn, together with his court and standing army, to the east behind the Mount of Olives, and Absalom enters Jerusalem as the victor.

David has almost allowed himself to be cut off by Absalom's attack on Jerusalem from the south. Among his following, both morale and equipment (weapons, food) leave much to be desired, as they try to reach the Jordan through rough and uneven terrain. If Absalom is clever, he will take advantage of the situation and give chase immediately, so that he can capture David and his retinue before they manage to escape across the natural barrier of the river. This is exactly the advice given to Absalom in the council of war that he convenes immediately after his arrival in the capital. The formidable counselor Ahithophel, who behind the scenes was the political heavyweight of the David regime but who has now put his money on the prince and his coup, puts it like this in 17:1-4:

> "Let me pick twelve thousand men and set out tonight in pursuit of David. I will come upon him when he is weary and disheartened, and I will throw him into a panic; and when all the troops with him flee, I will kill the king alone. And I will bring back all the people to you; the man you are after equals the return of all the people; the

entire people will be saved." The advice pleased Absalom and all
the elders of Israel.

This is simple and businesslike language without stylistic flour-
ishes and without flattery for the prince. Its point is clear: we
have to act swiftly, Ahithophel says, and moreover we should
have the sense not to spill blood unnecessarily. It is better if
Absalom eliminates only the deposed king, and gives his following a second chance by proclaiming a general amnesty after
the decision has been made. This is a better start for a new regime than leaving your subjects with a lot of smoldering resentment about the many who have fallen. In the first instance,
everybody is indeed agreed about the wisdom of this strategy.

Then, however, Hushai steps forward. He pretends to be a
defector, but we know that David has instructed him (15:34) to
act as his agent in the capital, and that primarily he is to try and
undermine Ahithophel's counsel. Apparently, Absalom himself
is not yet satisfied, or feels insecure, and first wants to hear what
Hushai has to say, 17:6: "This is what Ahithophel has advised.
Shall we follow his advice? If not, what do you say?" Then
Hushai speaks, with the following verbal fireworks, vv. 7-13:

> "This time the advice that Ahithophel has given is not good....
> You know that your father and his men are courageous fighters,
> and they are as desperate as a bear in the wild robbed of her whelps.
> Your father is an experienced soldier, and he will not spend the
> night with the troops; even now he must be hiding in one of the
> pits or in some other place. And if any of them fall at the first at-
> tack, whoever hears of it will say, 'A disaster has struck the troops
> that follow Absalom'; and even if he is a brave man with the heart
> of a lion, he will be shaken—for all Israel knows that your father and
> the soldiers with him are courageous fighters.
> So I advise that all Israel from Dan to Beersheba—as numerous as
> the sands of the sea—be called up to join you, and that you yourself
> march into battle. When we come upon him in whatever place he
> may be, we'll descend on him [as thick] as dew falling on the
> ground; and no one will survive, neither he nor any of the men
> with him. And if he withdraws into a city, all Israel will bring ropes
> to that city and drag its stones as far as the riverbed, until not even a
> pebble of it is left."

This is totally different than the advice of his competitor! In the
first paragraph, Hushai puts much stress on David's experience

as a warrior, who especially when cornered is at his most dangerous. His message is the exact opposite of Ahithophel's: do not act in haste, because the fortune of war may change. In this way, Hushai gains time—time, we realize, which is crucially important if David is to escape across the Jordan in one piece.

In his second paragraph (vv. 11-13) Hushai connects space and time, and through flattery plays on the prince's ego. Absalom will first have to call up a people's army, and that alone will require at least a week.... Next, the speaker uses three or four metaphors to overwhelm the new king: the sands of the sea are an image of numerousness, and at the same time an allusion to the promises made to the patriarchs; next, there is the dew which in the morning covers everything, and finally the awesome exaggeration of the city being pulled down and dragged into a riverbed. Absalom's personal vanity is tickled when Hushai suggests that the new king, with his splendid physique, will be a great inspiration to his troops by leading them into battle himself.

All this sounds attractive, but the objective spectator, who has the advantage of prior knowledge (Hushai is a spy), wonders whether most of this is not plain bombast. Which of the two counselors is going to win the competition? Moreover, is it possible for us who are outside the narrated world to arrive at a judgment as to who is wrong and why? The council of war, in any case, allows itself to be persuaded, as v. 14a tells us: "Absalom and all Israel agreed that the advice of Hushai the Archite was better than that of Ahithophel." But then v. 14b follows, consisting of only one compound sentence constituting a radical intervention on the narrator's part:

> Yahweh had decreed that Ahithophel's sound advice be nullified, in order that Yahweh might bring ruin upon Absalom.

Here a lot is happening at the same time, in spite of (and also because of) the fact that this sentence does not form part of the stream of sub-actions, but consists in information. Here we get the voice of the narrator himself, who, being omniscient, has consulted Heaven and now shares the result with us. Moreover, his communication anticipates the outcome of the battle, and hence is a *prolepsis,* i.e. a tool only sparingly used by good narrators. By casually slipping in the word "good," the narrator guarantees that we are left in no doubt as to the quality of both counsels. Ahithophel's advice was sound all right, we now know, and so the opposing plan of Hushai's is "bad" in the sense of "destructive for Absalom and his throne." The writer considers it so important that we should be quite clear on this, that by exception he himself spells it out for us. This loses him a powerful trump card, that of suspense. We now share his fore-knowledge about the outcome of the entire rebellion, and are not unduly anxious when the spy Hushai in 17:15-22 sees to it that the decision of Absalom's war council is communicated to David, and his two messengers narrowly escape arrest. In ch. 18, too, all suspense has gone as regards the outcome of the military confrontation in Trans-Jordan; all the writer can do is to tell the story in such an attractive way that at least he can convey the tension in the question, *how* is it going to happen? And how will David take the downfall of his son?

From the intervention in 17:14b we may deduce that some-times the narrator will prefer certainty for his readers over cre-ating and exploiting suspense. At the same time, "Yahweh's de-cree" annuls another aside from the narrator (16:23), which has made us fear the worst for David's chances:

> In those days, the advice which Ahithophel gave was accepted like an oracle sought from God; that is how the advice of Ahithophel was esteemed both by David and by Absalom.

Here we have a rare—one might almost say blasphemous—comparison: the word of the human being A enjoys the prestige of a veritable oracle (word of God). The verse makes very clear what Hushai was up against on his own! I will return later to Hushai's rhetorical fireworks and his position, when I discuss characterization and points of view.

The program of the book of Judges

I will discuss two more examples of prior knowledge affecting a large amount of text: Judges 2 and 2 Samuel 8. Our under-standing of the book of Judges as a whole is to a large extent determined and controlled by two paragraphs of more than normal importance. One is a programmatic paragraph that presents a cyclic scheme for the era of the Judges (roughly the 12th and 11th centuries BCE); the other is the only paragraph in the book to exhibit this model in its perfect form.

In English, there is a difference between "Then John would cycle" and "Then John cycled." The first phrase indicates a custom, the second phrase refers to something that only happened once. The sentence containing "would" is an example of repetition in the past. We also find this in the text of Judg. 2:11-19. It tells us that during this period, history basically follows a depressing cycle of six phases: Turning away from God through idolatry—God's wrath—oppression of (part of) Israel by an enemy—the people crying out to God for help—God sends a savior—peace in the land. However, besides repetition in the past tense, this text has another striking characteristic: it looks forward to the narrated time covered by chs. 3–21. The paragraph is a prolepsis (= anticipation) and thus also a striking case of providing the reader with prior knowledge.

This model of six phases governs the narrative material until the Samson cycle, but is especially recognizable at the outer edges of the episodes about Ehud, Deborah, Gideon and Jephthah (Judges 3–8). As the book moves on, the regularity of the cycle is progressively more affected as the atmosphere gets more and more somber and perverse. Without a central authority— "in those days there was no king in Israel"—the chosen people lapses into crime, anarchy, civil war and total chaos (Judges 17–21).

The six-step cycle is demonstrated in its entirety in the paragraph about one of the early judges by the name of Othniel, from the tribe of Caleb. This is the text of 3:5-11, which is so short that it is largely composed of the fixed formulas from the scheme. The converse of this is that there are hardly any individual traits to be found. Here, the writer's intention is once to show the pattern of 2:11-19 compactly and perfectly, with the first judge as an example. In this way, we are manipulated and prepared for everything that is to come. In other words, it is our task to fit the later judges into, or contrast them with, the basic pattern.

When for instance we read the conclusion of the actual Gideon cycle, we easily recognize in 8:28 the final formula from the scheme (peace in the land), but at the same time we understand from v. 27 that even within his own cycle the hero sows the seeds of new disasters. Next, in 8:29-32 and 33-35 we get the verses that build the transition to the long and bloody story of Abimelech:

> (8:27) Gideon made an ephod [of the captured gold] and set it up in his own town of Ophrah. There all Israel played the harlot after it, and it became a snare to Gideon and his household.
> (28) Thus Midian submitted to the Israelites and did not raise its head again; and the land was tranquil for forty years in Gideon's time.
> (29-32) So Jerubbaal son of Joash retired to his own house. Gideon had seventy sons of his own issue, for he had many wives. A son was also born to him by his concubine in Shechem, and he named him Abimelech. Gideon son of Joash died at a ripe old age, and was buried in the tomb of his father Joash in Ophrah of the Abiezrites.
> (33-35) After Gideon died, the Israelites again played the harlot after the Baalim, and they adopted Baal-berith as a god. The Israelites gave no thought to Yahweh their God, who had saved them from all the enemies around them. Nor did they show loyalty to the house of Jerubbaal-Gideon in return for all the good that he had done for Israel.

Notice how 29-32 form an AB-B'A' sequence: on the outside, there is the information about house and grave and the designation "son of Joash" which impresses upon us how much Gideon is part of his family; inside these, the contrast between the "many wives" (viewed in the light of Deut. 17:17 this is not exactly a compliment to Gideon!) and the one concubine. The difference between 70 acknowledged sons and one marginal son in Judg. 9:2 quickly becomes a dramatic contrast that will lead to carnage. Now we see how 8:27 relates to ch. 9: Gideon sows the wind and reaps the whirlwind, albeit posthumously. After 8:28 (concluding stage) and 8:33-34 (beginning of a new cycle: apostasy), the model of the six phases makes us expect a new period of invasions from abroad, and thus we are confronted with a negative climax: the tyranny now comes from inside, from the dynasty of the very man who did (deep in his heart) and did not (in his words) want to be king, and who in 8:26-27 set the wrong example. Not until 10:6-8 does a new cycle get under way, in which foreign nations again play a part.

David's conquests

In 2 Samuel 8, too, foreknowledge is used, this time of a completely different nature. This is a comprehensive list of David's conquests, which has been placed at the end of a section that consists of two groups of stories. The first group (2 Sam. 2–5:16) tells us how David, who soon after Saul's death has become king of his own tribe of Judah, establishes a united kingdom comprising all the tribes of Israel, among other things through a pact with Abner. The second group (5:17–8:18) covers the final consolidation of David as sovereign. The conquests (ch. 8) form a fitting conclusion.

At the same time, however, the writer has in this way also acquitted himself of his task as historian. This suits him very well, as in the fourth part of the Samuel books (2 Samuel 9–20 and 1 Kings 1–2) he wants to concentrate on the court and on the established King David. In advance, he has swept all expansions of the realm that David has achieved in the second half of his 40-year reign into one pile: the list of ch. 8. This leaves his hands free for what is sometimes called David's court history. This refers to David's moral and religious fall against the backdrop of the Ammonite war (in 2 Samuel 10–12), after which the king loses the initiative and finds himself permanently overtaken by events: he loses his grip on reality because others (especially his sons, who reproduce his own criminality through sex and violence) present him with one problem or deceit after another.

Points of view

Our knowledge of a narrated situation expands if we keep asking ourselves whose perspective we are actually being given. I will give a modest but compelling example, 2 Sam. 15:19-20. When David sets off on his march towards the east, his general Ittai, leading 600 Philistine mercenaries, also starts to move along with his troops.

> And the king said to Ittai the Gittite, "Why should you too go with us? Go back and stay with the king, for you are a foreigner and you are also an exile from your country. You came only yesterday; should I make you wander about with us today, when I myself must go wherever I can? Go back and take your kinsmen with you."

The narrator does not refer to the speaker by his proper name of David, but calls him "the king." This is in flagrant contrast with the second "king," in the clause "stay with the king." The reader may be confused for a moment: to whom does this speech refer? Yet as soon as we ask ourselves whose point of view is represented here, there is room for the discovery that this second "king" refers to the rebel Absalom, in spite of the fact that this is a speech of David's, who has no intention of giving up his throne without a struggle. Thus the speaker David shows how he has identified with the interests of Ittai and his troops. Now that he is robbed of his power, he is so loyal as to restore freedom of choice to his mercenaries: it is better for their fortune and their future to offer their services to the new king. (Eventually, Ittai outdoes his sovereign in loyalty and insists on following David on his hazardous journey.) By means of the first "the king" the narrator himself has given us a hint as to his own position in the confrontation David–Absalom: he still sees the fugitive as the king, and goes on using that title (vv. 21a, 23, 25a, 27a; cf. 16:2a, 3a–5a, 14).

"Behold"

The term *point of view* covers different perspectives. One of the simplest forms has directly to do with "seeing." A character looks up and suddenly realizes, "Why, there goes X" or "What do you know, such-and-such is going on here." The interjection is the signal that the spectator's discovery and amazement are being introduced. What immediately follows is the observation by the characters themselves, often in their own words. In Hebrew, the word used is *hinneh*, often translated by "lo," or "behold." Some short examples:

> 2 Sam. 15:24 [after Ittai has sided with David and they have crossed the Kidron Valley, with its symbolism of humiliation and death,

right below the East wall of Jerusalem] And *lo*, Zadok came also, with all the Levites, bearing the ark of the covenant of God.

15:32 When David came to the summit [of the Mount of Olives], where people would prostrate themselves before God, *behold*, Hushai the Arkite came to meet him with his coat rent and earth upon his head.

In these two texts the narrator's words exactly cover David's viewpoint in the literal sense: the character's *perceptual point of view*. The king looks up and is pleasantly surprised to see the priests and his friend Hushai, who by turning up there show him their support. The two encounters that follow, on the summit of the Mount of Olives, are also narrated mainly from David's point of view: 16:1-2 and 16:5ff.

The same word "behold" (*hinneh*) is often used to draw attention to something. In Genesis 27 the writer puts it on the lips of a character four times, thus turning it into a series:

> v. 2 [Isaac to Esau] *"Behold,* I am old; I do not know how soon I may die." [Then follows the command to go and hunt some game, and prepare a dish with it, in order to receive the blessing.]
> v. 6 [Rebekah to Jacob] *"Listen,* I heard your father speak to your brother Esau" [after which the mother relates the commission, and discusses her counter-proposal with Jacob.]
> v. 11 [Jacob's answer to Rebekah] *"Behold,* my brother Esau is a hairy man, and I am a smooth man. Perhaps my father will feel me, etc." [Jacob foresees a "technical" difficulty and does not want to be found out too soon, but does not have any conscientious objections against the deceit itself....]
> v. 26-27 [Isaac is using practically all his senses to find out who is there before him. He eats from the dish Jacob serves him, but is still uncertain.] Then his father Isaac said to him, "Come near and kiss me, my son." So he came near and kissed him; and he smelled the smell of his garments, and blessed him, and said: *"See,* the smell of my son is as the smell of a field which Yahweh has blessed! May God give you ...."

This type of series is a form of establishing connections, and hence an invitation to the reader to work out the interrelations between these passages. The signal *behold* appears at regular intervals in vv. 2, 6 and 11 and has the modest function of signposting information: the speaker imparts some information and then arrives at a plan. This trio, however, culminates in a climax. The fourth occurrence signals the peak when Isaac, torn between the contradictory data of hearing and feeling, finally makes a decision, impressed by tasting and smelling. He submits to his task and blesses the son whom we know to be the wrong one (morally speaking, and in the short term) and yet the right one (in the long term, as it were from the perspective of Providence).

The series, however, is not finished yet. In the scenes of the counter-blessing and the winding-up by Rebekah, the signal "behold" is also used:

> v. 37 [Isaac to Esau, who appears too late] *"Behold,* I have made him your lord." [In vv. 39-40 we then get the counter-blessing for Esau.]
> v. 42 [Rebekah warns Jacob] *"Behold,* your brother Esau wants to satisfy himself with revenge. Now therefore, my son, obey my voice; arise, flee to Laban my brother in Haran ...."

This signal of attention, information and observation largely corresponds with the division into six scenes that, as we have seen, always have one parent talking to one child. So, in Genesis 27 "behold" also has a structural function by contributing to the ordering of the dialogs.

At the end of Judges 4, "behold" is used twice. When the battle is over and we have passed the collectives (the armies), there are two scenes for individual characters: the escaped general Sisera with Jael, who kills him (vv. 17-21), and lastly the arrival of his pursuer Barak at Jael's tent, vv. 22-23. The first signal "behold" is a hint from the narrator who draws our attention to Barak's appearance; the second is the exact marker of the observation by the character. The meeting between Barak and Jael is as sobering as it is revealing, because when Barak enters the tent the sight of the dead Sisera leads him to the conclusion that there is no honor for himself in this any more. The beginning and the end of the dramatic conclusion have been marked by the signal word *hinneh*. The second "behold" is an ironical climax for us, but an anti-climax for Barak:

v. 22 [in v. 21 Sisera dies, killed in his sleep] And *behold*, as Barak pursued Sisera, Jael went out to meet him, and said to him, "Come, and I will show you the man whom you are seeking." So he went in to her tent; and *lo,* there lay Sisera dead, with the tent peg in his temple.

Conceptual and emotional points of view: Ittai and Hushai

In its literal sense, the concept of perspective or point of view is simple and may be pinpointed in the text relatively easily. Other forms in which this concept is used require more alertness and training; I am referring here to emotional and conceptual perspectives. These go deeper than mere observation. The way real-life people of flesh and blood view things is usually determined by self-interest, socio-economic position, talents, background and education, desires and plans, and this series of factors is by no means exhaustive. The same applies to many characters (people on paper). They, too, will usually view their situation in a specific way, through a specific type of glasses. They are rarely neutral or objective.

The conceptual and emotional point of view may be aptly illustrated with the example of David, who has to flee and is willing to relieve his general Ittai from his duties towards him. By suggesting that Ittai "stay with the king" (i.e. Absalom!), David suspends his self-interest in a gesture unusual for him, and identifies with the uncertain situation of the mercenary who, being an exile from Gath, has nowhere to go. The sequel is pleasant: precisely by giving up this commander and his regiment, David wins them back and is assured of their unconditional and personal loyalty. The writer gives this a specific form and space by having Ittai speak in 2 Sam. 15:21:

> Ittai replied to the king,
> "As Yahweh lives and as my lord the king lives,
> wherever my lord the king may be, whether for death or for life,
> there your servant will be."

This is no less than an oath, the strongest and most binding language available, and it is being taken not only on God's life, but also on the king's—a flattering parallelism. Apart from the opening of the oath, its content is also clearly structured by two or three pairs. By the comprehensive life/death (a figure of speech called a *merism*) the speaker indicates that he will follow his lord in all situations imaginable. Their fates will be identical, hence the mirroring of "wherever...may be" and "there...will be." The message conveyed by these symmetries is one of unity and inseparability. That is the emotional, but also the military and political point of view of this professional soldier.

The most important window on the characters' emotional and conceptual perspectives is their own words, at least if they are not deceiving us or their conversation partner. We remain alert, and should always weigh speeches against the character's actions. In this, foreknowledge may guide us. Take for instance Hushai, who in 2 Sam. 15:32-36 is told by David not to join him in his flight, but instead to return to the lion's den in order to frustrate the duo Absalom–Ahithophel. The time aspect of v. 37 is revealing: "And so Hushai, the friend of David, reached the city just as Absalom was entering Jerusalem." This is a case of synchronism (concurrence) that stimulates us to accommodate David's and Absalom's comings and goings in one and the same outline of narrated time. Hushai and David have separated on the summit of the Mount of Olives, and the king disappears from view from the city, on the other side of the hill. If we assume that it takes Hushai half an hour to return to the eastern gate of the city from there, a reasonable estimate, logical reasoning will lead us to the conclusion that the Absalom who reaches the southern gate at that moment must have appeared on the southern horizon half an hour before—at the time of the David–Hushai conversation. In short, Absalom has just missed seeing his father move away over the Mount of Olives with his own eyes! What he would have done then is not hard to guess; Ahithophel's advice would have been superfluous.

I will now trace how Hushai approaches Absalom, continuously keeping track of the point of view at every stage. In 2 Sam. 16:15-19 their meeting is described; there are two levels of knowledge, as Absalom does not know that (from his point of view, and as regards his pursuit) Hushai is a traitor, whereas we do. What Absalom does know is that Hushai is "David's friend," which understandably makes him suspicious. Thus, Hushai's first task is to dispel that suspicion before he can think about his next subversive moves.

> When Hushai the Archite, David's friend, came before Absalom,
> Hushai said to Absalom, "Long live the king! Long live the king!"
> But Absalom said to Hushai,
> "Is this your loyalty to your friend?
> Why didn't you go with your friend?"
> Then Hushai said to Absalom,
> "Not at all! I am for the one whom Yahweh and this people and all the men of Israel have chosen, and I will stay with him.
> Furthermore, whom should I serve, if not David's son?
> As I was in your father's service, so I will be in yours."

It seems a little superfluous for the writer to call Hushai again "David's friend," but if in the apposition of the first clause we hear the writer's perspective, this changes matters somewhat. Moreover, this repetition (it has been mentioned in 15:37 already) is functional, as it is a hint to the reader: look how this friendship is being tested in the conversation with Absalom. The attraction of this scene, then, is its extreme ambiguity. Absalom's position is completely normal and exactly what we expect. He has the right to ask awkward questions and test Hushai's loyalty. Halfway through the scene, the word "friend" has sounded three times. Hushai is going to match this with a different trio: God/people/soldiers, ostensibly to symbolize his new loyalty. From the perspective and to the ears of the conceited Absalom, Hushai's answer sounds brilliant. He seems to be acclaiming Absalom's reign when he calls out the formula "long live the king"—twice, in fact. Moreover, the prince thinks he is the subject of the lofty sentence about election that Hushai presents him with. Yet, we realize that all Hushai's words cannot really annul or exclude his true loyalty to David. When Hushai says "Long live the king!," deep inside him this still means: "Long live King David!" And even his final clause may still be interpreted as pro-David: just as I used always to be loyal to David, I will continue to serve his interests even when you are king.

Hushai has passed his first test all right, but the text does not say whether Absalom thinks so too. What it does say, in 16:20, is that Absalom consults the man whom Hushai has to beat,

Ahithophel. Absalom's silence after Hushai's speech should not
be dismissed lightly. It may mean that Absalom does not want to
commit himself for the moment, and that the new king defers
the decision to trust Hushai a little longer. Hence, together with
Hushai we move to the second and crucial test, where in the
presence of Absalom he will have to outdo the strategy recom-
mended by his formidable opponent.

This big speech of 17:7-13, Hushai's trial by fire as an orator,
has been discussed earlier from the perspective of knowledge
levels. Yet it also deserves attention as regards the competing
points of view. The task that Hushai has to accomplish after
Ahithophel's correct advice (go after the fugitives immediately
and only capture David) is a daunting one: he has to further
David's cause while making it appear that he is serving Absalom's interests, and moreover manage really to convince the
prince himself. As we have seen, he succeeds by means of fireworks, flattery and overawing his audience.

At the basis of this masterpiece there is an even more oner-
ous test, the trial by fire that the writer has set himself. What he
has to do is even trickier. Through his narrator he not only has
to make Hushai speak in such a way that Absalom (within the
story) becomes completely convinced that his proposal (calling
up a people's army, massive warfare) is better than Ahithophel's
sound words, but also in such a way as to make Absalom's giving in seem credible to us, the readers, in spite of our knowing
better. That is, the speech also has to have characteristics that
enable us (above the story) to prick the bubble of Hushai's
rhetoric and diagnose it as bombast and deceit. In short, the
writer has to reconcile the irreconcilable. As this is a hazardous
enterprise, and as we run the risk of being mesmerized by the
verbal fireworks in about the same way as Absalom is, the writer
prefers to play safe by including a signal (17:14b) that ends all
ambiguity and spells out for us what is "good" and what is
"bad"—i.e. what serves the interests of Absalom's coup and
what does not.

The ambiguity makes some demands on the reader as well.
We will only perform our task correctly in 17:7-13 (Hushai and
Absalom), if we attach two mutually exclusive interpretations to
the speech, and at the same time realize that there is only one

text. One reading should develop all pro-Absalom meanings, the other follow the anti-Absalom track. Within the story, the interpretation the prince gives to the rhetoric and the interpretation that we (with Hushai in his secret *persona* of David's friend) accord it are two closed circuits that do not touch or disturb each other. At the story–reader communication level ("outside" the story) we are both inside the separate circuits, understanding and sympathizing, which is not simultaneously possible, and outside these, reconciling the irreconcilable in our own way; for us, there is still the challenge of the text that has remained a single whole.

More points of view: Gideon again

When the narrator himself is at work, that is, speaking, his communications appear to be objective: events tell themselves. Yet, as soon as we try to enrich our understanding of the text by asking about points of view, we will often find that the narrator's text covers more than one perspective at a time.

In Judg. 8:24-25, Gideon, after his refusal to become absolute monarch, asks the people to pool the booty from the Midianites. From his action, melting down the gold into an idol, it becomes clear what his motives were. First, however, the writer drily notes in v. 26:

> The weight of the golden earrings that he had requested came to 1,700 shekels of gold; this besides the crescents and the pendants and the purple robes worn by the kings of Midian, and besides the collars on the necks of their camels.

Whose point of view is this? Our first thought would be the narrator's, who apparently feels he has to play the part of a public notary by providing an exact inventory of the spoils together with what the various items are worth. But why, exactly, would he do that? If we have to leave "aside" the pretty trinkets listed after the weight of the gold, why does he mention them with the same pedantic completeness? This can only be explained if we consider that Gideon's point of view, too, is covered here. We then realize that the narrator has used his apparent dryness to underline Gideon's greediness. The judge is fascinated by the glamour of the gold and the splendor of the royal paraphernalia.

He is especially fascinated as moments before he himself has renounced the status of king. It's in his blood, and Gideon tries to make up for the damage (I wish I were king after all) by rapacity, and next—and much worse—by the mock-piety of casting a divine image, something which to the true Yahweh worshipper is anathema. Succumbing to the temptations of materialism, the leader sows the seeds of subsequent idolatry and all the disasters resulting from it—see above.

Going back one step in the text, I again exploit the possibility of reading a character's point of view in a seemingly objective communication by the narrator. In 8:21 he concludes the report about the war of liberation with two actions on the hero's part: "Gideon killed Zebah and Zalmunna [the two Midianite kings] and he took the crescents that were on the necks of their camels." Our first reaction to this paratactic sentence structure is mystification: what is the point of the weird detail about the ornaments when Gideon is bagging the biggest prize of all? Is the writer justified in mentioning the taking of the crescents on the same level as the execution? My answer would be that he is: these baubles represent Gideon's fascination with royalty, and form the first indication that he will be mesmerized by their material glamour. The narrator has promoted them to a position equal to that of the execution, because they represent the field of vision of the grasping Gideon and are the objects of his obsession.

The narrator's value scale

This reading of Gideon's true desires takes us to the level of *values*. I am not concerned here so much with the characters' value scales. Enough tools have by now been presented for the determination of the values by which a character is driven or fixed. The weighing of words and actions that we have to do in order to get at these values sometimes takes patience and subtlety, but is comparable to the considerations I mentioned under the heading of "knowledge." Much more important, even crucial, is *the narrator's value scale*, and here we find ourselves up against the problem—or rather, the challenge—that he is rarely willing to disclose the "moral of the tale" at the end of his story. Good narrators are usually frugal with this; something should be left to guesswork. In fact, this process of weighing and guessing might be the very job the writer wants us to do. This draws us more actively into the story, so that we participate in the never-ending debate between various interpretations. In this way, we educate ourselves further, while the story, through the moral, legal and religious challenges arising from its unique events, confronts us with the question of what we are prepared to accept, and what not. So, the world of the text and that of the real reader touch, and regularly even collide for the benefit of our progressive awareness.

The exercises we have done so far about plot and hero, time and structure, are largely preparatory work with respect to the essential question we usually ask ourselves when we are reading texts we consider important: what exactly is the view of the writer? What faith or ideology inspires him, or rather, inspires this text? Apparently, the text exactly matches his intentions, given the fact that he has released it, sent it out into the world. I will now stop looking round inside the arena where the characters' opinions, prejudices, desires and plans collide, and consider the arena itself, which as such is a linguistic structure and is determined by the preferences, belief structures and interests of the writer.

The biblical writers have at their disposal a range of tools with which they convey their values to the reader. These forms and techniques may be arranged along a scale that runs from very clear and explicit to vague, implicit, and well-hidden. A good narrator does not want to make things easy for us by sermonizing himself all the time. He knows that in that case his text would be reduced to the level of didactics. He also wants to make us think, and the best way to do this is to speak indirectly and implicitly. This is why in many stories we are forced to be patient, to read and re-read sensitively. We must first get plot and structure clear before it transpires, or before we can tentatively point to, where the ideological focus is or where a judgment has been incorporated. I will not say much about the various ways in which the writer leaves his judgments implicit, partly because space does not permit this. In a guide such as this it is more practical to concentrate on that half of the scale that contains the explicit signals.

Abimelech and Jotham

In Judges 8, the writer concludes the Gideon cycle proper with v. 28. Immediately before that we have heard Gideon's last action, melting down the captured gold into an idol, which he places in his own town. "All Israel played the harlot after it there, and it became a snare to Gideon and to his family." It is not hard to recognize a judgment in these words; two of them are explicit enough: "snare" and "harlot." The latter has been used twice in the same way in this context, as a metaphor to indicate unfaithfulness; see 2:17 and 8:33. Moreover, this figurative use occurs at the religious level, the most important level by which to judge Israel. And if you look up "snare" in a concordance, you will find that it is used sparingly but cuttingly—it is a strong condemnation, cf. for instance Deut. 7:17 and Judg. 2:3, and moreover reserved for idolatry. The disapproval expressed in v. 27 corresponds well with the cyclic view that is presented as early as ch. 2 in the programmatic section, and which pictured a cycle of extensive misery starting with Israel's apostasy.

In addition to strong criticism of Gideon's pretensions, the narrator also shows appreciation of his leadership. In 8:34-35 he parallels Gideon's merits to what God has done as Israel's savior. In this way, he textualizes or makes visible a double standard, faithfulness to God and faithfulness to the God-given leader. Both forms of loyalty, but especially the latter, are decisive criteria in the evaluation of the experiment that starts off the monarchy in Israel: the tyranny of Abimelech, the long story of Judges 9.

From the mouths of the writer as well as the main speaker Jotham we hear applications of the concept of retaliation, in its positive form of loyalty after services rendered, and in its negative form of unfaithfulness leading to divine retribution (*nemesis*). On his way to the key passages vv. 23-24 and 56-57, which frame the second half (downfall of Abimelech and his city), the writer decides to express a value judgment even before the carnage takes place. When he introduces the collective that, financed by the temple of Baal-berith, constitutes the gang with whose help Abimelech perpetrates his coup, he calls them "worthless [lit.: empty] and reckless men." Thus these gentlemen are disqualified from the start, and the reader is informed of the writer's opinion at an early stage.

This helps us to listen in good faith to Jotham and his big speech of vv. 7-20. This is Gideon's youngest, the only one to escape the massacre, who wants to analyze the event thoroughly and in very principled fashion before extracting himself from pursuit by the tyrant (and from the spotlight of history). After the famous fable about the trees wishing they had a king (vv. 8-15), Jotham measures the behavior of the town of Shechem by the criteria of loyalty and retribution: almost every line of his application of the fable, in vv. 16-20, testifies to this. He foresees that this incredible evil will trigger off an objective mechanism of disaster in which both parties, the town and its tyrant, will be crushed. And this is exactly what happens later. Verses 23-24 contain the narrator's text with which the writer supports Jotham: "Then God sent a spirit of discord [...] to the end that the crime [...] might be avenged," and in v. 57 he reveals the true character of Jotham's speech ("And so the curse of Jotham [...] was fulfilled upon them"): it is nothing less than a curse (especially taking into account vv. 15 and 20), fulfilled by God himself. How much the writer himself is committed becomes clear from the aspects of time, knowledge and values contained in vv. 23-24: they look ahead, give away the trump card of the outcome, show the narrator's omniscience and disclose the value judgment of God himself.

Belial

An explicit value judgment on the part of the narrator may be found in those passages containing the name of Belial. The Hebrew *b^eli yaal* literally means "without profit," but its meaning is several times more serious: it refers to the destructivity that results from a total disregard of God and his commandments. Sometimes, but always at a carefully chosen moment, the writer will call a person or group "son of" or "men of" Belial. This gives us security, as we now know what he thinks.

An important example is Judges 19. Every now and then a militant feminist will stand and declare in all seriousness that the writer of the "Outrage in Gibeah" must himself be as depraved and macho as the unsavory and callous riffraff appearing in the story. Why is this a blunder—one apparently resulting from prejudice? Because it is based on such a superficial and incorrect reading that the striking signal in v. 22 has been overlooked. The narrator leaves us in no uncertainty about his position, by saying immediately upon introducing the collective from Gibeah that these were "men of Belial" (JPS: a depraved lot, RSV: base fellows). That should be enough for the good listener; before and after this, the writer's policy is to let the facts speak for themselves. In our time of literature and reading we, too, prefer an ex-internee from Auschwitz to tell us his experiences soberly and let the facts speak for themselves, rather than using a tearful, indignant or melodramatic style.

The children of Belial also appear in 1 Sam. 10:27 and 2 Sam. 20:1. In the latter instance we have to do with an individual who, like Shimei, belongs to the tribe of Benjamin, i.e. the frustrated origins of the doomed first king, Saul. This Sheba son of Bichri profits from the great political blunder that David commits upon his return (preferment of Judah, 19:11, 41-43) and exhorts the people to secession. The writer is not enthusiastic about this, as this character, too, is disqualified upon his introduction in 20:1: another "scoundrel." When we combine this judgment with the trump-card-and-anticipation in 17:14b (about God's decree that Ahithophel's advice would be nullified), our conviction grows that in principle the writer remains supportive of the Davidic dynasty, however critical he may be of its founder.

And what is his opinion of the first king? When Saul has been presented to the people by Samuel, and they have acclaimed him with a heartfelt "Long live the king!", the prophet dissolves the general meeting. Then it says in 1 Sam. 10:26-27:

Saul also went home, to Gibeah,
accompanied by upstanding men whose hearts God had touched.
But some scoundrels said:
"How can this fellow save us?"
So they scorned him and brought him no gift.

But he pretended not to notice.

This final note contains a clear and strong contrast. There are supporters and opponents, and both groups are described in judgmental terms. Introducing the factor God in v. 26 favors the supporters—in fact, they are a bit like Saul himself, because what happened when he started on the journey back after his anointing? God "gave him another heart" (10:9), which moreover brought him into a sort of prophetic trance. The other group, however, the opponents mentioned in v. 27, should be classified under Belial. With this value judgment the writer betrays his strong disapproval of the opposition to the first king. He himself is at least moderately in favor, as he goes on with a text stressing Saul's glory as a charismatic leader. Through the delivery of Jabesh, Saul, inspired by the Spirit, attains the impossible (ch. 11).

God and the demand for a king

What, then, is the relation between God's value scale and the writer's? At first sight, we would be inclined to think that they are identical. However, things are not that simple. The average believer and the traditional churchgoer assume that if God considers something good or bad, the writer will agree with him. This is based, however, on two identifications that cannot be maintained: firstly, the contention that the character "God" in the biblical text is the same as the supernatural being (the metaphysical entity God) the churchgoer believes in, and secondly, that the writer of course has no choice but to serve this God.

The God of the books of Samuel is not exactly the same as the God of Moses, the great orator from Deuteronomy, and something else entirely than the God of Ecclesiastes. Add to this the fact that the God of a devout Jew or Christian will always be different and greater than the *image* that anyone has of God. And the Bible is more, and different, and richer than even the best authorities imagine it to be. So let us start from scratch and not immediately lock the narrator of the Hebrew story inside our assumption that he, the maker of the character God, entertains the same values. I will illustrate this with the issue of the monarchy.

The crucial text about the monarchy as a form of government is 1 Samuel 8–12: five stories that together constitute an act in an extensive composition. Samuel's judgeship is nearing its close, and this honest administrator is in danger of being succeeded by his two sons, who unfortunately are corrupt. Partly because of this, the people are now demanding a king. Who thinks what? The text immediately presents us with wholehearted disapproval by the prophet; but as an advocate of the institution of judges he is of course a party and hence not objective at all. To begin with, he refuses to confront his sons' corruptness, as we can gather from his lachrymose words about them in the center of 12:2. The text, however, goes on and in 8:7-9 gives the floor to God. The Lord supports Samuel in his utter disapproval by equating the request for a king with idolatry, the strongest accusation God can make! Things are not looking too good for the monarchy project. Moreover, God feels personally deserted: "it is me they have rejected as their king" (v. 7). Where does this leave the narrator?

God's speech is not over yet. We are perplexed to hear that in v. 9 he does after all command Samuel to appoint a king! What is more, God repeats this in v. 22! What are we to make of this? Indeed, we are here confronted with a formidable contradiction, and we should be careful not to massage this away through our own clever reasoning. As yet, the writer's position is far from clear. Would it not be better to read on first, and not venture an opinion until the end of the race (after ch. 12)?

The portrait that the writer paints of Samuel remains consistently anti-monarchy; it can be found at the beginning, middle and end of the act (i.e. in 1 Samuel 8, in 10:17-27, and in ch. 12, which really starts at 11:14-15), and the prophet continues to act crabby. He is rather in a huff that his excellent performance as a judge apparently makes no difference to the people. His long speech in 1 Samuel 12 about the principle of the new constitution is full of frustration, resentment, pedantry and obstinacy. However, this will not help him: his Lord has commanded him to appoint a king, so he will have to do so. If it is impossible to retain an exclusive theocracy (God the only king), then he had best suggest a form of inclusive theocracy: a human king who is not above the law, but expressly subjected to the law of God as king.

In the two colorful stories that have been positioned between the three national meetings, i.e. 9:1-10:16 and 11:1-13, we are presented with a sympathetic portrait of Saul, who at first is baffled at his unexpected calling, and next, with the aid of God's spirit, organizes an amazing liberation. The writer keeps him outside the resentful and embittered atmosphere surrounding the old prophet. In addition, at the end of ch. 10 he betrays, by means of the judgmental "Belial," that he considers Saul's opponents no more than scum. And what about God himself? He twice inspires Saul with his spirit, from which we can deduce that God himself changes his mind and creates an opening so that He, albeit under certain conditions, can agree to the new form of government.

The writer's value scale is roughly that of the fundamental paragraph 17:14-20 in Deuteronomy. He too is writing at a time when the monarchy has been around for centuries, about the seventh century BCE, according to the specialists. In the passage from Deuteronomy, the monarchy is seen as a fact of life: something that is just there, and is all around us, something you have to live with despite its frightening shortcomings. If only the king would observe all these conditions: no polygamy, no gold and silver (unlike Gideon!), no treaties with Egypt, but study and observance of the Torah—then the monarchy would be acceptable. The position in Deuteronomy is not "no, unless," but cautiously positive: "yes, if." And the writer of 1 Samuel 8–12 hardly feels called upon to resolve for God the contradictions He is wallowing in...

9

Stories organized

Act, cycle, book

So far, our attention has been primarily concentrated on the single story, the so-called literary unit. Actually, however, there is hardly a story in the Bible that stands on its own. A unit of narrative prose is always part of a sequence, a link in a chain, and these chains can themselves be distinguished at three levels: *(a)* a group of stories, usually about five or six, which may be called an *act*, *(b)* a *cycle* of stories, often consisting of three to five acts, and *(c)* rarely, an entire Bible book comprising several of these acts. Because of the fact that the single story forms part of these greater wholes, it need not always have a plot of its own, and discussing the theme will in that case only be possible if we go up one or two levels and read the entire act or cycle first. In the first half of this chapter, I will discuss these higher levels, and in the second half go on to the macro-plot that is active there.

The act: a group of stories

The first section of the book of Genesis, also called the Primeval History, consists of two such groups. They are easily distinguishable, as they are marked by a parallelism: both end in a long genealogical register, Genesis 5 and 11:10-26 respectively. The first group, Genesis 1–4, covers the creation as the beginning of everything, plus two fundamental horizontal relationships in our lives: that between man and woman (in the Paradise story, Genesis 2–3) and that between brother and brother (and by association: between man and his fellow human beings) in Genesis 4. The second group tells of Noah, his sons and the

Deluge (Genesis 6–9 and 11:1-9). The many data from the genealogical registers in chs. 10 and 11:10ff. demonstrate how the human race scatters over the earth. Against this broad background, the "line of Terah" (the label for the Abraham cycle) starts in 11:27. Only a few verses further down (in 12:1) a narrow but strong searchlight hits the figure of Abraham, and this concentration of the election by God will from then on continually determine the focus of attention until the end of the Hebrew Bible.

The stories about Gideon (with the one about his son Abimelech as negative climax), Jephthah and Samson constitute three acts from the book of Judges. The finale is an act as well, comprising chs. 17–21: the corruption of a Levite in 17 and 18, the outrage in Gibeah in 19, and culminating in the quest at national level (exterminating Benjamin, chs. 20–21) that is the result of the appeal by the Levite in 19.

At the beginning of 1 Samuel, biblical scholars get hold of the wrong end of the stick by thinking that chs. 1–3 form the first series, and that ch. 4 is part of a unit 4–6 about the Ark of the Covenant. The Ark, however, is in ch. 4 merely an object or attribute, and the two defeats Israel suffers there in the war against the Philistines are the fulfillment of the oracle of doom that was given to Eli at the end of ch. 2. Moreover, they have overlooked the internal structure of 1–4 as well as the striking frame around this act.

This first act in Samuel has been composed on the pattern ABAB, as it alternates the birth and rise of Samuel with the corruption and downfall of the priestly dynasty of the Elides. The story of Hannah, the fulfillment of her heart's desire after years of barrenness, and the special destiny of the baby Samuel are related in ch. 1, and are crowned with her thanksgiving song (2:1-10), some two or three years later, when she hands over the boy to Eli and the temple. Story 2, in 2:11-36, describes the corruption of Eli's sons, and ends in a formidable oracle of doom. In story 3 (= 1 Samuel 3) Samuel receives his call as a prophet through a revelation at night, in the temple, and in story 4 (ch. 4) a double defeat on the battlefield wipes out the Ark and the sons of Eli. The conclusion is remarkable: one of Eli's daughters-in-law, shocked by the bad tidings from the front, gives birth to a child but herself dies in labor. With her last breath, she defines the state of the nation: Inglorious (Ichabod), and leaves that as the name for her child. This scene of birth and name-giving at the end of the B-line is the counterpart to Samuel's birth and the extensive name-giving by Hannah at the beginning of the A-line; an impressive frame around the act as a whole.

There are two short Bible books, true gems, that both consist of one group of stories: Ruth and Jonah. In Ruth the (medieval) division into chapters is correct for a change. Chapters 1 and 4 have a polar relation: the bitterness of famine and death characterizes Naomi in 1, and is relieved by the sweetness of Ruth's marriage to Boaz and her motherhood in 4. Inside these, Boaz and Ruth meet: in ch. 2 on the field during the day, in ch. 3 on the threshing floor during the night. This results in an AB-B'A' pattern.

The book of Jonah—the only narrative book in the series of twelve known as the Minor Prophets (or *Dodecapropheton*)— consists of four stories. They are grouped around his psalm (Jonah 2:1-9) and twice show a quest that more or less founders on Jonah's kooky mind and his piousness. From his books he knows that God is merciful, but he cannot really internalize this or rejoice in it. Sent by God to the north-east in ch. 1, he tries to escape on a ship to the west. God corrects his route by means of a "great wind" and a "great fish," and has him spewed out on land. Again, Jonah is commanded to go to Nineveh, which makes the beginning of ch. 3 into a parallel of the opening of ch. 1; I suggest readers find out for themselves how this reluctant prophet messes up this second quest. In any case, the conversion of Nineveh takes place in spite of rather than thanks to Jonah...

The cycle or section

The book of Genesis contains four cycles or sections. They are marked by a curious word (*toledoth*), which literally means "begettings" and in our translations has been rendered by "generations" or "history:" it occurs five times as the introduction to a genealogical register (for readers who like details: 5:1; 10:1;

11:10; 25:12 and 36:1) and five times as the heading to an act or cycle (6:9; 11:27; 25:12 and 37:2; only the first occurrence has been shifted to the epilogue of the Creation story, 2:4a).

The second cycle in Genesis is devoted to the person who for Jews, Christians and Moslems is the Founding Father of the Faith, Abraham, and runs from 11:27 through to 25:18 (the *toledoth* of Ishmael constitute the final paragraph).

Immediately after this, the writer skips a generation by starting on the cycle of Jacob in 25:19 (labeled "*toledoth* of Isaac"). This section is a triptych, and is not hard to mark off. Using the criteria of space and traveling, we see:

Gen. 25–28	Jacob's birth and his youth in Canaan
Gen. 29–31	Jacob starts a family in Haran, living with his uncle Laban
Gen. 32–35	Jacob returns to Canaan

In the first act, Jacob fights for the prime position and robs Esau of his birthright and paternal blessing. In the third act, he is confronted with his deceitful nature, but receives God's grace in the mysterious nocturnal fight at the Jabbok, after which he reconciles himself with Esau by symbolically returning the stolen blessing to him. In the middle part we see Jacob living the life of a shepherd, spending twenty years in Mesopotamia. He learns hard lessons there—the deceiver deceived, etc.—but acquires two wives, many children and herds of cattle.

The whole of this section is invaded by a chapter about the previous generation, and a chapter about the next generation. Genesis 26 contains a few scenes with Jacob's father Isaac, and in Genesis 34 there is a story about Dinah and her brothers, that is, Jacob's children. By their positions, each at a distance of one chapter from the boundaries of the Jacob cycle, these units function as hooks by which as it were Genesis 25–35 is fastened inside the composition of the book of Genesis. To put it differently: the generations are intertwined. Section 4 is taken up by the Joseph cycle.

The first section of the books of Samuelconsists of 1 Samuel 1–12. The first act presents the rejection of Eli and his dynasty, plus the election of Samuel. The second act, 1 Samuel 5–7, follows the Ark on its wanderings and its return, and Samuel as the ideal judge. The third act is devoted to the inauguration of the monarchy. The introduction of the king at the same time puts an end to Samuel's judgeship. (He himself has several more years to live, and continues in the capacity as a prophet that had been granted to him in ch. 3.)

This change of leadership is in the second section followed by the change Saul–David. It is a long text, 1 Samuel 13–31 plus 2 Samuel 1, containing many embarrassing episodes for the first king. Its theme is the dynamic interaction of a rising and a falling line: Saul's rejection and downfall are intersected by David's rise. Saul's downfall is a veritable tragedy, and is concluded with a poem of homage and love: the dirge that David devotes to the deaths of Saul and Jonathan on the battlefield, 2 Sam. 1:19-27. A structural analysis shows that this song is the exact middle of the composition, with strong thematic links to the poem right after the beginning (Hannah's song about God's power in 1 Samuel 2) and David's long poem just before the end (2 Samuel 22). From this point of view, the book of 1 Samuel should have ended with David's dirge in 2 Samuel 1.

The dynamics in the Samuel books can be represented by three pairs of names, each covering different generations and a changing of the guard: Eli : Samuel = Samuel : Saul = Saul : David. The rejection of Eli, together with the calling of the young Samuel, requires four chapters, the takeover that Samuel *contre coeur* has to agree to in favor of the first king gets eight chapters (i.e. acts 2 + 3, = 1 Samuel 5–12), but the third change is huge as regards the amount of text and hence the attention that the writer accords it: it contrasts 1 Samuel 13–31 (Saul's downfall) with the whole of 2 Samuel (the book of King David).

The fourth section of the Samuel books is a quartet of acts on the AB–B'A' pattern. The inner pair is a sub-cycle in David's life devoted to prince Absalom, i.e. 2 Samuel 13–14 starring Absalom as avenger, and 15–20 about his rebellion. Framing these two acts are 2 Samuel 9–12 about David's moral fall, and 1 Kings 1–2 about Solomon's accession. These two acts are dominated by Nathan, Bathsheba and Solomon and their relations with the king. None of these three is present in the intervening chapters, and neither does Absalom figure in 9–12.

Longer Bible books as prose compositions

The final level up is that at which cycles are organized into compositions that sometimes coincide with an entire Bible book. This is the case with Genesis and Exodus. As we have seen, Genesis has four sections. The last section is about Joseph and his brothers, i.e. the generation after Jacob/Israel, the eponymous ancestor. The two halves of the book of Joshua (stories and descriptions of tribal regions, respectively) together with the five acts of Judges probably form a single composition as well. This is certainly the case with the two "books" of Samuel: they contain four sections (including 1 Kings 1–2). The fact that Joshua plus Judges have not been combined into one book has a purely technical reason: 2000 years ago they did not fit on a single scroll of parchment. The same applies to the two "books" of Samuel and 1–2 Kings. The subject matter and text of 1 and 2 Kings also form a single composition, which should be a single book: from Solomon up to and including the catastrophe.

The macro-plot

The single story is called a literary unit, as it is the first level at which a text may largely be understood as an entity in itself. Yet, we just climbed up to the next level, that of the act, and from there we have gone even higher up, to two more levels. This layered structure of the text makes it into a hierarchy.

a. The lowest levels, those of sounds, words, and sentences, constitute the field of traditional grammar, as this does not go beyond sentence structure. These layers we may also call the texture of the story or poem. They are also the realm of style: each element has been put there by the writer with an eye to its contribution to the whole, chosen for reasons of thematics and effective communication.

b. The higher levels are those that transcend the sentence, and form the subjects of text grammar and structural analysis. First there are the three steps leading from the sentence up to the story: sequences (paragraphs with narrator's text) or speeches (if of reasonable size), scenes or story segments (as for instance the six in the story of the deceit of Isaac), and story. Next, we get the three layers of act, cycle, and composition of the book (if extensive).

The Hebrew storytellers must have received excellent literary training, as time and again they demonstrate a strong preconception of form, and consummate mastery of it at all these levels. A sound interpretation of a biblical text must start by taking all these levels seriously and sound them out one by one as regards their specific characteristics and functions (a series of analyses for us to carry out), and then relate the various layers "vertically" to each other in order to understand how they work together as a single entity (synthesis). At the levels above the single story I will now turn to the macro-plot.

Abraham

My first example is the cycle about the first patriarch, Abraham. Let me first remind the reader of the parallel between Genesis 5 and 11:10-26. These two genealogical lists or family trees, of Adam and Shem respectively, share the main characteristic of enumerating generation after generation, but only through the names of the father and the firstborn son. They each do this ten times in a pattern that is so fixed as to become monotonous. Then, however, comes a remarkable deviation that indicates the end of the list, and serves as a signal that something special is going to follow, and that the actual storytelling will be resumed:

5:32   When Noah had lived 500 years,
         Noah begot Shem, Ham, and Japheth.
11:26   When Terah had lived 70 years,
         he begot Abram, Nahor, and Haran.

Thus, the ends of the lists themselves form a parallelism, as suddenly the preference for the firstborn has gone and both verses contain a trio of names. The stories that follow offer their own justifications for this.

The prologue of the cycle about Abraham, 11:27-32, can be recognized by its caption: "this is the line (lit.: begettings) of Terah." We hear about Haran's early death (v. 28), about the marriages of Abram and Nahor, and we suspect that the purpose of this information, with the writer leaving out all description of Abram's youth, has again to do with continuity through off-spring. Next, we get a curious detail about Abram's wife. Apparently it is important, as it is presented in two static clauses of information rather than one (v. 30): "Now Sarai was barren, she had no child." These clauses mirror each other, as many poetic lines do in the Bible (a phenomenon called *parallelismus membrorum*). Even if you have cursorily leafed through the Abraham cycle only once, you will recognize the "lack" (and the problem) here from which a plot so often springs. How can Abra(ha)m prevent his genealogical line from dying out, if he cannot expect any children from his wife?

The narration proper of Abraham's life starts at ch. 12, but this character has by then reached the age of 75. His wife must long have been menopausal (cf. 24 years later Gen. 17:17 and especially 18:11-13). The famous opening of the unique election, the start of ch. 12, is a speech by God that puts the problem of continuity in an acute, almost cruel form:

> Yahweh said to Abram:
> "Go forth from your native land and from your father's house
>   to the land that I will show you.
> I will make of you a great nation, and I will bless you;
>   I will make your name great, and you shall be a blessing.
> I will bless those who bless you,
>   and curse him that curses you;
>   and all the families of the earth shall bless themselves by you."

This typography with the indented lines is an attempt to show the poetic articulation of the half-verses; there may be two bi-cola plus one tricolon. The style is elevated, and indeed as compact as Hebrew poetry usually is. Its contents, however, must be torture for the husband of a sterile woman! Can this be some sick joke on God's part? Abram says nothing of the sort and obediently sets out. This is a radical farewell, as he leaves behind everything that was familiar to him, at an age when people usually do not want change. Once Abram has arrived in Palestine, God adds another promise to the one about numerous progeny: the promise that this land of Canaan will belong to him and his offspring (see 12:7 and especially 13:14-17).

These two promises constantly recur in Genesis: every patriarch receives them from God. Thus this Bible book, which is the foundation of the Jewish and Christian Holy Scriptures, accords a fundamental meaning to the elementary coordinates of time and space by hallowing them. Worldly time receives meaning and becomes manageable because God announces and monitors the concatenation of the patriarchs, and the continued existence of the chosen people. And space becomes meaningful through a centripetal arrangement: this dynasty is the central one, God says, and the other peoples will be grouped around it.

The macro-plot of Genesis 12–25 has now become visible, but the action of the Abraham cycle has hardly got under way yet. A long arc of immense tension grows that keeps the stories together through to Genesis 21, when Isaac is born. It even stretches further: shortly after this birth, God pronounces a new "Go forth" that introduces what for Abraham will be his greatest ordeal—Genesis 22 contains the horror (whoever would think of something like that?) of the Binding of Isaac, the recently arrived and only son of Abraham and Sarah. Once the sacrifice of Isaac is concluded, and the father has retained his son by renouncing him, the cycle is soon finished: only two stories in the strict sense remain, about Sarah's death and about finding her successor (a bride for Isaac!) (Genesis 23–24).

The macro-plot of Abraham's narrated life, then, is a long-drawn-out quest which supposes that the object of value at the end of its trajectory is the arrival of a physical son to Abraham and Sarah. The problem now, however, is: who is the hero of this quest? This question opens a double possibility. Our first answer will probably be: surely, Abraham himself? The patriarch is certainly not a flat character, as he is not only obedient and completely trusting towards God, who incidentally explicitly "reckons this his merit" (15:6!), but he also has some experience of despair and distraction; he sees no way out of the combination of old age and sterility, which is completely understandable. These feelings he expresses most strongly in ch. 15. God reacts with a remarkable manifestation of the twofold promise of land and progeny, through a nocturnal and frightening vision.

Sarah tries to find her own solution, and by way of her servant Hagar arranges an adoption that hardly has the desired effect (Genesis 16 and 21:8-21, the stories about Ishmael and his mother). Then, Abraham enters the hundredth year of his life. This is going to be the turning point. God concludes a pact of circumcision with him (in 17) and announces two matters: individual life (birth of a son) versus collective death (the destruction of Sodom and Gomorrah). Both events take place within the same year, albeit in reverse order: in Genesis 19, the region near the Dead Sea is destroyed; in 21 the long-awaited birth follows. There is another contrast with death: during her pregnancy, Sarah stays with her husband in the Philistine town of Gerar, where the king's court is stricken with collective sterility (a form of death that Abraham and Sarah themselves have had to confront for a long time!), Genesis 20. The hundredth year of the patriarch's life is so unique that it takes up no fewer than five chapters of discourse time: Genesis 17–21. It is no accident that it forms the central panel of the entire cycle.

The question of the hero of the macro-plot makes us consider an alternative answer: might it be God? Isn't it he, after all, who takes the initiative of 12:1-3? It is he who speaks promises; he creates collective death and miraculous birth; he intervenes when Hagar has been sent into the desert by Sarah and seems condemned to death; he confronts the patriarch with ordeals, etc. In this view, Abraham ends up as the favored character who receives the object of value.

The entire cycle will benefit if we do not pin ourselves down to one line of approach, but read and interpret it completely from the angle of God's pursuit, and then read it again from the angle of the life and expectations of a non-comprehending, but trustful Abraham. This double reading is made possible by the fact that God here regularly appears as an acting character (an *agent*), showing initiative and spectacular interventions. This is not at all obvious; in the next two cycles, those about Jacob and about Joseph and his brothers, God's participation in the action is already much reduced. Consequently, in these cases it is possible to determine unambiguously who is the hero.

The fact that the Abraham cycle is determined by a powerful macro-plot does not mean that the individual stories always have to do without a plot. I will discuss two clear situations from the *dénouement*, Genesis 23 and 24. In ch. 23 Abraham is the hero, negotiating with the Hittites of Hebron. He has lost his wife and now wants to have a burial place as a legal and permanent possession. A decent grave for Sarah is the object of value to which the trajectory of his quest takes him. Genesis 24 is an attractive sequel, as this time the "object" of value is finding a kinswoman for Isaac, to fill the gap left by Sarah. Abraham is the sender; his servant is the hero; and the quest, a literal search, takes him to distant Mesopotamia. In addition, the object of this one chapter, endogamous marriage, is a consequence of the macro-plot and what is at stake there—the continuity of the family line, and the fulfillment of God's promise of numerous offspring—as well as a contribution to it, and a manifestation of it. (A little later, history seems to repeat itself; it is striking how the Jacob cycle starts with the same problem of sterility: Rebekah, Isaac's wife, is also barren, 25:21. Only after 20 years of marriage does God show mercy towards her, and she feels new life in her womb; these turn out to be two little boys who, while still inside the womb, already begin their bickering...)

The three stories filling the block of material Genesis 12–13 also have plots of their own. Abram wants to settle, but is immediately faced with three dangers and complications he will have to overcome: in 12:1-9 it is a famine that forces him to travel on, in vv. 10-20 Pharaoh's household threatens to swallow his wife, and in 13 Lot is so assertive (read: shameless) as to reserve the best part of the land for himself. In the last two cases, Abram can only pass the test thanks to intervention (12:17) and encouragement (in the promise, 13:14ff.) from God. In ch. 14, too, survival is the issue, and here "being the hero" for Abraham really does mean waging war and liberating his cousin Lot from the hands of the enemy. He manages to pull in this object of value, and the final two paragraphs (vv. 18-20 and 21-24) relate how two kings from the area express their respect for him. Their words emphasize how much prestige Abram has gained with his campaign. Melchizedek's blessing is

of considerable benefit to Abram, but he does not let himself be
taken in by the other king's offer.

Jacob

The cycle about Jacob has a powerful macro-plot, dictated by
the pushing ego of this obsessive careerist. Both inside and outside the womb he wants to be the first, if necessary by means of
deceit and the radical tearing apart of the family quartet. During
his sojourn as a shepherd abroad, Jacob again tries with all his
might exclusively to be a winner, again if necessary by means of
deceit. His uncle Laban gives him a taste of his own medicine
when Jacob wants to marry his youngest daughter, the beautiful
Rachel. He cleverly arranges matters in such a way that Jacob is
first stuck with the oldest daughter, the spurned Leah, and subtly adds: we do not do things that way here, giving the younger
sister in marriage before the older (39:26). The words "older"
and "younger" hint at the intrigues around the bowl of lentil
stew (which cost Esau his birthright) and the blessing of the
blind father, and even at the sting in the tail of the prenatal oracle (25:23). By means of the fast-change routine in 29:23ff.
where uncle has eliminated Jacob's eyesight as a factor (we remember Isaac's eyes!), Laban has maneuvered his nephew into
another seven years' hard labor...

  On his return from Haran, Jacob finds that there is no way
in which by some trick he can avoid the confrontation with his
brother, and hence with his own bad conscience. He is seized
by mortal fear (32:7-13), is certain that his brother is still full of
anger and bloodlust, and half-heartedly tries to buy him off (vv.
14-21), an attempt that founders on his surprising loneliness and
the attack on him at the Jabbok (vv. 22-32). There, this rock-
hard ego dies in a mysterious struggle with a man whom a later
poet (the prophet Hosea) called an angel of God. The hero receives a new name, i.e. the new destiny and identity of "Israel,"
and discovers he can confront his dark side by taking the responsibility for his misdeeds, and ask Esau personally and openly
for forgiveness. In 33:3-11 he bows deeply seven times before
his brother, as he would for a king—a prostration that is a reversal of what their father had said in the blessing in 27:29!—

and symbolically returns the stolen blessing. This is a paradoxical conclusion to the macro-plot: by renouncing the object
of value that for half a lifetime had been the focus of his fana-
tical endeavors, Jacob-Israel breaks the spell of the "I" and its
desires, and opens the way to his true identity and self-respect.
He who gives away his life, will keep it; remember the way
Abraham retains Isaac's life by renouncing him.

Absalom's rebellion

As a last example of the subject of macro-plot I will discuss Absalom's rebellion. If we were to write this down ourselves, we
might go about it as follows: provide some background on Absalom first and mention his desire for power, then describe the
beginning and the first success of the coup, and only at the decisive battle turn the camera round and give some attention to
the camp of the victor David. If we now look at the text of 2
Samuel 15–20, the difference will make us more aware of the
writer's line of approach. In chs. 13 and 14 he has painted a
portrait of a powerful, stubborn personality, which ended in a
merely formal reconciliation between the father and the fratricide, returned from exile. The chilliness of this reconciliation
(just compare 14:33 to Esau's warmness towards Jacob in Genesis 33) bodes no good.

The central act of the rebellion, which comprises no fewer
than 16 scenes, does start with the four years' careful planning
of the coup: by conspicuously taking a personal interest, Absalom makes himself popular with numerous subjects, 15:1-6, and
proclaims himself king in Hebron, the capital of Judah, where
David himself had started his reign (vv. 7-12). But how does
the writer go on after that? Immediately there is a surprise: the
literary unit that follows this opening, 15:13-31, is not given to
the prince and his advancing army, but to David who in great
haste organizes the escape of his standing army and the court,
and marches off with these groups in perfect order, down
through the bed of the river Kidron, and up the Mount of Olives. What is more, the camera remains with this party, although it seems to be losing, for three more scenes: David's
encounters on the mountain top with Hushai, Ziba and Shimei.

In 16:14 the fugitives are granted some rest, by which the writer has given himself the opportunity to finally pan back with his camera.

The first half of the sixth unit (16:15-23) moves back about an hour in narrated time, in order to get Hushai and Absalom together in Jerusalem, and at the same time brings up the issue of Ahithophel's prestige through his first advice. The second half of the story (17:1-14) describes the Ahithophel–Hushai duel in front of Absalom's national council, with the familiar result in 17:14 and the disclosure on the writer's part. This marks the end of Absalom's central position. In 17:15 Hushai informs the two priests' sons, who have remained behind as pro-David messengers, of the situation; the rest of this unit 17:15-22 is already devoted to their departure and takes us back, by way of their hazardous but successful escape, to David himself at the Jordan. After this, the focus (the camera) will not leave David's camp any more.

In other words: only two out of the 16 segments refer to the rebel's camp! This quantitative aspect alone justifies the supposition that the narrator's loyalty has remained with the other party. In terms of a macro-plot: the act devoted to the rebellion does not grant the macro-plot to the prince who is chasing after the throne as valuable object. Rather, the macro-plot has been awarded to the fleeing father and his trajectory. Hence, the quest here does not relate to the question whether Absalom gets what he wants, and neither is this prince the (narratological) hero of the piece. Already at a very early stage the quest goes to David. When we reread ch. 15, we are struck by the surprising purposefulness with which in the first hour of his flight he already takes steps to ensure his military survival and his political return.

In 15:16 (end) he leaves behind ten concubines, "to mind the palace." In vv. 27-28 David unrolls as it were the cord of the field telephone: the young men Jonathan and Ahimaaz are to remain on standby in order to bring him news later of the machinations in the enemy camp; he also informs Hushai of this in v. 36. Hushai himself, one end of the line, is David's main trump card for his survival: his friend has to put a spanner in Absalom's works by discrediting Ahithophel. On the spiritual

side, David shows an excellent attitude towards the fathers of
the two young men, vv. 25-26. These are Zadok and Abiathar,
the highest-ranking priests, and David hits the right note by
saying:

> Take the Ark of God back to the city.
> If I find favor with Yahweh,
> He will bring me back
> and let me see it and its abode again.

Like Hushai, they are not allowed to travel with David, but
have to return with the precious attribute that is the Ark (a
portable sanctuary). But they are allotted this task in a speech
with which David abandons his fate and puts it into the hands
of God. The courage necessary for this also enables David
seemingly to hand over the Ark to the enemy. He understands
that if God does not want it, Absalom will not be able to benefit from it. All these details illustrate that the true quest has been
given to David and should read: how will the king manage to
nullify this formidable attack on his throne?

10

The collaboration of prose and poetry

The distinction between poetry and prose in classical Hebrew is radical in principle rather than practice. The definition of *narrative prose* is strongly dependent on the plot, that is, that form of organizing the material which earlier I have called decisive. Yet this plot-wise arrangement of the linguistic material is in itself a clever intertwining, observable only to competent readers, of two ordering principles: sequentiality and thematics. The story offers a series of events, actions and speeches that obey the chronological order. Incidental interruptions of this succession-determined stream by a flashback or an anticipation are no more than exceptions proving the rule. At the same time, the flow of events and dialogue constitutes a series of elements that have all been marked thematically: every word, sentence and paragraph has been selected or constructed to contribute to the story's thematics. There is no unnecessary ornamentation, not even a description (of a landscape, someone's appearance, etc.) purely for description's sake; everything serves the plot. The circumstance that Esau is very hairy and Jacob is not is in Genesis 27 a crucial factor in the deceit practiced on the blind father. At the same time, it is a small obstacle, which makes it interesting for the writer: he takes care that Rebekah and Jacob overcome it, and in this way he can also expose their scheming and lack of scruples.

Two differences

The *poetry* in the Hebrew Bible, on the other hand, refuses on principle to be controlled or determined by the articulations, constrictions and corresponding rules of plot and chronological sequence. The reader who has been reading Judges or Kings and then turns to a page from the three longest and most famous poetical Bible books (Psalms, Proverbs and Job) will immediately notice this.

A quick look at the neighbors will also be illuminating for our exploration of the radical difference between biblical prose and poetry. All around the Israel of antiquity, narration in verse is quite common. The Greeks have Homer; the Mesopotamians, who for more than 2000 years spoke Babylonian or Assyrian (Semitic dialects, cognates of Hebrew, Aramaic and Arabic), have Gilgamesh, Erra and other epic poems; and even Ugaritic (14th and 13th centuries BCE, older sister to "the language of Canaan," i.e. Hebrew) had its epic poetry to communicate the stories of Aqhat, king Kirtu or Daniel, and the Baal cycle. From a literary point of view, in its historical context biblical Israel is rather conspicuous by not having written and left any epic poetry.

If you take another look at a psalm or the book of Job, you will immediately notice another radical difference; this is a distinction that has to do with prosody. In the poetic books, the clauses are seldom longer than one line, and moreover are usually grouped in twos, and frequently even in threes. In Job and Proverbs, these pairs or trios usually coincide with a biblical verse. (We will now have to put the entity called "biblical verse" between parentheses for a moment. The so-called biblical verse is largely a practical and liturgical unit, varying immensely in length: it can contain from one to as many as ten clauses. The delineation of these units is of much later date, and was meant to ensure correct recitation in the synagogue.) In this chapter, the term "verse" has the literary and prosodic meaning of "full poetic line." Such a full poetic line almost always consists of two or three short lines ("cola") that have a compact formulation, and thanks to a network of repetitions often run parallel to each other. What follows here is a complete poem, with a length of one strophe and made up of three verses in the technical sense:

> Adah and Zillah, hear my voice,
>   ye wives of Lamech, hearken unto my speech:
> for I have slain a man to my wounding,

and a young man to my hurt.
If Cain shall be avenged sevenfold,
truly Lamech seventy and sevenfold.

These are three so-called bicola, that is six half-verses (six printed lines in our translations), making up Lamech's song of revenge, Gen. 4:23–24. The holy number seven is excessively multiplied by Lamech, who is here addressing his wives, and the number that he boastfully and proudly reserves for himself, 77, has the connotation of "boundless." The first verse is dominated by maximum parallelism, as every single element of one colon has a counterpart in the other. This balance receives a slight shift in meaning in the middle verse, as the element of "young man," compared to "a man," introduces an escalation of the revenge. This slight break of the (balance of) synonymy quickly reaches a climax in the final verse, where the braggart completely outdoes his father.

The strict discipline that controls real verses is of a quantitative nature and can be described in metrical terms. The half-verse runs from two (long) to six (short) words, and has a rhythm of two to four stresses. Lamech's song has these dimensions (in the original language):

words:	2+2 + 2+2	stresses:	4 + 3
	4 + 2		3 + 2
	4 + 3		3 + 3

The balance between the half-verses and that between the verses, then, has here been based on a strictly applied system, but I should add immediately that most poems have been constructed slightly more freely by their poets. The increase in figures towards the end in itself indicates that we are nearing the climax. Note that the final verse has seven words—it would be bending matters too much to put this down to coincidence.

To summarize: the principal difference between poetry and narrative prose is based on both negative and positive characteristics. Negative: the poet could not care less about chronological order and plot. There is no epic poetry. Positive: his clauses conform to rules of quantity and meter; on an average, they are more compact and make even more intensive use of all sorts of devices for varied repetition.

The difference undermined: prose turning to poetry

So much for theory; we now turn to practice. The literary genius of the prose writers resists compartmental thinking, and refuses to follow the sharp distinctions drawn by theory, with its propensity to pedantry. The literary production of biblical Israel has managed to transform this rigid demarcation into a gradual fade-over: there is a sliding scale from prose to poetry. A few examples: the oracles—the prophecies proper—that we find everywhere in the books we know as Writing Prophets (the Big Three: Isaiah, Jeremiah and Ezekiel, plus the *Dodecapropheton*) are all poems. However, although books such as Isaiah, Joel and Amos almost exclusively consist of poetry, the oracles in Jeremiah and Ezekiel are introduced and linked by prose texts, and there are passages in which the prose/poetry distinction can hardly be made, or not at all.

The sliding scale also figures in Ecclesiastes, that almost heretical manifestation of the "wisdom" genre. Wisdom was an internationally known and popular genre in the ancient Near East, and the classical collection of this in Israel is the book of Proverbs. However, there are two heterodox representatives as well: the books of Job and Ecclesiastes, which expose the standard views of wisdom turned cliches by the devices and aphorisms of their own wisdom. They undermine the system from within. Ecclesiastes—a Greek translation of Hebrew *Qoheleth,* "Preacher," the misleading name of an author who did read and admonish, but was not a preacher in a congregation—is the only philosopher among the biblical writers. He collects a wealth of observations and reflections which, as radical explorations of the human condition, appear very modern and offer a ruthless analysis of the contingency and transience of this world. Sometimes, this late thinker (around the third century BCE) quotes verses from the standard wisdom literature in order to refute them; sometimes he makes his own verses and alternates them with longer prose sentences. However, the variation alone suggests that the distinction is not very fruitful within the framework of this disconcerting little book.

The same applies to my third example. In Nehemiah 9, another late text, we find a summary of Israel's history together with God. Many verses could easily be shown to be good poetry; of other verses I would say that they have the length and more relaxed rhythm that goes with argumentation, i.e. prose. Yet, a mature reading of this chapter would benefit from not being locked into a black-and-white scheme, a rigid division of the text into poetic lines rather than prose. The hybrid form chosen by the writer relativizes, or even mocks and annihilates the distinction.

I will now return to the first half of the Old Testament, to the narrative books of Genesis through to Kings. I see two main reasons why the distinction between prose and poetry should be obscured, massaged away or emasculated; these reasons differ in character, as one (a) is descriptive, and the other (b) explicative.

(a) The prose writers like to vary their prose with poetry at well-chosen moments. We regularly come upon a fragment of poetic art, maybe just a single verse or strophe, and sometimes even poetry of a sizable length is inserted: a series of sayings, or a poem that accommodates a group of for instance six or twelve strophes into two to four stanzas and easily takes up an entire page in our translations. So much for this description; questions of why the writers would do this, what might be the function of this alternation of verse and prose, examples, etc. will all be explored later.

(b) Not only does the text contain poetry that may be read as a more or less independent unit, such as for instance Lamech's song of revenge, it also regularly happens that the language used by the writer condenses during narration, somehow becomes more compact, and suddenly proves capable of being scanned. This observation, which can only really be made in the original text, leads me to an explanation of the fact that actual literary practice undermines or transcends the sharp distinction between prose and poetry.

This explanation starts with the observation that the narrative style itself is rather laconic, and usually expresses itself in short clauses. The vast majority of sentences in Hebrew contain two to eight words. Moreover, they are usually linked into sequences by *parataxis* ("... and ... and ... but ... and then ..."), at least in the supporting text, that of the narrator himself. Compound sentences are clearly in the minority. All this contributes to an apparently simple and compact style, and it is not surprising for the reader to find that the writer easily constructs parallelisms and groups of clauses of about equal length (read: brevity) that may be scanned perfectly. Take for instance the beginning of Genesis 21; I am printing vv. 1-2 ("biblical verses") right away as verses (= poetic lines), in the first place by indenting:

v. 1 a   Yahweh took note of Sarah
   b   as he had promised,
   c and Yahweh did for Sarah
   d   as He had spoken.
v. 2 a   Sarah conceived and bore
   b   a son to Abraham in his old age,
   c   at the set time of which God had spoken.

In this arrangement (v. 1 two bicola, v. 2 one tricolon) we soon note that the forms of repetition serve a few parallelisms. The content of 1a is identical to that of 1b. In v. 2 this is different: the sequential ordering becomes visible, "conceived" ... "bore," as the story has to get under way (as we would say)—a vivid expression that hints at the linear dynamics. In the original language, the number of stresses is exactly what it would be in poetry: 3 + 2, 3 + 2 (in v. 1), 3 + 3 + 4 (in v. 2). In vv. 3-4 the parallel construction is continued: "... his newborn son, whom Sarah had borne him" and "Abraham circumcised Isaac (...), as God had commanded him." This last clause is the fourth already to refer back to God's earlier verbal intervention. In v. 6, the key word "laugh," from which the proper name Isaac itself has been derived, is doubled. And the writer provides a fitting end by giving the last word to the elated mother. This is a speech that may be perfectly scanned as 3 + 3 + 3 stresses, i.e. a tricolon:

7a   "Who would have said to Abraham:
7b   'Sarah does suckle children!'
7c   yet I have borne a son in his old age."

In this way, the end doubles back to the beginning, as in 7c Sarah exactly echoes the words of the writer in the center of v. 2. This is not for nothing, as the phrase "old age" draws our attention to the miracle, in the same way as the sub-clauses about God's pronouncements hammer home the fact that God's word will be fulfilled and will shape history. The various forms of repetition and condensation all have their specific purposes: to emphasize, accentuate, highlight the main points, etc.

These effects are found already at the story–reader communication level. What, then, is the use of all these repetitions, paired constructions and powerful rhythms providing cohesion to sentences? In short, what is the use of this condensation? We will be able to determine this by first going up one level in the hierarchy of the text, so as to be able to survey the paragraph as a whole, and then go on up to the level of the Abraham cycle as a whole. We then realize that vv. 1-7 as a paragraph itself is a form of condensation: a node in the macro-plot. From the beginning of the story proper (God's command, the beginning of Genesis 12) the old couple's life is dominated by the painful question: will God be able to fulfill his promise of numerous offspring? And if so, how? Both the couple's quest and God's attain their objects of value at Isaac's birth. Gen. 21:1-7 is the paragraph and at the same time the literary unit presenting this fulfillment. The plot has now reached its *dénouement*. In order to mark this precious moment, the writer accentuates and charges it by means of his poetic devices. The condensation he executes here turns the literary unit into the shortest of the cycle—quite a contrast to the almost idyllic breadth of Genesis 24, where Isaac finds a bride, or the shocking details of the embarrassing ch. 19 (Lot in and after Sodom)!

What, then, are the characteristics of poetry from a more content-orientated point of view? What is it that poetry offers? It is never narrative, but always strictly lyrical. We are confronted with the present of an "I" (sometimes a "we") who admires, jubilates, laments, complains, professes, gives thanks, admonishes, or puts wisdom in the form of proverbs. The lyrical voice that we hear is always fully involved in its present, and speaks of its present. In story-telling, this is quite different: almost every narrator operates at a great distance (in time, sometimes spatially or culturally as well) from his material. The reader also feels this distance, and may turn it to his advantage, as it does not carry a negative connotation. We benefit from the distance because we can use it as a form of reader's license. The hustle and bustle we

are confronted with, the passions and especially the reprehensible violence are more manageable, thanks to this distance.
However committed an attitude we would like to adopt, we are
sitting in our armchair, and this is essential for the story reader:
we have the time to consider everything at leisure, put it away,
reread it, and take our own time to answer such questions as:
What do I think of it? Is this acceptable? Would I permit myself
that sort of behavior? What would I myself want from war,
love, power, partners?

This distance is lacking in poetry; its immediacy has two
faces: either it seems to address the reader with great directness,
or it is spoken by a voice (the lyrical I) that directly addresses
God, the king or a fellow pilgrim with praises, thanks, re-
proaches or supplications.

Embedding

Formally, the poetry discussed in this chapter is embedded
within the body of prose. This means that every poem has the
status of direct speech, i.e. character text. The size of these poems shows considerable variation, as is also the case in the poetry collection of the (book of) Psalms. The length of the verses
relieving and enriching the prose runs from one to 70 poetic
lines. Usually, the poetry is very short, and the interpolated
poem is no more than a single poetic line or one strophe (2 to 4
verses).

This embedding can for instance be found after Judges 4,
when the writer has told us about war against the Canaanites
and about their iron chariots. Next, in ch. 5, he gives the floor
to his main characters Deborah and Barak for an impressive and
colorful song of victory, which exhorts the people to thank
God, and parcels out praise and blame to the surrounding tribes.
In the middle, for a moment the song takes on the character of
a duet in which the man and the woman, as leaders, are firing
each other up: "Awake, awake, O Deborah! [...] Arise, O Barak" (v. 12).

Poetry embedded in prose has various functions. It articu-
lates the material, contains a lesson, or offers a point; it intensifies the meanings already hovering in the air or implicitly pres-

ent in the surrounding prose; or it formulates a conclusion in order to add a point of its own to the prose. The poetry embellishes and enriches or intensifies the prose, and is usually conspicuous, like a pearl within its setting. These functions are largely subservient to the prose, but sometimes the situation is reversed and we find it is the prose that has been geared to the verses.

A splendid example of this is the oracles of the professional diviner Balaam. This Aramean man has been hired at great expense by the king of Moab, on the other side of the Dead Sea, to put a curse on the passing Israelites. An expert craftsman will be able to do this with lethal effect, which is exactly what King Balak is after. Balaam is granted a small cycle of his own in the book of Numbers, or rather an act of his own, Numbers 22–24, a good three pages in translation. This narrative prose ends, and attains its true force, in the four poems that Balaam speaks. To his own horrified amazement he there does the exact opposite of what he had traveled such a long way to do: he finds himself forced by the true God to bless rather than curse this unique people and its tents, and to Balak's fury Balaam explains in verse that witchcraft will not harm Israel. These poems are in Num. 23:7-10 and 18-24, 24:3-9 and 15-25. They contain 7, 11, 12 and 13 verses respectively, i.e. an increasing series. The last poem is in two parts, one containing 8 pro-Israel verses, while the other part loosely lists some sayings against its enemies.

This embedded poetry can be divided into very short units, which because of their small size cannot do more than emphasize or intensify the prose or provide it with a significant node for the plot, and longer units, substantial poems that partly have come from elsewhere. In 2 Sam. 1:18, for instance, we hear that the writer got David's dirge from the Book of the Upright. This title is mentioned only once more, in Josh. 9:13, and we can only suspect that it is some sort of national poetry collection from which the writer is quoting here.

The very short units

The shortest units contain a single verse or strophe (2 to 4 verses). Neither in the Hebrew manuscripts, nor in most translations have they been typographically indicated as such (for instance by indentation). This is a pity, as the reader now has to be reasonably well-trained in order to be able to recognize them. It is to be hoped that future Bible translations will make these little gems visible in a more systematic way.

My first example is at the same time one of the first applications of separate poetic lines within the body of prose. Moreover, its subject is fundamental: what exactly is the essence of man? In Genesis 1:27 there is a single strophe, containing the verb "to create" that is characteristic for God:

> God created man in his own image;
>> in the image of God he created him;
>>> male and female he created them.

The sixth and last day of creation is the climax of the story in Genesis 1. Its text, vv. 26-31, describes man as the seal on the creation, and as God's steward on earth. This last aspect is then elaborated in the story set in the "Garden of Eden": the paradise story, Genesis 2–3. Our quotation is a tricolon with the predicate as a firm axis, a threefold "he created." The identity of image/image is followed by similarity-and-difference in the object: "him" becomes "them." This small shift indicates that one human being yet has a double essence: it is either man or woman, but being human is at the same time man–and–woman in their reciprocity. It is exactly in this duality or dialogical dimension that man—as suggested by the parallelism—is an image of God. That is no mean statement about our nature, and it is also a statement that immediately puts an end to any notion of woman as an inferior being. Indirectly it offers us some idea of God's dialogical nature.

Before the plot of the paradise story has really got under way, we are told in 2:18-24 in a more strictly narrative form what the situation is as regards the duality of the essence of man. After God has made man and woman from the one human being (vv. 21-22), the man first says, in recognition: "This at last is bone of my bones, and flesh of my flesh." Here again we see word pairs and parallelism. His second sentence is also a poetic line, circular this time, and the typography shows that there are seven words in the original language:

this (being) / shall be called / *'isha* (woman) /
because /
from the *'ish* (man) / was taken / this (being)

Notice that the explanatory word "because" occupies the pivotal position in an abcxc'b'a' pattern. The ring around it is the word play *'isha*/*'ish* (cf. our man/woman). In the middle of each half-verse we find the predicate in the passive voice, and the outer ring is based on identity: this (being) = this (being), a feminine demonstrative pronoun referring to Eve. This is half of a two-line poem. The dialogue and the mutual commitment of man and woman are expressed in the compelling shape of a concentric symmetry, in order to show exactly how "being human" is essentially twofold and reciprocal.

The subsequent instances of poetry in the first section of Genesis make up three curses. In Gen. 3:1-7, the start of a remarkable plot, we meet serpent–woman–man, and in vv. 8-13 God questions the man–his wife–the serpent. Following that, God pronounces curses against the serpent (3:14-15), the woman (16) and her husband (17-19). We thus have three chains of three characters, connected by two reversals. We have already looked at Lamech's song of revenge in Genesis 4.

In 1 Samuel 15 there is the story of Saul who is commanded to proscribe the detested Amalekites, i.e. exterminate the tribe completely. When he then takes away the best of the cattle in order to sacrifice it to God—Saul has his own definition of piety—and moreover spares his counterpart Agag, the enemy king, the wrathful deity sends the prophet Samuel to him. Samuel pronounces a formal oracle of doom against Saul and his disobedience; this text, vv. 22-23, is a strophe of four verses (eight cola = half-verses) expressing the final rejection of the first king. Moreover, what Saul has neglected to do, the prophet does himself: he cuts Agag to pieces "before Yahweh." First, however, he addresses a poem to the prisoner; although it contains only one line, it is totally crushing. I am giving a word-by-word translation here, so that the structure is easily recognizable:

| 33b | Just as | / women | / made childless | / your sword, |
| 33c | so | / will among women | / be made childless | / your mother! |

Apparently, this king was an awesome warrior who on his many raids knew no mercy. Maybe he thought that he and his mother were exceptional, but this verse puts the parent back in the category where she belongs: "among women." Unexpectedly, she is put on a par with those others who Agag had previously thought were to be found only on the other side: in the camp of his enemies. Now, however, this one woman will suffer the same fate and wail like the others.

The cruel and clever aspect of this short poem consists in a manipulation, a rhetorical trick that explodes like a bomb inside Agag's belly. The structure is based on parallelism: abcd//abcd. However, the syntactic structure of this verse, which is just a single compound sentence, is such that the listener, Agag, after having heard seven of the eight elements, still is not sure what the point is going to be, and still less realizes what is being said to him personally. And by the time he hears element 8, "your mother," he can only get the message by thinking hard: he will have to combine the words "mother" and "childless," and then deduce that he himself will be killed. But because he has had to put together this jigsaw himself, inside his head, he cannot escape its message. Here the structure works like a precision lock that only functions and relentlessly snaps shut with the last element: abcd–a'b'c'... d'!

On his way to the conclusion of the second half-verse (point d') the king will nevertheless have smelled enough rats. The frame "just as ... in the same way" bodes no good; it is a signal of symmetry, but the symmetry is that of *vendetta*. This pattern is a rhetorical way of suggesting that the execution of this king is the obvious and objective counterpart of the countless murders he was boasting about. It is the "mischief hatches, mischief catches" order of law. If we survey the poem as a whole, we also notice the sinister effect of the positioning of the elements "your sword" and "your mother" in corresponding positions at the end of the lines. Are they not totally alien to each other, as one represents death and the other represents life? The beauty of the cruelty is finally found in the fatal inversion of subject and object: the many women have certainly become objects, even victims, of the warrior, and the subject position that the single woman gets in the other half-verse will not give her any satisfaction or feeling of power...

The longer poetic units

The longer passages in verse are not hard to find, as the translators print them in the typography that is so familiar from the book of Psalms etc. I will just mention those in Genesis through to Samuel: Genesis 49 (the Blessings of Jacob), Exodus 15 (The Song of Moses at the Reed Sea), the oracles of Balaam in Numbers 23–24, Deuteronomy 32 and 33 (didactic poem about the future, plus blessing of the tribes by Moses), Judges 5 (the Song of Deborah), 1 Sam. 2:1-10 (The Song of Hannah), 2 Sam. 1:19-27 (David's lament over Saul and Jonathan) and 2 Samuel 22 (King David's Song of Thanksgiving, a variant of Psalm 18). There is hardly any poetry in the books of Kings. The poems mentioned here each have a much more important function than enlivening the body of prose. A discussion of one or more of these poetic chapters belongs in a book on "Poetry in the Bible" rather than here. I will limit myself here to some remarks and suggestions, in which I will not lose sight of the prose–poetry relationship.

1. There are two spectacular pairs that form a sort of duet between prose and poetry. One is chs. 14 and 15 of Exodus, which both describe the miracle of Israel escaping through the bed of the Red Sea, while the Egyptian army pursuing them is swallowed up by the waters. Exodus 14 has the narrative, ch. 15 the lyrical version, the Song of Moses at the Reed Sea. The other pair is Judges 4 and 5, which is concerned with the victory over Sisera and his army, in the same order of prose (Judges 4) before poetry (Judges 5).

Biblical scholarship has hardly come to grips with these duets, and regularly returns to gnaw on the question of whether the prose or the poetry version is the older. It does not seem a very fruitful approach to me, as it is rather like the silly problem of what was first, the chicken or the egg. I do not have much time either for the romantic who says: Ah, the poetry is older of course, so basic, you know.

The real question is how to approach these pairs creatively, while at the same time respecting them as a pair. There is every reason to get our first information about the events at the Red Sea and those along the banks of Kishon (the brook traversing the Plain of Jezreel) on the wavelength of prose, and then, knowing the outcome and impressed by the divine intervention, enjoy the variations, the passions, the exclamations and the colorful *vignettes* presented to us in verse form by the lyrical "I" of Exodus 15 (Moses) and Judges 5 (Deborah and Barak). The reciters of these poems are leading characters from the preceding stories, and when we hear their sung version of these deliverances it is not our job to confront the first narrators with the outlines, or all sorts of details, from their poems: we are neither lawyers nor schoolmasters. Let us instead be thankful that we can enjoy the differences.

For a couple or a small group of readers (for instance a Bible class) it can be an exciting and instructive assignment to discover the differences between the roles of Barak, Deborah, Sisera and Jael in the prose and poetry chapters, by comparing, drawing up lists of characteristics, and mutual discussions, and then try and determine why this should be so: what difference in view and emphasis is responsible for these shifts. Some building blocks for this investigation: in Judges 4, Sisera is important, especially when, exhausted, he arrives at Jael's tent, but in 5 he is mentioned only briefly and does not get a part to play. In 4, Barak is viewed critically and ironically by the writer, which obviously is not the case in Judges 5 (he is one of the singers). And take a look at the two versions of the murder by Jael in the two texts. The differences and similarities are intriguing.

For readers who want to do this comparative analysis it is useful to have an idea of the structure of the poem, which is tightly interwoven and complex. There are 50 poetic lines making up 20 strophes. These units are themselves grouped into seven stanzas, which in turn have been divided into three sections: vv. 2-8, 9-23 and 24-31. Here I am only showing the section (numbered I, II and III) and stanza levels (arabic numerals):

I	1) vv. 2-5	exhortation to a hymn, intervention by God
	2) vv. 6-8	before the battle: stagnation, internal problems
II	3) vv. 9-13	exhortation to a hymn, mobilization
	4) vv. 14-18	advance; praise for two, blame for four tribes
	5) vv. 19-23	the battle proper, nature takes part,
		the enemy flees, curse upon Meroz
III	6) vv. 24-27	highest praise for Jael; she kills
	7) vv. 28-31	Sisera's mother and her ladies:
		their illusions of victory and spoils

Notice how the notion of "blessing" opens sections I and III, and how the contrast between blessing and curse frames section II.

I will also sketch the structural outline of the Song of Moses. The rigorous construction of a staircase parallelism occurs in three places within Exodus 15: vv. 6, 11 and the second half of v. 16. The repetitions of this figure have been strategically distributed, and mark the division of the poem into four parts: the first section (vv. 1-5) is a hymnic prologue which opens in v. 1 with a theme, the two parts of which (God's majesty and his action) are elaborated in vv. 2-3 and vv. 4-5 respectively. In the second stanza (vv. 6-10) these subjects are treated in more depth: God's mighty arm, the water, the enemy. In the third stanza (vv. 11-16), besides God's guidance (11-13) we get the contrast between the one people that is delivered and the many peoples that become eyewitnesses and tremble (13-16; note how the many are surrounded by the one people, by means of v. 13 and v. 16). The conclusion is short, a strophe and a half, and already speaks of the settlement of the chosen people in Canaan, the destination of the long journey that started in Egypt, and even looks two centuries ahead by speaking about Mount Zion (without explicitly mentioning the name) and the temple in v. 17—an even more striking destination.

2. Another pair, with a different connection, are Genesis 49 and Deuteronomy 33. The series of proverbs, usually one strophe per tribe, in Genesis 49 functions as a solemn conclusion to the book; what little prose follows in ch. 50 joins this form of closure, with the death of Jacob and the reconciliation of the brothers. In 49, Jacob the speaker—as the forefather of the people of Israel he is the pre-eminent patriarch—employs poetry as

the perfect instrument of definition: he formulates his sons' essence, who here are both individuals and ancestors of dynasties. The fact that there are many more verses for Judah (Gen. 49:8-12) and for Joseph (vv. 22-26) is significant. They are the two great tribes of the future Israel, established in Palestine. Moreover, Judah is the tribe that will produce David and his dynasty. There is a political side, too, to these proportions.

In Deuteronomy 33, the most authoritative leader from the history of Israel takes over the role of speaker-above-the-situation from Jacob. This series of proverbs, together with the concluding prose section of Deuteronomy 34, concludes the Torah, the so-called "five books of Moses." Again a productive comparison is possible, this time with Genesis 49, if we just leave both texts their dignity instead of playing them off against each other.

3. The huge mass of prose in the middle of the so-called Deuteronomistic History, the books of Samuel, is supported by three pillars of poetry. These pillars have been strategically positioned at the beginning, in the exact middle, and near the end. These are the Song of Hannah in 1 Samuel 2, David's lament over Saul and Jonathan in 2 Samuel 1, and the great Song of Thanksgiving by the established King David in 2 Samuel 22. The existing biblical commentaries are all shockingly negligent in performing an elementary interpretative task: they do not make the connection between these three supporting poems, in spite of three striking aspects:

(a) more than half of Hannah's vocabulary returns in 2 Samuel 22,

(b) the final verse of her song ends in the same rhyme as the final verse of 2 Samuel 22, i.e. "his king" and "his anointed," and

(c) all three poems are thorough explorations of one and the same semantic field that is of primary political, psychological and spiritual importance: that of power and strength.

The first and last poems are in a major key, as the One who alone is mighty has brought deliverance and power to his Anointed, i.e. the king. The song that occupies the structural center, being a dirge, is in a minor key. Yet it has a formidable dynamic force because of its relations with the power theme. The second of the three stanzas (2 Sam. 1:22-23) looks back on the distant past and praises Saul and Jonathan as heroes. The power they had then now forms a tragic and for the poet almost insupportable contrast with their impotence of yesterday and today: their bodies are on the slopes of Gilboa (vv. 19-21 and 24-27, the surrounding stanzas). A creative reading connects these poems and understands that they are power stations and sources of inspiration for the narrator. *C'est la force des choses dites qui meut l'écrivain*, and in the same way as David makes himself a channel of the forces that come to him from the hills of Gilboa (shock, grief, anger), the writer who created the character David and gave him voice, is also moved by those forces; we in turn may also decide to expose ourselves to the full and immediate force of this poetry.

11

The New Testament

The narrative art of the New Testament can be found in the four Gospels and the Acts of the Apostles. These books have been written in the Greek of the Hellenistic world and the first century CE. All of them move around two landmarks: the person of Jesus Christ and the group of texts that for Jesus, his disciples and the writers of the Gospels and the Letters constitute the Holy Scriptures: the Hebrew Bible. Paradoxically, we can only speak of the Old Testament after a New Testament has been written and recognized as a canon.

The Gospels by Matthew, Mark and Luke are also called "synoptic," after the Greek word *synopsis* which literally means "combined view." They have so many encounters and scenes from the life and work of Jesus in common that to a large extent they run parallel, and thus may be easily printed in three parallel columns. The RSV clearly indicates these parallel texts, so that readers may easily locate corresponding paragraphs. The synopsis offers a unique opportunity to put the dialectics of similarity and difference to work.

If you read through a Gospel, you notice immediately that, being a story about Jesus' life, it is a unity. Mark and John only write about the adult Jesus, while Matthew and Luke take great pains over his youth, each devoting his own overture to the birth of Jesus. The Passion especially (Jesus' arrest, trial and execution) has a powerful structure as a tight sequence of dramatic moments. In the long run-up to this impressive finale, however, we get the impression that the composition consists of a disjointed series of often short paragraphs, each containing its own speech, incident or encounter, like beads on a string. This impression of a loose structure is not wrong, but it falls far short of doing justice to the stories of the New Testament, where just as

in the Old Testament every word has been selected deliberately
and has been given its place in relation to many others, directed
by a creative and controlled narrative art. Here, too, every detail
serves the whole composition.

When we reread the story carefully, we will notice more and
more signals inviting us to a search for hidden but no less firm
lines of coherence. First of all, various Hebrew motives and
techniques are still operative. The short units often exhibit the
devices we have become familiar with: alternation of dialogue
and narrator's text, *inclusio* and the use of key words, indications
of time and space functioning as boundaries, etc. Secondly,
there are many quotations from the Scriptures (which I'll just
call the Old Testament), which in the eyes of the characters
have unassailable authority and the interpretation of which is
hotly debated. The narrated world is totally Jewish: circumcision, Sabbath, fig tree, the owner of the vineyard, the temple
roster, etc.—there is Old Testament material everywhere. I have
selected the Gospel of Luke as practice area, and will discuss
various examples.

Luke and the Hebrew Bible

The words "and it came to pass," which in the Old Testament
often mark the start of a new scene, are still around in the Gospels. Luke uses them about 40 times, usually with the same purpose of marking the threshold of a new moment. In the KJV
they are fortunately still there, thanks to literal translation. On a
few occasions they form a trio by constituting the beginning of
three consecutive paragraphs or scenes: thus in 5:1, 12, 17 or
the series 7:11 and 8:1, 22. Another of these threesomes occurs
in 9:18, 28, 37. Such series contribute to a greater coherence, a
background against which deviations from the scheme become
interesting. The last element of the trio 11:1, 14, 27 does not
mark a beginning, but a conclusion. Something similar also happens in the overture, when Zechariah has finished his service as
a priest in the temple: "and it came to pass" in 1:23 forms an
inclusio with 1:8a, where he comes on duty. In this way, the first
story in its strict sense (Lk. 1:8-23) has been clearly delineated.
Luke 3 starts with a different application of this phrase when

John (the Baptist), who is to prepare the way for Jesus, has grown up. The first verse is historiographic *tour de force*; it lists an impressive array of names from current political reality, but this is a purely ironical piece of dating, as the importance of these top brass totally evaporates when compared to what is happening here:

> In the fifteenth year of the reign of... [here the names of the Roman emperor Tiberius, his manager Pontius Pilate—the very governor who will hand Jesus over in ch. 22; then the tetrarchs and two priests] ... *the word of God came to* John the son of Zechariah, in the wilderness.

Thus, the Roman empire and its hangers-on are being made secondary in importance to the history of the Word. This will hardly be a surprise to readers who have passed 2:1. That verse is the beginning of the famous Christmas text: "And it came to pass in those days that there went out a decree from Caesar Augustus, that all the world should be enrolled." Readers who remember David's census in 2 Samuel 24 will have their own ideas about it. Luke has a plan of his own. He has to get Joseph and Mary to Bethlehem, so that Jesus can be born Judean, and even be born in David's birthplace. To this end, the emperor Augustus himself (blissfully oblivious of this) has to do Luke's dirty work...

Finally, "and it came to pass" is used in a special way in the last chapter, after Jesus has risen from the dead. Before this, it has not been used by Luke for a long time (not since 19:29 and 20:1), but here it occurs three times, and not once as a threshold. Its function, then, here in 24:4, 15 and 30 is to draw attention to contact: the women at the empty grave see two heavenly creatures, and Jesus himself appears to the shaken disciples. Only the contact with the two "men" that remind them of the resurrection ("why do you seek the living among the dead?") and with Jesus personally can save the women and the disciples from mourning, perplexity and disbelief, and only then will it be possible to send them out into the world with the Glad Tidings.

Another, very Old Testament signal occurs about 50 times in Luke. This is the word "see!" (*idou*, the direct successor of the Hebrew *hinneh*). The narrator mostly uses this to mark a new character, and to mark how he or she enters Jesus' field of vision; see for instance 2:25 (the old Simeon); 5:12 (a leper) and 18 (a paralytic); 7:12 (a dead man) and 37 (a woman who has sinned); or 10:25 and 23:50 (Joseph of Arimathea). It is no coincidence that the final chapter should contain a trio of these; first, the narrator gives the two "men" (angels) an *idou* in v. 4, then in v. 13 the two disciples on the road to Emmaus, and finally, "see" introduces the last verse spoken by Jesus, v. 49.

In speeches the word occurs about 30 times, and then usually indicates the salient point in the speaker's argument. In 1:20 the archangel Gabriel, whose announcement of the birth of John meets with incredulity on the part of the father-to-be, stresses the point that Zechariah will be struck dumb during his wife Elisabeth's pregnancy. In 1:31 and 36, "see" is the signal from the same angel which marks the coming of both John and Jesus. Mary answers in v. 38 with her own "see," and while she pronounces a formula of obedience, she links the word to an original application of "be:" "Behold, I am the handmaid of the Lord; let it be to me according to your word." In 2:34 Simeon uses "see" for the two remarkable verses in which he defines Jesus' importance as a catalyst in Israel.

Luke's overture is a rich collage of Old Testament words and motifs. For instance, a line can be drawn from the beginning of 1 Samuel to both pregnant women: to Elisabeth, because she, like Hannah, had remained childless, and to the Mary of 1:46-55. Her song of praise, known as the Magnificat, was inspired by the song Hannah sang in 1 Samuel 2 when she handed over her little son Samuel—a Nazirite, dedicated, like John, to God—to the temple.

The unit 1 Sam. 2:11-36 describes the corruption among the priestly dynasty of the Elides, but is interrupted three times by a note about the growing Samuel, vv. 18, 21b and 26. Luke competes with this, and grants a similar set of three to the pair John and Jesus, 1:80, 2:40 and 52. He, too, gives these notes strategical positions, on the boundaries of passages of text. Both in Luke's text and in 1 Samuel 2, his source of inspiration, the third element of the series is the climax:

- Young Samuel, meanwhile, grew in esteem and favor,
  both with Yahweh and with men.
- And Jesus increased in wisdom and in stature,
  and in favor with God and man.

Other antecedents for the comprehensive pair "God and man" are Gen. 32:28b (divine recognition of Jacob's determination and strength) and Judg. 9:9b/13 (the delicious produce of the olive/vine, in Jotham's fable). The Gospel writer knows his Scriptures very well!

This chapter is a plea for connective reading, for tracking down the connections that hide in the seemingly disjointed and often short paragraphs, in both Matthew and Luke some 150 in number. I will follow four strategies for an integration of the material: (a) the questions about plot, quest and valuable object, (b) the signals about structure and articulation, (c) a lateral reading to exploit the synopsis, and (d) the metaphorical view.

Narratological analysis

The *main questions of narratology* remain the first to be addressed: who is the hero, what is his quest, what does he want to achieve, and how have his action and pursuit been shaped as a plot? How are the various themes distributed along the linear axis of the story? Of course, Jesus is the hero of the Gospels, in both the narratological and the spiritual sense. However, as soon as we start to follow the axis of action or pursuit, he proves to be a strange sort of hero. The question of what is the quest, and what Jesus is after, will clarify this. From the beginning, Jesus is purposefully on his way to the "self-emptying" (*kenosis*, a term from Paul) which will be his death: the cross. Whoever carries out a quest is actively seeking. There are enough striking moments when Jesus himself comes into action. Sometimes he takes the initiative for a healing, sometimes for an act of forgiveness or expelling a devil. It is, however, much more remarkable how often and in what ways Jesus *is being* sought. His road to the cross and the resurrection is invaded dozens of times by other people's agendas and quests. Jesus is a wanted man:

– Jesus is asked to bring cures or relief, by the seriously ill and the possessed. He is a *healer* who by the laying on of hands or transmitting ethereal and magnetic forces—see Lk. 8:19 and especially 8:43-47—works miraculous cures. The writer often notes the reactions of the bystanders: awe and shock, sometimes praise to God.

– Jesus is wanted by scribes and Pharisees for testing on at least two points: is his behavior in accordance with the law; does he for instance observe the Sabbath rest? And does he, in his capacity as an interpreter, handle the difficult passages in the Scriptures correctly? Jesus proves himself to be an excellent exegete, and often parries the catch questions by which the others try to trip him up by showing himself a teacher with unusual insight into the true spirit of the letter.

– Finally, Jesus is wanted in a criminal sense: enemies from the realms of politics and religion are persecuting him. The combined forces of the Roman authorities and the jealous leaders of Pharisaic Judaism prove his undoing and sign his death warrant. The parallels between the four Gospels are especially close in this last phase of the Passion.

The man who gives people back their powers and their positions as subjects by raising them from the dead, now himself becomes the object of killing. What, then, is his quest, and what is the valuable object at the end of the trajectory followed by the hero Jesus? We have to give more than one answer to this, in view of the richness of the text. The first one, however, should certainly be: the valuable object that Jesus' life leads to is the Cross and the Resurrection, i.e. the paradoxical duo of death and victory over death. The finale of the Gospel story is the Passion. There, we discover what is the true or ultimate achievement (*actio*) of the hero: *passio*. Jesus' being a subject is his total surrender, that is, his becoming completely the object of others, of enemies; and becoming an object here reaches the extreme of his becoming a victim, so that John the Evangelist can call him a sacrifice: the Paschal Lamb who ends all animal sacrifices.

A different solution to the problem of the quest is one entirely in the spirit of the writer: what matters is the fulfillment of the Holy Scriptures. Luke elaborates on this in all sorts of ways.

Already in the preliminaries about the two births, the word "fulfillment" itself regularly occurs: see the end of 1:15, 20, 41b, and 2:27; also 1:45, 65, 67, 2:39. His subject matter, too, is full of it: announcements by the angel and words of scripture that are fulfilled; Elisabeth and Mary in whose wombs children are growing, and who experience the fulfillment of motherhood; the characters Zechariah, Elisabeth, Mary and Simeon who are filled by the Holy Spirit and eloquently glorify God, John's parents even in two long poems of programmatic importance. After the overture there are moments when Jesus' quality as the Redeemer (cf. 4:21) or his authoritative forgiveness of sins (7:47-49) are justified through the Scriptures; finally, his ultimate action, the *Passio*, is also traced to these. In short, we have reached the fullness of time.

The concept of the Scriptures as matrix of the many meanings of Jesus Christ and his actions makes for an aspect of retrospection in the Gospels, of leaning on what has been revealed. Yet, at the same time the story also has a powerful forward impetus. The hero himself announces his suffering three times, long before the text has arrived at the finale. There is "preparation" in various ways: John the Baptist prepares the way, disciples have to prepare Jesus' royal entry into Jerusalem (19:29ff), and a little later, the Passover meal which becomes the model for the sacrament of Communion; Jesus prays fervently while he looks ahead to his end. Further, there are strong signals of direction marking Jesus' trajectory—a journey through Galilee and Samaria, on his way to Judea, to end in the capital and the temple; they are especially in 9:51-53 (note the threefold "face," preserved in the KJV) and the pivotal points 13:22, 17:11 and 19:28ff. The eye always looks "up" to Jerusalem. Finally, there are striking anticipatory terms such as the unique words "departure" (*exodos!*) in 9:31 and "received up" in 9:51, with their balance of death and resurrection. All the time during the journey, the hero realizes that he will end up in Jerusalem for trial and execution, and that his ultimate action will be sheer passion. Meanwhile, the disciples are being prepared by their master Jesus for their future task, that of preaching and healing. Towards the end, the forward impetus is so strong that it bowls over the finishing post of Luke's Gospel, as it were, at the very moment (the final paragraph) that the disciples are being made apostles by the Resurrected One and are being sent out into the world to spread the Glad Tidings. This is why Luke decides not to stop there: he adds another whole book, the Acts of the Apostles, containing his report of how they (especially Peter and Paul) disperse and preach all over the world.

Structural analysis

The second strategy of connective reading is establishing the *structure* of the Gospel. The long trajectory from beginning to end does not exactly make this easy. The continuous succession of incidents and encounters, and the colorful cast of characters crossing Jesus' path—sufferers and maniacs, magistrates and ordinary folk, scribes and disciples—do not offer a criterion for an efficient *structuration* of the text. Neither is there a compelling development of themes, between Luke 4 and 21. In cases like these it is sensible to limit oneself to those signals that are elementary, but never insignificant: the system of time and space coordinates. The report about Jesus' life and work is to a large extent a journey as well (an itinerary).

Part I, Luke's overture, contains the stories of Gabriel's two annunciations and the births of John the Baptist and Jesus; next, there is the double reception of Jesus in the temple of Jerusalem, first as a baby by Simeon and Anna, and twelve years after this in the circle of the scribes; finally, there are the activity of John the Baptist and Jesus' genealogy (cf. Matthew 1). Most of Luke 1–3 is set in Judea, that is, in Jerusalem and Bethlehem, and three scenes are even set inside the temple. The question now arises whether 4:1-13, the temptation in the wilderness, still belongs to the overture or already forms part of the body of the Gospel.

At this point, I gratefully turn to a three-part model from literary theory that is unsuitable for many biblical stories as these are too compact and laconical, but is certainly illuminating in the case of the Gospel. This is a model devised by the French semiotician Greimas, who says that the hero has to pass a test three times. In the first test (the *épreuve qualifiante*) he has to

prove himself as a hero, in the second (the "decisive one") he
makes his name, while the third (the *épreuve glorifiante*) serves to
confirm his renown. A good example of the first test is Gideon,
who was first commanded by God to destroy one of the detested Baal's altars (Judges 6), before he can start on the real
work and the actual conflict, putting an end to the Midianite
occupation (Judges 7–8). With the action against the altar
Gideon does qualify as a hero, albeit by his own methods (during the night).

What about Luke? I propose to view the firm and impressive
way in which Jesus withstands the temptations of the Devil in
4:1-13 as Test One, by which Jesus proves himself as a hero. He
is afraid neither of the Devil nor the deep blue sea, so who can
touch him after this? Jesus is not taken in by any of the temptations thrown at him by his adversary, because he sees through
him. The weapon with which he sends the Devil packing is a
thorough knowledge of the Scriptures. Three times he parries
the attack with a quote from the book that is literally called the
"second Torah," Deuteronomy. His using the Scriptures in this
way now casts a new light on Jesus' discussion in the temple:
when he was only twelve years old he did a test there in the
presence of the rabbis (2:43-50) that itself was a qualification, or
a sort of adumbration of Test One, and a good preparation for
the argument with Evil.

Lk. 4:14–9:50 constitutes Part II, Jesus' activity in Galilee.
The opening is striking, as it is not for nothing that the writer
has Jesus start out in the town where he grew up. This takes
place in Nazareth, more precisely in the local synagogue, and
moreover, on a Sabbath: all telling signals. Before the end of this
section we have already come across the crass anticipations that
make up the first and second announcements of the Passion, and
moreover the crucial scene of Jesus' so-called "transfiguration on
the mountain," which already prepares him for his end.

Part III, Jesus' activity in Samaria, stretches from 9:51 to
19:28 and mainly consists of a travel report that is specific to
Luke: the synopsis shows that nothing of the material in Luke
10–18 has a parallel in Matthew and Mark. This section is so
long that it is usually subdivided into the segments 9:51–13:21
(IIIa), 13:22–17:10 (IIIb) and 17:11–19:28 (IIIc). Its thresholds

are terms of space, 13:22 and 17:11, which keep reminding us
of the main business, and of the destination of Jesus' traveling:
up towards Jerusalem. Just before the end of this large section
the old city of Jericho is the scene of two encounters.

Part IV makes up the rest, and consists of two halves. In
19:29–21:38, Jesus is already in Jerusalem; he fights the rabbis
and prophesies disaster for the capital. The Mount of Olives is a
good landmark, as it dominates the frame formed by 19:29 and
21:37-38. The second half is the Passion proper: 22 describes
the Last Supper and Jesus' arrest after Judas has betrayed him; in
23 we get Jesus' trial and death on the cross; 24 is about the
empty grave and the apparition of the Resurrected One. The
crucifixion I interpret as the decisive test (Two), and the resurrection as the test and the proof of Jesus' glory (Test Three).

An outline of this structure would look as follows:

I	Overture and preparation: mainly in Judea	1–4:13
II	Jesus' activity in Galilea	4:14–9:50
III	Jesus' activity in Samaria	9:51–19:28
IV	Finale: back in Judea: Jesus in Jerusalem	19:29–24

A division such as this helps us to formulate new questions and
test new insights. We might, for instance, be led to suppose that
there are special links between the overture and the finale
proper (22–24). Indeed there are, and of varied character. First,
there is of course the fact that the Gospel is wrapped up by the
polarity of the birth and death of the hero. Next, both outer
sections describe his appearing in the most hallowed spot in the
land, the temple. In Luke 1, the angel appears twice, in 24 there
are two heavenly beings at the empty tomb. In 1:33 Jesus' destination is indicated, on David's throne: "And he will reign over
the house of Jacob for ever, and of his kingdom there will be no
end." Jesus is a rather unusual king, as he categorically refuses
what few would refuse: when the (second) greatest power in the
world, that of Evil (personified as the Devil), makes him the
attractive offer to rule "all the kingdoms of the world," he says
no, 4:6ff. In the finale, when he has been nailed to the cross, the
inscription reads "King of the Jews".... Thus, Jesus' rejection of
power has ended in total powerlessness. In the overture we
meet three women; in the finale there are three beneath the

cross and at the tomb, mentioned by name. The poems in the overture describing Jesus' task are answered by the fulfillment. Zechariah's incredulity and perplexity receive their counterparts in the incredulity and perplexity of the men of Emmaus and the other disciples (Luke 24); the awe and praise of Mary and the shepherds in the manger find a continuation in the awe and worship of the apostles at the end of 24.

Lateral reading

The synopsis, the parallelism between the texts by Matthew, Mark and Luke, enables us to perform a *tour de force* of literary involution. The *dialectics of similarity and difference* find a unique and powerful application in the New Testament. Here, we may enrich linear and circular reading with "lateral" reading: while we are allowing a verse by one of the three writers to sink in, it is almost always illuminating to look sideways, and weigh the parallels offered by the other two. The parallel text is rarely identical; there is usually some striking variation. Moreover, not finding a parallel is instructive, too: it means we have hit on what is specific to the Gospel writer we are reading, what is exclusively his own material. Thus, Matthew has a sermon on the mount, Luke does not; in Lk. 6:17-49, however, there is an address in a field, which is much shorter. The story of the Good Samaritan or the parable of the Prodigal Son are specific to Luke, i.e. lacking in the other Gospels.

The purpose of this *lateral reading* and comparing is to bring the picture we have of a particular Gospel more and more into focus. It would, however, be a colossal blunder to play off one text against the other, for instance out of a desire to know "who exactly is the one actual, historical Jesus." However legitimate this desire, it can never be satisfied. These stories have not been written to silence or refute others, nor to satisfy modern notions of verifiability or "historical reliability." Each writer wants to be heard and judged on his own merits; each story has its own internal truth. Thus, the New Testament offers in its four Gospels a spectacular polyphony in which each voice contributes its own accents and themes.

I will demonstrate this lateral reading and the new application of the dialectics of similarity and difference in a few passages from Luke. The Devil presents Jesus with three problems: (1) turn stones into bread; (2) worship me, and I will make you omnipotent; and (3) throw yourself down from the temple gate; if angels carry you, you have proved yourself to be the Son of God. However, Matthew gives these in a different order: 1–3–2! The question now is: what good (i.e. structural or thematic) reason did Luke have for the order he uses? We see the answer dawning when we consider the outline of 4:1-13:

> v. 1-2a: And Jesus, full of the Holy Spirit, returned from the Jordan, and was led by the Spirit for forty days in the wilderness, put to the test [RSV: tempted] by the Devil.
> ... [vv. 2b-12: three "temptations"] ...
> v. 13: And when the devil had ended every trial [temptation], he departed from him until an opportune time.

As opposed to the water that is characteristic for John's specific activity, baptizing, we now have the dry emptiness of the wilderness. This space, and the number 40, are symbolic: they refer to the election of the people of Israel, who, led by Moses, spent 40 years in the desert and there became Yahweh's partner in the covenant. This suggests that Jesus' abstinence and loneliness in the Judean desert (see also 1:80!) are conditions for a new beginning and a new election. The key word "temptation" alerts us to the fact that the scene has been wrapped up inside an *inclusio*. The frame, then, is "testing"—we can sense Greimas grinning offstage. Now, Jesus' third answer to ward off the Devil is a prohibition from Deut. 6:16, "You shall not put the Lord your God to the test." Thanks to the order Luke selected, the idea of "temptation," the crucial point of Jesus' last refutation, borders on the frame 2a + 13. In this way, the writer indicates what he considers to be the essential point. Moreover, the prohibition is in third position as it completely takes the wind out of the Devil's sails. Luke's decision is radically different than what the other writers are doing. While they celebrate Jesus' success against the Devil by bringing on angels (Mt. 4:11 and Mk 1:13) in honor of the hero, Luke remains focused on the seriousness of the situation. Matthew answers the double "temptation" in Lk. 4:12-13 with a double "serve" (Mt. 4:10-11)—a completely different atmosphere.

Luke exploits the idea of "temptation" in special ways. In addition, he links it several times to the speech act that may strengthen Jesus and his disciples: prayer. In the finale, Luke uses the word "temptation" again with a structural effect, as a frame for another scene; this is the terrible night Jesus spends in the garden of Gethsemane, before his arrest and death sentence: 22:39-46. Notice in which direction the aspect of worry is pointing this time:

> And he came out, and went, as was his custom, to the Mount of Olives; and the disciples followed him. And when he came to the place he said to them, "*Pray* that you may not enter into *temptation*." And he withdrew from them about a stone's throw, and knelt down and *prayed,* "Father, if thou art willing, remove this cup from me; nevertheless not my will, but thine, be done." And there appeared an angel to him from heaven, strengthening him. And being in an agony he *prayed* more earnestly; and his sweat was as it were great drops of blood falling down to the ground. [Then] he rose from *prayer,* he came to the disciples, and found them sleeping for sorrow, and he said to them: "Why do you sleep? Rise and *pray* that you may not enter into *temptation.*"

What, then, is temptation? A good answer to this has already been given in Lk. 8:13, and forms the climax of the parable of the sower. The text in 22 answers this by the word "sleep," and Luke is the only one to add, in a mild explanation: for sorrow. Sleeping is closing one's eyes; it is an image for avoiding reality: the disciples cannot handle the confrontation with tomorrow's reality and drop off. Jesus understands this, even though he is full of fear himself. He reaches out to his followers, as he is worried that they may be led into temptation and therefore points to the power of prayer. They could pray for themselves, in the same way as Jesus prays for himself.

The power of Jesus' own prayer is so intense that an angel descends to support him. This is a counterpart or a sequel to 9:31, as we shall see. We also recognize the words: "Thy will be done"—this is the sentence of total submission and obedience from the Lord's Prayer. The scene in which Jesus teaches the disciples this prayer by saying it for them, Lk. 11:1-13, opens with a triple use of the word "pray," and the shortened form of the Lord's Prayer in Luke (vv. 2-4 in that chapter) ends with the other key word "do not lead us into temptation"—the same link again. Most of the verses in Luke that contain "pray" are specific to this writer, see 1:10, 3:21, 5:16, 6:12, 9:18, 28, 29, 18:1, 10f. Moreover, when Jesus prays, this is often in solitude, see 5:16, 6:12 and 9:18.

Sometimes Luke organizes a mountain as the place of action when Jesus is praying: 6:12, for instance, has the combination mountain–prayer–night (just as in Gethsemane). While in Matthew the most important mountain is that of Matthew 5–7 (the Sermon on the Mount!), in Luke the mountain of the transfiguration is unique, thanks to a vocabulary that makes Luke's version totally different than its parallels (Mt. 17:1-9 and Mk 9:2-10), and thanks to connections with other highlights. The text is Lk. 9:28-36.

> And it came to pass about eight days after these sayings [= the first announcement of the passion!] that he took with him Peter and John and James, and went up to the mountain to pray.
> And it came to pass, as he was praying, that the appearance of his countenance was altered, and his raiment became dazzling white. And behold, two men talked with him, Moses and Elijah, who appeared in glory and spoke of his departure [*exodos*], which he was to accomplish at Jerusalem. Now Peter and those who were with him were heavy with sleep, and when they wakened they saw his glory and the two men who stood with him.
> And it came to pass, as the men were parting from him, that Peter said to Jesus, "Master, it is well that we are here; let us make three tents, one for you and one for Moses and one for Elijah"—not knowing what he said.
> As he said this, a cloud came and overshadowed them; and they were afraid as they entered the cloud. And a voice came out of the cloud, saying, "This is my Son, my Chosen; listen to him!" And when the voice had spoken, Jesus was found alone. And they kept silence and told no one in those days anything of what they had seen.

In the first place, the position of this episode is significant, just before the end of Part II and exactly between the first and the second announcement of the Passion. The triple "And it came to pass" determines the rhythm of this passage, and "behold" is clearly the indication of surprise. Matthew and Mark open with "after six days," but Luke has "eight;" why? In this way, he can make a connection with two other places where he is (again) the only one to have the same number: the circumcision and naming of John and Jesus, 1:59 and 2:21.

With a view to the end—the word *exodos* is unique in the New Testament—Jesus is given assistance from heaven, from the two greatest figures in Israelite religion. Their conversation with Jesus is a preparation completely missed by the disciples. They see nothing, as they have fallen asleep again. Who are they? Exactly the same trio that shortly before that witnessed a miracle: Jesus' raising a girl from the dead, 8:49-56 (a scene that ends parallel to 9:36b: silence on their part). Their sleeping now prevents them from realizing that this miraculous resuscitation might well constitute a message that helps them to accept the unacceptable—Jesus' death on the cross. They wake up and see the two visitors; their seeing, however, is no knowing.

Peter might not know what he is saying, but that does not mean he is wrong: he creates the series Moses–Elijah–Jesus, which as theology is not bad. The voice from the cloud is no other than the voice from 3:22; it is the Holy Spirit confirming the election that took place back then, at the Jordan. Jesus' being alone is an echo of 9:18. This run-up (9:18-21) to the prediction of the end also creates a sequence: three mistaken interpretations of Jesus' identity, with the fourth, Peter's, the correct one.

Jesus' prayer is so intense that it gives him a heavenly aspect ("glory," i.e. majestic radiance). His clothes become dazzling white, *exastrapton* in the original language. This choice of words takes us straight to a precious moment in the final chapter, at the empty tomb. The women who want to attend to his body with myrrh and spices do not find him, but "behold, *two* men stood by them in dazzling [*astraptousei*] apparel." If you see the connexion with Luke 9, you will at the same time have received a discreet hint about the identity of these two men. They cannot be mortal, as they possess divine knowledge: Jesus has risen from the dead, they tell the frightened women. The two who have given heavenly support and knowledge to Jesus as regards his "departure" from life, now explain to his followers that he has also departed from death; see, isn't the tomb empty?

Luke uses the Greek root *astrap-* in two more places:

10:18 (Jesus to the 70 whom he is sending out and instructing:)
I saw Satan fall like lightning from heaven.
17:24 (Jesus is addressing his disciples about the day of the Son of Man:)
For as the lightning flashes and lights up the sky from one side to the other, so will the Son of Man be in his day.

A spectacular image, which places the appearance of Christ diametrically opposite the power of Evil; these verses form a pair that we pass on our way from 9:29 (the mountain) to 24:4 (the empty tomb) and show a clear polarity.

Reading metaphorically

Reading imaginatively is also *reading metaphorically*. Having the courage to apply a metaphorical view changes the world; I remind the reader of David who saw an animal in Goliath and made history. We are actually invited to a metaphorical reading of the Gospels by the Gospel itself, in the first place thanks to the presence of parables. Just as a sentence acquires a figurative dimension by the presence of an image, a literary unit (a scene, a story, a speech) produces the same effect by being a parable. We can enter into this parabolic dimension of Luke's Gospel by starting with simple things: 8:4–15 and 15:1–7 contain parables that Jesus tells the disciples, and for which he immediately supplies an explanation. The stories Jesus tells in 10:30–36 and 18:9–14, about the Good Samaritan and about the prayers of the Pharisee and the tax collector, can hardly be called parables, but are rather examples (*exempla*) of morally or religiously desirable behavior. In both cases, the conclusion (10:37 and 18:14) is the moral, that is to say, the text itself contains the indications for a correct explanation and understanding. Thus, the boundary between the parables and the non–parabolic is fluid, and this aspect enables us to reread with a metaphorical eye all sorts of incidents that in the first instance seemed literal. Jesus himself does this in 5:9–10 by placing Peter on the intersection of "fishing for fish" and "fishing for people." And compare how illness and doctor fade from the literal into the figurative in 5:31.

The metaphorical dimension pervades the text like yeast. Surprisingly enough, we may observe this in the one passage from Luke that seems utterly boring: Jesus' family tree in 3:23-38, an enumeration of ancestors that connects Jesus to the beginning of creation. Note the last step in the list of names: "... the son of Seth, the son of Adam, the son of God." After 76 links all told, which we take literally (biologically, that is), the last link is name no. 77 (a number that itself is the result of literary and symbolic involution) and connects "Adam" (Hebrew for man, even) to God as his child. This is a clear metaphor, which reflects on the entire preceding chain, and thus also makes the connection between Jesus and God the Creator metaphorical. This effect teaches us also to be careful using the title "Son of God" for Jesus.

A third case of metaphorics "introduced" by the text itself, that is, made internally visible, I observe in Lk. 8:52-54. Jairus' daughter is dead, everyone knows this (v. 53); but Jesus in his own words turns this into "sleep" and "raises" her by saying to her what you would say to someone sleeping: "get up" (v. 54); and so it happens. In the vicinity there is also a boy who is raised from the dead in the same way, 7:14-15, and the texts in which someone is exhorted by Jesus to "arise" from a condition similar to death (paralysis etc.) are not far away either: Lk. 5:24 and 6:8. These four passages all occur as early as Part II (Jesus' activity in Galilee).

Jesus has led the reader in making the transition sleep/death, through his use of language. At the same time, however, by retrieving the boy and the girl from death he anticipates his own end and its surprising sequel, the Resurrection. This makes their deliverance an adumbration of Jesus' own resurrection, by which he takes the sting out of death. Thus, what he takes from death is what it always has, everywhere in the mortal world: the last word, to put it in language terms. Luke himself expresses this by devoting his last words (ch. 24) to the Resurrected One, and to the reception he gets among the followers: incredulous at first, then elated and grateful.

The idea of "preparation" is another gold vein for metaphorics. Its first application determines the significance of John.
He is to prepare the way, and a prestigious verse from Deutero-
Isaiah is his legitimation, Lk. 1:76 and 3:4. Chapters 1 and 2 also
mention preparation in 1:17 and 2:31. In 14:17, a meal is prepared, as part of a central parable about a host whose invitations
meet with refusals three times, so that finally (as the climax of
another 3 + 1 model) he welcomes beggars and blind men. His
repast adumbrates *the* supper in every Gospel: the Passover meal,
Jesus' last supper with the twelve. At that occasion Peter claims
to be willing to suffer prison and death for his master, but Jesus
predicts his triple denial, 22:33ff. This counterpoint contrasts
with the moments scattered through the journey when Jesus
himself is preparing his disciples for the kingdom of God, and
their mission as apostles.

Preparing the disciples takes us to a metaphorical network
that also affects the reader, that of vigilance, waking up, sleep,
and death. Jesus stimulates the disciples to be vigilant and remain
always alert, 12:35-40 and 21:34-36. Their awakening and rising
in Gethsemane (22:46b) parallels Jesus' rising in v. 45a. We now
remember how they woke up with a shock on the mountain in
9:32. Sleep is an image or herald of death. Jesus passionately
pleads for the clear, wide-awake open-mindedness of little children, 9:48, 10:21 and 18:15-17. He and his disciple/narrator
point to what this yields: a view of the kingdom of God. What
exactly is the difference between disciple and reader?

12

The reader's attitude

Ten productive questions; suggestions for further reading

The proper reading attitude

In the Introduction I have explained how completely defense-less the text is against any form of abuse. For the text, the reader is either a blessing or a curse. Much depends on our attitude. We may decide to work on our open-mindedness, and constantly adapt our picture of the text while we are reading. Curiosity is a great asset, self-criticism is even better.

Reading properly is always active puzzle-solving: comparing elements, checking on a character's history, sometimes consulting an atlas or a Bible handbook. Asking questions is more important than committing ourselves to answers. Uncertainty means that one is still open for change and substitution; certainty may soon turn to hardening. Being able to work with such simple but basic narratological tools as plot, hero and points of view is much more important in the encounter with the Bible than being devout.

All this may also be formulated in negative terms: what are our biggest traps? To mention a few:

a. Our desire to know: after some reading and searching we like to have a finished interpretation in front of us and are (too) easily satisfied with a total picture based on only partial observation of the textual characteristics. In this way we commit ourselves, and forget to check our results rigorously against the text itself once more, some time during the procedure.

b. We allow our energy and attention to be sucked up by the historical world that is connected to the origin of the text and was the immediate cause of its being written. That reality, or the reality of whichever century, has a different mode of being than a story as a creative but finite string of language signs. Do not be tempted to speculate on "how it really was," there and then, so far away and so long ago, in that utterly alien culture. The story accommodates these far horizons in its own way, but never exclusively consists in referencing them. Through the medium of our attention and our act of reading, it constructs its own world in words, which has only a tenuous and indirect contact with what is irretrievably past and gone.

c. An insidious form of delusion is the spectacles we ourselves are wearing: our unspoken hopes, expectations; our preconceived notions about Moses, Jesus and ancient Israel; and especially our prejudices, beliefs and unshakeable convictions. Fixed ideas about aspects of faith and the world will influence, lead and regularly impede us, even unconsciously. The Bible is so complex that it differs by definition from any religious belief, no matter how exalted our own creed or value scale may be. Only by keeping an open mind and by asking questions can we discover *how* different the Bible is. The Bible is not a picture book for our own ideas, which we open only if we want our opinions confirmed, or our vanity tickled. Nor is it a box of prooftexts.

This book is an exercise in grasping the overall shape of a text, and in reading from within. There is an old rule that says: the whole is more than the sum of its parts. I have tried to make this insight truly operational, so that at many levels it becomes practical and manageable for readers. From the viewpoints of creation and knowledge, proper reading and literary experience, the whole has priority over the parts: it comes first in the writer's mind, and it is the beacon for which we set course while, in our reading, we travel past many details.

Ten productive questions

The following questions, ten groups rather than ten separate questions, will be useful while reading narrative texts, for instance from the list of 110 stories following this chapter.

1. Who is the *hero*? What is your reason for thinking this (remember the criteria of presence, initiative, and the executor of the quest)?

2. What does the *quest* consist of? What is the hero after, i.e. what is his object of value? Does he attain his goal, and if not, why not?

3. Who are the *helpers* and *opponents*? Besides characters, factors, situations or personality traits also qualify. Are any *attributes* (objects) present? What do they contribute? Do they have a symbolic added value?

4. Can you feel the *narrator's* presence anywhere in the text? This will apply especially in the case of information, comments, explanations or value judgments on his part. Can you point to these instances of the writer speaking? Where is the writer less obviously present (for instance in his deliberate arrangement or composition of the material)? Does he usually make his own statements at strategic points in the text?

5. Does the narrator keep to the *chronology* of the events and processes themselves? If not, where does he deviate, and why do you think he does that? Try and get an idea of the discourse time/narrated time ratio.

6. Where are the gaps where *narrated time* has been skipped, and are there cases of acceleration, retardation, retrospect and anticipation? Assuming that the writer inserted them at the right points: why are they where they are? What is their relation with the context?

7. Is there a clear *plot,* or is the unit you are reading more or less without a plot of its own, because it forms part of a greater whole? What, then, is the macro-plot there?

8. Where are the *speeches*? Are there many of them? Have speeches been left out where you would expect them?
    What factors influence the character who is speaking, what self-interest, background, desires, expectations?
    Congruence: do the characters' words match their actions? If not, how come?
    Does the text contain indications of the *writer* supporting or approving of his character?

9. Is there any particular choice of words that strikes you?

Any other characteristics of *style or structure?* Take them seriously, and keep pondering them, guided, for instance, by such questions as "what does this contribute to plot or characterization?"

10. *Boundaries*: what devices are used to demarcate a unit? (Consider the data regarding time, space, beginning and end of the action, entrances or exits of the characters.)
    Can you make a *division* of the text (divide it into smaller units)? By what signals are you guided? Try and find other signals or markers, which may possibly lead to a different structuration. To what extent does the division clarify your view of themes or "content?"

Suggestions for further reading

Readers who want more, or who would like to know more about narratology, may want to turn to the following titles first:

Frank Kermode & Robert Alter (eds.), *The Literary Guide to the Bible*, Cambridge, Mass.: Harvard University Press, 1987. This is a collection of essays (co-published by Fontana, London, reasonably priced, and also available in paperback) by some 25 authors, providing introductions to most of the biblical books (Old and New Testament); see for instance Alter himself on the Psalms and poetry, John Drury on Mark and Luke, Kermode on the Gospels of Matthew and John, and myself on Genesis.

In the following titles the subject is only the Old Testament:

Robert Alter, *The Art of Biblical Narrative*, New York: Basic Books, 1981.

Shimon Bar-Efrat, *Narrative Art in the Bible*, Sheffield: Almond Press (Journal for the Study of the Old Testament, supplement, 70), 1989.

Readers who would like to dig a bit deeper, and who are not afraid of a little Hebrew or a few transcriptions, I would recommend the following titles, listed by subject:

—For the composition of the Abraham cycle: my article 'Time and the Structure of the Abraham Cycle' in *Oudtestamentische Studiën* 25 (1989), pp.96-109.

—For the Joseph story: James Ackerman, 'Joseph, Judah, and Jacob,' *in Literary Interpretations of Biblical Narratives*, Vol. 2, edited by Kenneth R.R. Gros Louis, with James S. Ackerman, Abingdon, 1982, pp.85-113.

—For the underlying time frame of 1 Samuel 27–31 + 2 Samuel 1: my article 'Structural Reading on the Fracture between Synchrony and Diachrony,' in *Jaarbericht Ex Oriente Lux* 30 (1987-88), pp.123-136.

—J. Cheryl Exum, *Tragedy and Biblical Narrative*, Cambridge: Cambridge University Press, 1992.

—And a series of three books on Deuteronomy through to Samuel by Robert Polzin; they share the common subtitle *A Literary Study of the Deuteronomic History*, and are called respectively:

Moses and the Deuteronomist, New York: Indiana University Press, 1980.

Samuel and the Deuteronomist, San Francisco: Indiana University Press, 1989.

David and the Deuteronomist, Bloomington (Indiana): Indiana University Press, 1993.

Next, some theory may be found in

—The introductory chapters of Parts I and II of my tetralogy *Narrative Art and Poetry in the Books of Samuel*, Assen: Van Gorcum 1981–1993. (Part I, 1981, has as its separate title, *King David;* Part II, 1986, is called *The Crossing Fates.*).

Further literature (for students and advanced readers) may be found in:

David M. Gunn & Danna Nolan Fewell, *Narrative in the Hebrew Bible*, New York: Oxford University Press, 1993, and in:

Duane F. Watson & Alan J. Hauser, *Rhetorical Criticism of the Bible, A Comprehensive Bibliography with Notes on History and Method*, Leiden: Brill, 1994.

For an overview of ways of reading the New Testament, reference may be made to

Stanley E. Porter (ed.), *Handbook to Exegesis of the New Testament*, Leiden: Brill (New Testament Tools and Studies, 25), 1997.

A fuller treatment of the application of recent literary approaches to the New Testament is

Stephen D. Moore, *Literary Criticism and the Gospels: The Theoretical Challenge*, New Haven: Yale University Press, 1989.

A concise practical introduction is

John M. Court, *Reading the New Testament*, London: Routledge, 1997.

For the reader who knows Greek and who would love a long soak in the technique and ring structures of the Gospel of John, I would mention

George Mlakuzhyil, S.J., *The Christocentric Literary Structure of the Fourth Gospel*, Analecta Biblica, 117, Rome: Pontifical Biblical Institute, 1987.

The next 110 stories

With some hints to assist further reading

Here follows a list of stories for further reading. They come in groups, as stories in the Bible usually do. For some groups, characteristics and sometimes an outline have already been discussed. I will take this opportunity to print the correct structure of some of the larger texts, hoping in this way to provide the reader with a useful reading guide. A slash (/) indicates the boundary between literary units (scenes, stories).

c. 19 units   *Abraham*
                 the main structure of this cycle:

frame: genealogical information = prologue 11:27-32

phase I	Gen. 12–14	(journey, promised land, Abram manages to hold his own)
phase II	Gen. 15–16	(crisis, stake: son? Nocturnal vision, adoption)
phase III	Gen. 17–21	(covenant = circumcision, announcements of birth and destruction; destruction, crisis in Gerar, birth, Hagar banished, treaty)
phase IV	Gen. 22:1-19	(crisis, sacrifice son? ordeal, blessing)
phase V	Gen. 22:20–24:67	(purchase of land, journey, Rebekah succeeds Sarah)

frame: genealogical information = epilogue 25:1-18

c. 16 units   *Jacob*
                 basic structure: three Acts

A   birth of the twins, two stories about deceit (Jacob acquires birthright and his father's blessing), departure/flight and revelation through dream in Bethel, Gen. 25:19-26 / 27-33 / 27:1–28:9 / 28:10-22

X   Jacob in Haran: works for his uncle Laban, 29:1-14 / 15-30 /
        29:31–30:24 / 25-43 / 31:1-21 / 22-55

A'   Jacob back in Canaan: 32:1-12 / 13-21 / 22-32 / 33:1-20 /
        35:1-15 / 16-29

c. 6 units   *Balaam*
                (Numbers 22:1-21 / 22-40; 23:1-12 / 13-26 /
                23:27–24:14 / 15-25)

4 chapters = literary units   *Ruth*

Note the opposition of chs. 1 and 4: in 1 there is famine and death, i.e.
the danger of the dynasty dying out, and the bitterness Naomi voices to
the women; 4 brings the fulfillment which makes the Ruth–Boaz marriage a new beginning; their fertility is an extension of Leah & Rachel,
Judah & Tamar: an extensive family tree is given. Naomi is comforted
and sung to by the women.

     Chapters 2 and 3 complement each other: 2 is set during the day,
on the field; ch. 3 at night, on the threshing-floor; both chapters have a
solid center consisting in a dialogue between the female and the male
hero, framed in both cases by Naomi's guidance.

A =   Ruth 1: famine and exile in Moab; the husbands die.
        Naomi returns to Judah embittered (Mara), Ruth does not leave
        her; the women of Bethlehem welcome them.

    B =   Ruth 2: at the beginning and at the end, Naomi takes care
            of Ruth,
         the story proper takes place during the day,
         on the harvest field; Boaz takes care of Ruth

    B' =   Ruth 3: at the beginning and at the end, Naomi takes care
            of Ruth,
         the story proper takes place at night,
         on the threshing floor, where a decked-out Ruth wakes Boaz;
         Boaz promises to start working towards a marriage

A' =   Ruth 4: during a legal procedure in the gate, Boaz scores off
        another candidate, buys land from Naomi and arranges his mar-
        riage to Ruth; when a child is born (ancestor to David!) the
        women bless the child and its parents—all's well that ends well.
        A genealogical table at the end extends the line from Boaz and
        Ruth to David.

12 units   *Gideon*

The structure I am giving here may serve as a guide to reading. There are 23 sequences, grouped in five main sections: Judges 6–8

I *preparation*

IA background	a) 6:1-6	oppression
	b) 6:7-10	oracle through prophet
IB assignment	a) 6:11-18	calling
	b) 6:19-24	sacrifice, miracle > altar
IC hero tested	a) 6:25-27	provocation: Baal's altar destroyed (night) (+ sacrifice on new altar)
	b) 6:28-32	Ophrah angry, Joash to the rescue, "Jerubbaal"

II *En route to the battle*

IIA God tested(!)	a) 6:33-35	armies, tribes called up
	b) 6:36-38//39-40	double test (fleece, night)
IIB army?	a) 7:1-3	God makes the first ...
	b) 7:4-8	... and (at the water) the second selection: 300 men

III *the night of the "attack"*

IIIA encouragement	a) 7:9-12	God: sneak up and listen >
	b) 7:13-15	dream + interpretation by Midianite soldiers
IIIB "attack"	a) 7:15-18	Gideon now instructing the 300
	b) 7:19-22	panic in Midianite camp, victory

IV *to/in Trans-Jordan: pursuit and death*

IVA dispute in Ephraim	a) 7:23-25	tribes in action, two generals killed
	b) 8:1-3	Gideon appeases Ephraim's anger
IVB way up	a) 8:4-9	Gideon passes through Succoth and Penuel
	b) 8:10-12	disperses the rest of the enemy, captures two kings, Zebah and Zalmunna
IVC way back/revenge	a) 8:13-17	Gideon cruelly punishes Succoth and Penuel
	b) 8:18-21	he speaks to the kings and kills them

V *conclusion: relation Gideon–people, king yes/no?*

VA rule?	a) 8:22-27	Gideon refuses supremacy, but ...
	a')	... collects spoils /gold > ephod, snare (v. 28, concluding formula)
VB transition	a) 8:29-32	Gideon, 70 sons plus one (Abimelech)
	b) 8:33-35	people unfaithful to God and Gideon

The paragraphs of 8:29-35 bridge the gap with, and prepare for, the big chapter Judges 9, the anti-climax after the Gideon act. This long and dark story about the town of Shechem and its tyrant Abimelech is the axis and point of gravity of the book of Judges.

c. 8 units	*Samson*
	Judges 13 / 14:1-10a / 10b-20 / 15:1-8 / 9-20 + 16:1-3 / 16:4-22 /23-31

5 units	*the introduction of the monarchy, 1 Samuel 8–12:*
	1 Samuel 8 / 9:1–10:16 / 10:17-27 / 11:1-13 / 11:14-15 + ch. 12

3 units	*1 Samuel 24–26*
	the hunter hunted: 24 parallel to 26, framing 25 (whether or not to shed blood)

16 units	*Absalom's rebellion, 2 Samuel 15–20*
	the concentric structure in two sequences:

A	preparation and outbreak of the rebellion 15:1-12
B	David flees from Jerusalem (10 concubines remain), crosses the Kidron, mourning procession 15:13-31

three encounters on the Mount of Olives, on the outward journey:

C	David–Hushai: espionage, thwart Ahithophel 15:32-37
D	David–Ziba: forage, Mephibosheth accused 16:1-4
E	David–Shimei: curses and stones from the Saulite camp 16:5-14

F	council with Absalom: advice by Ahithophel and Hushai 16:15–17:14

G   messenger scene: Jonathan & Ahimaaz escape, inform
           David, who escapes across the Jordan 17:15-22
H   preparation for battle; Israel defeated by the bush and
           David's army 17:24–18:8

H'   Absalom caught in an oak tree, killed by Joab 18:9-18
G'   messenger scene: Ahimaaz & Cushite inform David, David
           mourns Absalom's death   18:19-33
F'   Joab's harsh intervention, admonishes David. Judah's
           preferential treatment 19:1-15

           three encounters at the Jordan, on the return journey:
E'   David spares Shimei 19:16-23
D'   Mephibosheth justifies his actions before David 19:24-30
C'   Barzillai takes leave of his king 19:31-40

B'   David crosses the Jordan, quarrel Judah–Israel leads to
           secession; 10 concubines in Jerusalem 19:41–20:3
A'   the new rebellion led by Sheba ben Bichri put down by Joab
           (who kills Amasa) 20:4-22

5 units   *Jeroboam and the division of the kingdom*
             1 Kgs 11:29-40 / 12:1-24 / 12:25-32 / 12:33–13:32 / 14

6 units   *Elijah*
             1 Kings 17 / 18:1-15 / 18:16-46 / 19 / 20 / 21

5 units   *Jehu's coup*
             2 Kgs 9:1-15 /16-29 / 30-37 / 10:1-17 / 18-28

4 units   *Jonah*
             Jonah 1 / 2 / 3:1–4:4 / 4:5-11